CONTEMPORARY Barbie® DOLLS

1980 AND BEYOND

1998 EDITION

Bob Mackie's
Neptune Fantasy Barbie

CONTEMPORARY Barbie® DOLLS
1980 AND BEYOND

1998 EDITION

JANE SARASOHN-KAHN

Antique Trader Books
Norfolk, Virginia
Division of Landmark Specialty Publications

ISBN: 0-930625-84-6 (softbound)
0-930625-90-0 (hardbound)
Library of Congress Catalog Card Number: 97-74598

Manufactured in the United States of America

Published by

Antique Trader Books
Norfolk, Virginia
Division of Landmark Specialty Publications

To order additional copies of this book,
or to obtain a free Antique Trader Books catalog, please contact:
Antique Trader Books
P.O. Box 1050
Dubuque, Iowa 52004
1-800-334-7165

Front cover photograph: Escada Barbie doll (#15948, 1996),
based on a design by the Spanish couturier.
Back cover photograph: Portrait in Taffeta Barbie doll was designed by Robert Best.

This book is dedicated to the beautiful memory of

Polly Sarasohn

who believed that

This Girl Could Do Anything!

CONTENTS

PREFACE

Since the publication of the first edition of this book, the Contemporary Barbie® doll has greatly evolved. So has my own life, which shapes the lens through which I look at and appreciate the Barbie doll. In the interim, I have become a mother of an incredibly wonderful, sweet baby girl named Anna. She profoundly influences my relationship with the Barbie doll the way my mother influenced that relationship. I know that the invisible hand of Grandma Polly is eternally sweetening our playtimes. In this post-baby-boom household, a constant that links generation to generation is the Barbie doll.

JS-K
Summer 1997
On a laptop, somewhere over America

ACKNOWLEDGMENTS

Out of the proverbial blue, I received a call from a cable TV host planning a show on collecting Barbie® dolls. He needed someone to sit in the hot seat. That host was Harry Rinker, who has subsequently become my collectibles honesty broker (I was the one in the hot seat). Harry is the only person on the planet whose mission in life is to keep collectibles markets flowing and free, defending the rights and expanding the knowledge of collectors. It is fair to say that without Harry, this book would never have been written as it was he who said, "You've got to write a book." And it was Harry Rinker, Jr., who has created some of the most beautiful photographs of the Barbie doll ever published.

I thank Debbie Monroe, Vice President of Landmark Communications, for the opportunity to share my insights, ideas and the finer things in life. Thanks, too, to Jaro Šebek, the artist behind this beautiful book. Allan Miller, my editor, helped make my words sing.

Thanks, too, to all of the vintage doll dealers who have educated me and enriched my own collection over the years. Sandi Holder of The Doll Attic embodies the model of what good dealers provide collectors: access, good information and loads of fun. To Joe Blitman, Marl Davidson, and Kitty Stuart—thanks for helping me build a beautiful collection of Barbie dolls and for your friendship. These are real-life examples of how you can make true friends through a hobby.

Barbara and Dan Miller, publishers of the Miller's group of doll collecting publications, provided support, encouragement and knowledge through challenging times. Thank you for the long-distance early-morning cups of coffee.

Barbie doll's family at Mattel generously assisted me in gathering research and unearthing interesting stories about Contemporary Barbie. Lisa McKendall and Judy Schizas provided valuable counsel and direction. I thank Paulette Bazerman, Robert Best, Kitty Black-Perkins, Kim Burkhardt, Ann Driskill, Janet Goldblatt, Abbe Littleton, Larry Morgan, Anne Parducci and Cynthia Young for spending time with me. Danny Palumbo ably and patiently responded to my numerous requests for information. Lorraine Alkire navigated the manuscript through the labyrinth of legal review.

I warmly thank Barry Sturgill, most contemporary and creative of Barbie doll photographers, for adding his special touch to this book. Barry shot the new photographs that update and enhance the book with his own extraordinary, inimitable style.

I am blessed with a circle of wonderful friends. They challenge me, support me, and give me so much joy. I thank them: Constanza Erdoes Low, Betsy Jackson, Dave Peterson, Susan Steele, and the Wright Family. Carey Preston gets the Devon clotted cream award for finding the Franco-Italianate country house in England where I completed the manuscript of this book, overlooking sheep, the ruins of a magnificent manor home and spectacular gardens. Barbie never had it so good, even in her original Dream House! I also thank Jennifer Wayne, Internet Surfer Exceptionelle, who assisted me in my research. My circle of e-friends on the Internet (in particular, Fashion-Elle's), America Online, Compuserve and Prodigy also provided virtual collegiality.

Thanks to my sisters, Nancy and Margie, for letting me be number three in the line of "magnificent daughters." Because I was the baby, I was, to quote Paul Simon, Born at the Right Time to be in the first generation of Barbie doll consumers.

To Polly Sarasohn, I owe my love of life and my love of play, along with abundant affection, my first two Barbie dolls and a trunk full of 900 series outfits. She must be having one great giggle from her heavenly perch, watching me still playing with these vintage toys. To Charles Sarasohn, I owe my senses of integrity, intellectual curiosity and social justice.

Finally, to my life partner and best friend, Robert Kahn, I extend loving gratitude and never-ending hugs. He continually encourages me to do anything and everything I believe in. He really makes me feel that I can do anything.

JS-K, 31 August 1995 (revised August 1997)
Stevenstone
St. Giles-in-the-Wood
Devon, United Kingdom

INTRODUCTION

When Mattel began life in 1945 as a small giftware business, the company had $100,000 in sales in its first year. In 1980 (fiscal year ended January 31, 1981), Mattel had net sales of $916 million. By 1996, net sales reached $3.8 billion. Barbie dolls represent nearly one-half of the company's sales, twice the company's 1980 total sales figure.

Barbie doll, nearly a two-billion dollar baby to Mattel, celebrated her 35th anniversary in 1994. In 1997, Mattel is selling its one billionth Barbie doll, representing the most successful fashion doll of all time and one of the most powerful brands in the global economy. As overseas sales of the Barbie dolls expand beyond the 140 countries in which she is already sold—into and beyond emerging markets such as China, Indonesia and Russia—the market promises to double, and perhaps even triple, in the years ahead.

The average American girl has an estimated eight-plus Barbie dolls in her collection. Barbie dolls already reside in 99 percent of young Americans' homes. However, Mattel recognizes that both children and adults are consumers of Barbie dolls and related products. The adult market has become so important that Mattel sponsored a Barbie Festival at Walt Disney World in September, 1994. Thousands of collectors showed up for the event. This was not surprising: Adult collectors spent $65 million on Barbie dolls in 1993*, increasing to $175 million in 1995.

While a number of books have been published about Barbie dolls and accessories, none cover the Barbie doll comprehensively after 1980. The first generation of Barbie doll collectors played with the doll between 1959 and 1967. Many of these (mostly) women have become collectors of the dolls of their childhood. However, since the celebration of Barbie's 35th anniversary in 1994, legions of new Barbie collectors have entered the collecting fray—many with young children of their own, and they are sharing their childhood memories, and making new ones, in parallel.

These Barbie doll collectors, unless surnamed Rockefeller, Winfrey (as in Oprah) or Perot, have one thing in common: They cannot afford to buy every new Barbie doll issued by Mattel. In fact, if one wished to own every Barbie doll manufactured for the U.S. market since 1980 alone, in never-removed-from-the-box condition, a sizable cash sum approaching $75,000 would need to be invested.

A quick review of the comprehensive list in the Appendix illustrates that the roster of new Barbie dolls issued each year since 1980 gets longer and deeper; longer due to the sheer numbers of new dolls, and deeper in the broadening of market segments that Mattel is targeting. It is too simple to say that Mattel recognizes that there are two markets for Barbie dolls—children and adults. Even within those macro segments there are sub-segments of collectors. Some adults collect the high-end Bob Mackie dolls and porcelain examples; others specialize in bride and holiday dolls. Still others acquire every "career" Barbie doll and costume.

Festival Dolls. *Mattel gave these reproduction Barbie dolls to participants at the Barbie Festival in 1994. The highlight was this titian-haired ponytail, unavailable in the mass market.*

*SOURCE: *Brandweek,* December 12, 1994, p. 18

So whether specialist in "vertical" collections or dabbler across all types of doll themes, the contemporary Barbie doll collector must allocate available financial resources carefully.

My interest in writing this book is driven by my professional persona: I am an economist with a passion for information. As an economist by profession, I have two fundamental beliefs regarding markets:

1. A healthy, "perfect" market is based on the presence of a multitude of buyers and sellers.
2. A healthy market requires the free flow of information. More (good) information means a healthier market.

Prior to the Barbie doll's 35th year, the Barbie and associated collectibles market was highly imperfect. The vintage Barbie doll market was represented by relatively few sellers, lots of buyers, and relatively few sources of reliable information. Much of the information that was available was in fact written by dealers themselves, who can have conflicts of interest.

Through the years, Barbie has adapted her bathing suit styles to her times. From left: **Baywatch Barbie** *(1995),* **Malibu Barbie** *(1971),* **Bubblecut Barbie** *(1961),* **Sun Sensation Barbie** *(1993).*

Then, in 1994, when the Barbie doll's 35th anniversary was celebrated, several things happened in parallel:

◆ Mattel explicitly recognized and rewarded the Barbie doll collector with the company's first-ever national convention in Orlando, at Walt Disney World.

◆ Madison Avenue, the news media and daytime talk shows based content and hype on the Barbie doll and related topics, raising the profile of the 35th anniversary of the doll.

◆ The number of new Barbie doll collectors doubled (some say tripled). Some had rediscovered their baby boom childhoods; other non-baby boomers began new collections with "pink box" and/or mass merchandise Barbie dolls.

This book seeks to fill a gap in the Barbie doll collecting literature that tends to focus on the early vintage era of the doll. The intent is to provide collectors, both long-standing and new entrants into the arena, with a baseline of information on contemporary Barbie: those dolls produced after 1980. A primary objective is to provide this information with an eye toward freeing-up the collecting market, creating more informed consumers and more responsible dealers. Only in the balance of well-informed supply and demand can a healthy market exist. This will enhance collective enjoyment of the hobby for all of us in the long run.

*From American Airlines Stewardess (above) to **Astronaut Barbie** (below) in 35 years.*

Contemporary Barbie? Hasn't the Barbie doll always been contemporary since she was unveiled at Toy Fair in 1959? The fact is that it has always been the intention of Mattel's Barbie doll designers to have the doll reflect her times. Appearing as Barbie first did, so very pale and blonde in her zebra-striped bathing suit, the doll was a quintessential Fifties conception. But over time, Sorority Girl and Junior Prom outfits were joined by American Airlines Stewardess in 1960. We sweated with Great Shapes Barbie aerobicizing in 1980; went to the moon when Astronaut Barbie flew into space in 1974; and voted when Barbie [ran] for President in 1992. Since introduced, the Barbie doll has reflected the contemporary society in which she lived (or was played with). This was and still is art imitating life. "Art?" you say. Yes, art! Andy Warhol painted her, and the Museum of Modern Art, London's Victoria and Albert Museum, the Smithsonian Institution and the Oakland Museum all exhibited her. She has even had her own Hall of Fame in Palo Alto, California. And in December, 1995, the Liberty Art Gallery in New York City celebrated "Art and Barbie"—assembling works by some 50 prominent contemporary artists such as John Baldessari, Kenny Scharf, Andy Warhol and William Wegman; and architects Robert A.M. Stern and Emilio Ambasz.

This book provides a context of social history for *Contemporary BARBIE* and the colorful, sometimes twisted, ofttimes paradoxical, contemporary history within which the dolls were introduced in the United States. In the modern period of the Barbie doll, her global presence grew and she is well represented in both developed and emerging economies. However, the scope of this book is limited to U.S. domestic Barbie dolls in the contemporary period, leaving the Barbie dolls manufactured for non-U.S. consumption for another book. In addition, this book does not cover the prototypes or convention dolls that many *Contemporary BARBIE* collectors covet. Only dolls available on the mass market through national distribution (for the great bulk of collectors) are covered in this book.

One of the most limited Barbie dolls of the contemporary era, Gold Jubilee Barbie was issued in 1994 to commemorate the 35th anniversary of the Barbie doll. She was designed by Carol Spencer and was reportedly limited to 5,000 dolls.

Chapter 1

CONTEMPORARY BARBIE® HISTORY

This chapter describes the evolution of the modern Barbie doll using a timeline perspective for the *Contemporary BARBIE* era. Key real-world events which have shaped development of the doll are highlighted. These include events in politics, society, demography, the economy, and the arts (both the so-called "fine" and "popular" arts). This timeline should be kept in mind when reading the rest of the book because it sets the stage for understanding *Contemporary BARBIE* in the doll's modern historical and social contexts.

Before exploring the external events that provide a context and influence the modern Barbie doll, it is important to have some understanding of Mattel's corporate culture during the period. This book defines the contemporary era as beginning in 1980 and continuing to the present day. While the decade of the 1990s—when the adult collector market substantially boomed—has contributed to Mattel's success, the earlier years of the period were difficult times for the company.

It is worth first revisiting the 1970s, a period of new social attitudes, some of which did not bode well for Barbie. In 1971, the National Organization for Women began a formal campaign against Barbie with a press release that condemned advertising for the doll as sexist. By the early 1980s, many consumers had written-off the doll as, at a minimum, uninteresting; at the extreme, she was thought to be a sexist, poor example for children. (Such debates continue to the present day, and still appear occasionally expressed in Op-Ed pages, on television talk shows, in feminist manifestos and sociology Ph.D. dissertations).

To make matters worse, Mattel was devastated when the videogame craze of the early 1980s faded. Their venture into videogames had cost Mattel $403 million, and the company found itself headed into 1984 with a $394 million loss. Many Wall Street toy industry analysts believe that Mattel might not have survived the troubling early years of the 1980s if the venture capital firms E.M. Warburg, Pincus & Co. and junk bond king Drexel Burnham Lambert hadn't come together, in 1984, to pitch-in $231 million in capital to rescue Mattel from its videogame woes.

Mattel hit paydirt again in 1985 with its Masters of the Universe action toy line for boys. But the fad was short lived, leaving the firm with excess manufacturing capacity and a bloated corporate payroll.

Further complicating matters, between 1982 and 1987 Mattel underwent two major financial reorganizations and three reconstructed management teams. Sales in the period fell by 23% from their 1982 peak of $1.3 billion, and profits were erratic. In 1985, Hasbro overtook Mattel to become the world's largest toymaker. Between 1985 and 1987, Mattel lost $121 million, reflecting the restructuring, write-offs and some consumer indifference—even hostility—to many of the company's new toys (not just the Barbie doll).

A first generation international doll, from 1980. **Parisian Barbie** *wore a Follies Bergere-type costume.*

A re-energized board of directors, including representatives from the financial backers, counted on one man to bring Mattel out of the doldrums. That man was John Amerman, an ace consumer goods marketer who had originally joined Mattel in 1980 after successfully managing various brands including Ajax cleanser, Bromo-Seltzer, Listerine and Rolaids.

Prior to assuming the helm of Mattel as President and Chief Executive Officer in 1986, Amerman was head of Mattel International. During his tenure with that division, sales grew fourfold and, unlike Mattel's domestic operations, the international division had shown solid profitability.

Amerman downsized the company internally and focused on the two brands he believed could save the organization—Barbie and Hot Wheels®—brand names that by 1987 were 28 and 20 years old, respectively. He also established a tie-in with Disney on a toy line for infants and pre-schoolers; consolidated manufacturing in nine countries with among the lowest labor costs in the world; and convinced his own marketing staff that there was, indeed, a market for Barbie dolls beyond the long-held $10 price point. Finally, Mattel under Amerman developed the "We're into Barbie" advertising campaign for television. Amerman's multi-pronged strategy worked. Following a loss of more than $120 million on sales of $1 billion in 1987, Mattel reported a profit of $36 million on sales of $990 million in 1988, with Barbie ranking as the firm's biggest franchise.

1988 Happy Holidays Barbie—
one successful experiment.

HOW HOLIDAY BARBIE WAS BORN

John Amerman believed that there was pent-up demand for expanding Barbie dolls beyond a $10 price point. He recalled a staff meeting where he asked, "Why can't we sell a Barbie Doll for more than $9.99?" In response, Amerman said, "Everybody's face turned white. They held their heads for a while, then went to the easel with pointers and graphs and explained all the reasons why you couldn't do that. It all came down to being afraid of the retail buyer. I told our head of design and development to come up with the most elegant Barbie ever. I told the packaging people to develop the best package they could conceive. A week later, they gave me the hard costs. I said, 'Geez, we're gonna have to sell her for $19.99.' And that's how Holiday Barbie was born."

Amerman proceeded cautiously, shipping just 300,000 units in October 1988. "But they never even reached retail shelves," he said. "The clerks in the stores would buy whole cases and take them home for their family and friends or sell them for $50 apiece, so they became black-market items. When we saw that, we knew we had a bright idea."

The next year, the company shipped 600,000 Holiday Barbies retailing for $21.99. The company expanded the line each year, until it became a holiday tradition. In 1994, Happy Holidays Barbie retailed at about $34.99, and as of November 1995, the doll fetched over $100 on the secondary market. Amerman's 1988 intuition paid off for both Mattel and collectors of the Happy Holidays series.

SOURCE: "King Barbie," *Los Angeles,* August 1994, v39, n8, p62

Beyond his concept for charging more than $10 for a Barbie doll, Amerman and his team had other ideas that ultimately resulted in an expanded marketing strategy to attract even more adult collectors to Barbie dolls. These included working with Bob Mackie, manufacturing a line of porcelain dolls, and creating various themed lines of special edition dolls.

While Amerman is credited with turning Mattel (the corporate entity) around, Jill Elikann Barad played a key role in the resurgence of the Barbie doll line specifically. In the period since Barad took charge of marketing the doll in 1988, annual sales of the Barbie family have increased from $485 million to over $1 billion.

Jill Barad began working at Mattel in 1981 by pitching the sale of cosmetics for children. In 1985, Barad conceived She-Ra, Princess of Power, the first action doll for girls, as a female counterpart for the Masters of the Universe line. She-Ra, while short-lived, gave rise to a growing number of new ideas for the Barbie doll. (Note, some ten years later, the introduction of Flying Hero Barbie, with the look and feel of her predecessor, She-Ra.) Barad has been described as one of the top 50 women in American business. In 1988, *USA Today* dubbed her, "The toy industry's Princess of Power." And that was four years before Barad became Mattel's Chief Operating Officer in 1992.

In a very tangible way, then, this book covers the "Amerman and Barad era" of the Barbie doll. Given where the Barbie doll is in late 1995, collectors owe homage to both: to Amerman for his successful turnaround of Mattel through leveraging the Barbie brand in the latter 1980s; and to Barad for her continued focus on, and interest in, broadening the Barbie doll line.

THE SHORT LIFE OF SHE-RA

She-Ra was the sister of the Master of the Universe. Known as the Princess of Power, protector of the land of Etheria, she was among the first fashion/action dolls to have a world of characters to call her own. Her arch-rival, Catra, and fellow companions, winged horses, a unicorn and a comic book, were paraphernalia included in She-Ra's World.

She-Ra's alter-ego was Princess Adora.

SOURCE: *Working Woman*, September, 1985

WOMAN TO RUN HOUSE THAT BARBIE BUILT

Mattel picked a woman to run the house that Barbie built, making Jill E. Barad chief executive of the $3.6 billion toy manufacturer, arguably the most powerful businesswoman in the nation. When the 45-year-old Barad took over January 1 from 64-year-old John W. Amerman, she topped the very short list of women who headed Fortune 1000 companies. That sorority numbered only four.

Barad's rise has been rocket-like in an industry that is anything but child's play, accomplished partly with the help of the Barbie doll. Barad's appointment, though expected among toy industry insiders, stands out for what it indicates about the world of business: Although women, who make up 47% of the work force, can be found prospering in corporate America, they remain few and far between in the executive suites.

In 1995, the federal Glass Ceiling Commission reported that women accounted for just 3% to 5% of senior managers in major corporations.

SOURCE: *Los Angeles Times*, August 23, 1996, pA-1

Good reason to smile—Mattel's Jill Elikann Barad and John Amerman.

"I Will Survive" by Gloria Gaynor was the hot disco hit, and the first Black Barbie hit the floor in 1980 doing The Hustle and other popular dances of the time.

CONTEMPORARY BARBIE®
SNAPSHOTS: 1980-1985

This chapter, and the two that follow, highlight key Barbie doll releases based on annual Mattel Toys catalogs published from 1980 through 1995. As the chapter heading implies, this is a "snapshot" of the available offerings. It is not meant to be an exhaustive inventory of all dolls released each year, but is instead intended to provide a flavor for how the *Contemporary BARBIE* doll has evolved since 1980. The descriptive "snapshots" are organized chronologically by year, each with a Barbie-specific anecdote from the Mattel, Inc. Annual Report for that year.

For ease of reading, we have divided the *Contemporary BARBIE* period from 1980 through 1995 into three chapters—each covers a five-year period. Readers should note that the dates dividing these three periods have no special significance in Barbie doll history, and they do not define recognized or unique "eras."

1980
Mattel, Inc., says. . .

"Mattel Toys U.S.A. continued to demonstrate the strength of its principal consumer franchises, Barbie and Hot Wheels, with increased sales and profits in each of those lines.

"The Company's strong consumer franchises in continuing product lines such as the Barbie doll, Hot Wheels® and Preschool toys and the Intellivision™ Intelligent Television videogame/personal computer are more characteristic of branded consumer products than short life cycle or promotional toy products, and thus contribute to Mattel's established leadership positions."

(Source: 1981 Annual Report)

1980 • • • • • • • • • • • • • • • • •

◆ First group of female graduates from the nation's service academies include 61 from West Point, 55 from Annapolis and 97 from the Air Force Academy.

◆ The White House confirms a *Time* magazine account that reports First Lady Nancy Reagan continued to borrow expensive gowns from top designers for indefinite periods despite an earlier agreement not to do so. *Time* estimated that the borrowed fashions were worth in excess of $1 million.

The first Black doll named "Barbie" was designed by Kitty Black-Perkins. The doll had short hair and wore a long red lurex dress.

The big news in 1979 and 1980 was the introduction of both the first Black Barbie doll (#1293) and the first Hispanic Barbie doll (#1292). The Mattel catalog from 1980 enthuses about each doll.

"Black is beautiful, and Black Barbie® is a knock-out. She's ready for a night out in her fabulous body suit with a wrap-&-snap disco skirt. Little girls will love to pose Barbie. Her arms move and she twists at the waist. Completing the outfit, she comes with stylish hair comb/pick, stud, hoop & dangle earrings, modern necklace & ring, and shoes."

"Little Hispanic girls can now play with their very own Barbie®. Her pretty face accents her lovely dark eyes and long, dark hair. She has many glamorous poses—her arms move and she twists at the waist. Hispanic Barbie comes with fiesta-style dress and shawl, modern necklace & ring, choker with 'rose' stud, hoop & dangle earrings, and shoes."

The Hispanic Barbie doll's packaging featured both English and Spanish text. Not only was ethnicity being reflected by the advent of the "American" Black and Hispanic Barbie dolls, but the International line was introduced in 1980 as well. This year, the first International Barbie dolls included the Italian Barbie doll (#1601), the Parisian Barbie doll (#1600) and the Royal Barbie doll (#1602). The Italian doll was the first Barbie doll to use the Guardian Goddess face mold first seen in 1979.

The lead glamour doll of 1980 was Beauty Secrets Barbie (#1290). While Mattel did not celebrate the 21st birthday of the Barbie doll with a special issue, many collectors believe that this is the "official" doll of the 21st birthday. Beauty Secrets was promoted as having the longest hair ever on a Barbie doll (a distinction ultimately surpassed in 1993 by the Hollywood Hair Barbie). Beauty Secrets, a very "poseable" doll, continues to be popular with collectors today. The features of this doll included movable wrists and bendable elbows. When her back was pressed, the doll could comb her hair, brush her teeth, powder her face, and put on lipstick. She was therefore marketed as a beauty and hair play doll, and included lipstick, powder puff, hair dryer, toothbrush, two perfume bottles, wash mitt, compact with "mirror," comb, brush and clothing.

Kissing Barbie (#2597) would "kiss" when her back was pressed—tilting her head, puckering her lips, and making a kissing sound. With her special lipstick, she would even leave a tiny lipstick mark. Her pink floor-length dress was adorned with "kiss prints." This was the first Barbie doll to use a new face mold, known, appropriately, as the "kissing" face mold.

1980

◆ American entrepreneur Ted Turner founds the Cable News Network (CNN). Over the next few years, cable TV stations of many kinds proliferate.

◆ Jacqueline Cochran, the first woman to fly faster than the speed of sound, died at the age of 70.

◆ According to a report from the surgeon general, lung cancer in women is increasing dramatically and soon will overtake breast cancer as the leading cause of cancer fatalities among women.

Pretty Changes Barbie doll (#2598), another hair play doll, came with hairpieces and a changeable costume that allowed the doll to alter appearances. Her "natural" hair was a chin-length bob, and she was packaged with long blonde and brunette "falls."

The novelty of Sun Lovin' Malibu Barbie and friends were their "peek-a-boo" tans: When the top or bottom of the doll's bathing suit was removed, suntan lines could be seen. Each came with a monogrammed swimsuit and mirrored sunglasses, in the style of the time.

Rollerskating Barbie and Rollerskating Ken were the "king and queen of the roller scene," according to Mattel's promotion. While roller-skating had been a popular sport among children and teenagers for decades, Mattel capitalized on the trendiness of skating featured in popular rink and disco skating films of the time such as *Xanadu*, which starred Olivia Newton-John. The dolls featured plastic wrist straps so Barbie and Ken dolls could skate holding hands.

Other dolls marketed by Mattel this year were the Mork & Mindy™ character dolls, Starr™ and her high school friends, and Guardian Goddesses.

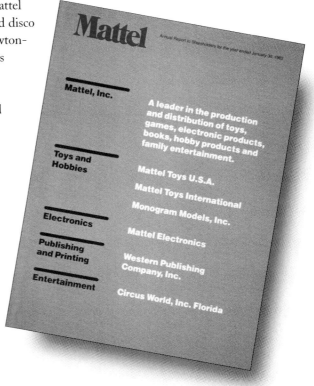

1981
Mattel, Inc., says. . .

"Barbie, the world's best-known fashion doll, is now in her twenty-third year. More than 135 million Barbie dolls, in various styles and costumes, have been sold worldwide since introduction in 1959, with new unit sales records set in fiscal 1982. . . .

"Mattel also utilizes the established Barbie franchise on non-doll related product introductions to gain more ready customer and consumer acceptance. During the past year, Mattel Toys U.S.A. introduced a line of Barbie Cosmetics intended for use in play by young girls who have traditionally associated with the Barbie name."

(Source: 1982 Annual Report)

1981 •

◆ President Reagan announces he will nominate Arizona judge Sandra Day O'Connor to serve on the U.S. Supreme Court, making her the first female justice on the high court.

◆ The video game Pac-Man shows up in every nook and corner of the country as the nation finds itself in the grips of Pac-Mania.

◆ MTV, an all-music cable channel, radically changes the face of TV. It takes to the air with its first video— "Video Killed the Radio Star"—by the Buggles.

The lead glamour doll this year was Golden Dreams Barbie (#1874). "She's golden. She's gorgeous. She's got the billion dollar look!" Mattel promoted. The doll came with Quick Curl hair and gold body suit with overskirt. Golden Dreams Barbie was both a glamour and a hair play doll: She came packaged with curling "iron," styling foam, two combs, hair arranger, two barrettes, brush and comb.

New International Barbie dolls were introduced in 1981, including the Oriental (#3262) and the Scottish (#3263). The Oriental Barbie doll was the first to use the new Oriental face mold.

The Barbie World of Fashion booklet illustrated the broadest range of Barbie dolls to date, from the Western Barbie to the glamorous Golden Dream Barbie and Christie dolls.

Golden Dream doll: blonde with fur coat (left); blonde (center); and Christie–Black (right).

This Golden Dream variation came with "big hair."

Western Barbie (#1757), dressed in a silver-trimmed western jumpsuit, cowboy hat and boots, came with a unique "autograph-signing" feature. This was accomplished through an autograph stamp, included with the doll, which attached to her hand. A second special feature was her ability to wink an eye, which she did when her back was pressed. Positioned as a western star, she came with small pictures of herself to "autograph" for her adoring fans. This was the first Barbie doll to use the new "winking" face mold, considered by many collectors to be among the least attractive face molds in all of Barbiedom. Her horse, Dallas, was packaged separately.

The first My First Barbie (#1875) appeared in 1981. She was—and to this day still is—marketed as an entry-level Barbie doll especially easy for younger children to dress. In addition, this doll helped prepare the young Barbie consumer for future hair play dolls since she was

Western Barbie
*winked and signed
her autograph.*

*This is the first **My First Barbie** doll, issued in 1981.
My First Barbie variation 1 (left), My First Barbie
variation 2 (right).*

designed with long blonde hair simply gathered into a ribbon. Carol Spencer, a Barbie doll designer with Mattel since 1963, developed My First Barbie. Mattel conducted market research in the late 1970s which revealed that the largest group of children playing with Barbie were four to six years old, although some children received their first Barbie as early as age two. Mothers in the focus group said that younger children had trouble dressing Barbie, so a new niche was identified.

Another key introduction in 1981 was the Happy Birthday Barbie (#1922), the first in a very successful themed series for Mattel. "What happens all year long?" Mattel queried. "Birthdays!" the company rightly surmised, and the Happy Birthday dolls have been successful for Mattel ever since. This doll was packaged with a "birthstone" ring and a booklet of party games. To carry the theme through, the Barbie doll also carried a gift box.

Carol Spencer, designer of My First Barbie for Mattel.

*"Happy Birthday to you!" the first **Happy Birthday Barbie** sings. She came packaged with gift and birthday story book.*

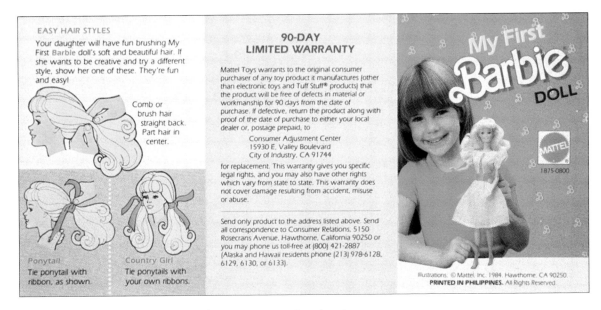

A booklet included with My First Barbie in 1981 introduced and explained the Barbie Experience to new, young Barbie doll consumers.

1982
Mattel, Inc., says. . .

"In the United States, traditional non-electronic toy industry sales declined slightly from $3.87 billion in 1981 to $3.68 billion in 1982. This sales decline—the first in eight years—was attributed to difficult economic conditions and a continuing shift in consumer purchases toward video game products. . . .

"Mattel Toys U.S.A., products offerings. . .include fashion dolls, featuring the Barbie® doll line in its 24th year. . . .

"The Barbie franchise was expanded throughout Japan following the successful 1981 market test by Japanese licensee Takara."

(Source: 1983 Annual Report)

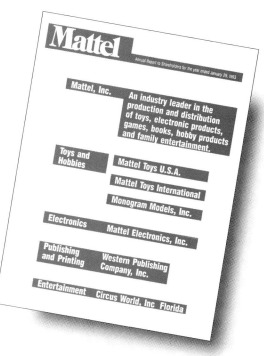

1982

◆ The booming video games industry receives a series of jolts in December, when the price of related stocks fell sharply in trading on the New York Stock Exchange. Issues of Mattel Inc., the industry's No. 2 manufacturer, dropped 2⅛, to 24 points. Mattel reopened trading December 10 and lost nearly one-third of the market value of its issues. Its stock declined by 7¼ to 16¾ on 2.6 million shares traded.

◆ *USA Today* debuts in the Washington-Baltimore area. Calling itself "The Nation's Newspaper," the new entry in American journalism relies on short, punchy articles and the heavy use of color.

The lead glamour doll was Magic Curl Barbie (#3856). "Look at Barbie®—
she's gone curly! She's got gorgeous hair you can curl, straighten, curl again!
And again!" the Mattel ads promoted. Magic Curl Barbie, dressed in a long
yellow puff-sleeved dress, had hair with chameleon-like properties: Her hair could go
from Dolly Parton style "big hair" to straight, sleek, blonde Christie Brinkley type
hair, to a curly style that Tammy Faye Baker had been known to wear in the 1980s.
Yet another hair play model, Mattel saw early-on that little girls never seemed to tire
of such dolls. The doll also came in Black Magic Curl Barbie doll version (#3989),
one of the first Black Barbie-named variations.

New International Barbie dolls in 1982 included the Eskimo Barbie doll (#3898)
and the India Barbie doll (#3897). The Eskimo doll used the 1981 Oriental face mold.

*Eskimo Barbie, costumed in warm, furry coat and
hood, was added to the International series.*

*Magic Curl Barbie was an early Black Barbie.
Her hair could be curled or straightened using
Magic Mist™ spray solution.*

The Pink & Pretty Barbie (#3554), new for 1982, wore a pink ensemble that could be magically transformed into over 20 "absolutely dreamy looks." A furry trimmed hat became a cape or peplum, and a fur boa could be used in many ways.

Fashion Jeans Barbie (#5315) mirrored the designer jeans trends of the year. Her back jeans pocket was emblazoned "Barbie" in pink embroidery, and pink

Pink & Pretty Christie
(and Barbie) came with 20 outfit "changes."

stitching accented the legs and pockets. Her fuzzy pink short-sleeved sweater was personalized as well. Her blonde hair was extra-long for the time.

The second My First Barbie doll (#1875) hit the market based on the initial version's "success story that went beyond even our expectations," according to the 1982 Mattel Toys catalog.

Hawaiian Barbie was introduced this year, using the 1972 Steffie face mold with a slight smile and open mouth. She was packed with a ukulele and windsurfer.

1982 •

◆ Ground is broken for a memorial to honor the 58,022 Americans killed in the Vietnam War. Maya Lin submitted the winning design for the Vietnam Veterans Memorial in Washington, D.C.

◆ Mattel Inc. announces in March that it will sell Ringling Bros. and Barnum & Bailey Combined Shows Inc. back to the unit's managers, for $22.8 million in cash.

1983
Mattel, Inc., says...

"Mattel's leadership in the toy industry is dramatically illustrated by the worldwide popularity of the Barbie doll, 25 years after introduction still the world's best-selling toy.

"Barbie, the best known and most successful toy product in history, celebrates her 25th anniversary in 1984.

"More than 200 million dolls in the Barbie family have been purchased around the world since 1959.

"More Barbie dolls were bought in the United States last year than there are little girls—14 million dolls for 11.5 million girls ages 3-9.

"The Barbie dolls, fashions, accessories and playsets stimulate a child's imagination and take her into a special world of her own.

"Mattel is the largest manufacturer of female apparel in the world. More than 20 million Barbie doll outfits are purchased each year."

(Source: 1984 Annual Report, for year ended January 28, 1984)

__Hawaiian Barbie__ was packaged with a windsurfer. She was made with the Steffie face mold.

The lead glamour doll was Twirly Curls Barbie (#5579). Capitalizing on previous successes with hair play dolls, Twirly Curls Barbie came with her own personal beauty parlor which included a special chair, barrettes, and Twirly Curler device. The doll was also available as Black Twirly Curls Barbie doll (#5723) and Hispanic Twirly Curls Barbie doll (#5724) versions.

Angel Face Barbie (#5640), new for 1983, came with makeup in its own case and hair accessories. She wore a Victorian-inspired dress with fuchsia pink skirt and white lace high-necked blouse with cameo brooch—"a perfect blend of yesterday and today," according to the 1983 Mattel Toys catalog. Cheesebrough-Pond's, cold cream king at the time, had a marketing tie-in with this doll.

This booklet covered the Barbie International Collection, the first edition of the International Barbie Dolls. Photos include: Parisian Barbie, Eskimo Barbie, Scottish Barbie, Swiss Barbie, Irish Barbie, Spanish Barbie, Oriental Barbie, Swedish Barbie, and Indian Barbie.

1983

◆ The Cabbage Patch doll creates pre-Christmas pandemonium. In a Pennsylvania store a woman suffered a broken leg in the push to get to the toy counter, where the toy department manager swung a baseball bat for protection.

◆ The final episode of "M*A*S*H," a long-running series on U.S. medics in the Korean War, was seen by the largest television audience to date for a non-sports program: 125,000,000 viewers.

◆ Astronaut Sally K. Ride becomes America's first woman in space as she and four colleagues blast off aboard the space shuttle Challenger.

In 1983, the new International Barbie dolls include the Spanish (#4031) and
the Swedish (#4032). The Spanish Barbie doll was the first to use the new
Spanish face mold.

Dream Date Barbie (#5868) set the trend for more glamour dolls later in the
decade (such as the JC Penney's customized dolls). Her hair was long and sleek,
and her red and purple ruffled gown came with a ruffle wrap that changed the
look of the outfit. The sequined top of the gown marked an early example of
sequins used on a Barbie doll fashion.

Horse Lovin' Barbie (#1757) continued the western fashion fad that persists
throughout the *Contemporary BARBIE* era. "Here come the dolls who love to ride
horses!" was the
introductory line
used to promote this
doll. Barbie came
equipped with
leather-like pants and
boots, as well as sad-
dlebags. Like the
Western Barbie of
1980, Horse Lovin'
Barbie also came with
an autograph stamp.

Crystal Barbie
*(right) was the
lead glamour doll
of 1984.*

Spanish Barbie
*(far right) wore a
lovely black man-
tilla and red dress.*

1984
Mattel, Inc., says. . .

"The United States toy industry sales in 1984 grew at a higher rate than in any year in recent history. Consumer purchases of traditional non-electronic toys were approximately 18 percent more than in 1983.

"Industry sales in 1985 and beyond will benefit from such demographic factors as the increasing birth rate, the larger percentage of first-born children, the increased disposable family income per child, the increasing incidence of three-parent families and the expanding population of grandparents.

"The popularity of Barbie extends around the world as little girls continue to enjoy role-playing with the Barbie family of dolls and accessories. Since her introduction in 1959, more than 250 million Barbie dolls have been purchased worldwide.

"Mattel's nationally-distributed Barbie and Masters of the Universe magazines are each expected to grow beyond the 1 million circulation mark in 1985."

(Source: Annual Report dated 12/29/84)

Barbie's 25th birthday was in 1984. This marked the last time the word "birthday" would be associated by Mattel with the period elapsed since Barbie's introduction in 1959. The press promoted this as "the year an American Legend turns 25." On Valentine's Day, 1984, Mayor Ed Koch of New York City named Fifth Avenue, "Barbie Boulevard." Tiffany & Co. commemorated Barbie's 25th anniversary with a sterling silver replica of the doll. At Toy Fair that year, hundreds of "Loving You Barbie" dolls adorned the Mattel Gallery.

The lead glamour doll was Crystal Barbie (#4598). The feature of this doll was her gown, made of a silver shimmery new fabric, and sparkly shoes (the companion Ken doll came with glittery socks). The doll was packaged with a child-size necklace for girls to wear, a feature that would be repeated with future dolls. The Crystal Barbie ensemble was the best-selling outfit to date in Barbie's entire ensemble.

Great Shape Barbie (#7025) represented the influence of aerobics and exercise on fashion. In addition to a turquoise spandex-style leotard and headband, she

1984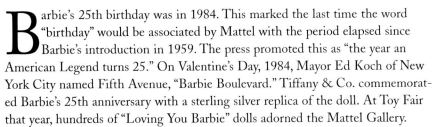

◆ The first black Miss America, Vanessa Williams, relinquishes her crown two months early after nude photographs of her are published in *Penthouse* magazine. She is the first pageant winner to give up her title.

◆ Democratic presidential candidate Walter Mondale chooses Geraldine Ferraro of New York to be his running mate. Ferraro is the first woman to run for vice president of the U.S. on a major-party ticket.

◆ Mattel gets rescue financing. Shareholders of Mattel Inc. approve a plan by which an investor group would put up $231 million for the ailing toy maker in return for a 45% share in the company.

*BillyBoy**'s **Le Nouveau Theatre de la Mode Barbie** poses on a Patron Original Christian Dior Paris design.*

came with a workout bag, striped leg warmers and ballet slippers. Exercises were illustrated on the package.

A new Happy Birthday Barbie (#1922) hit the market. Although numbered the same as the 1981 first version, this doll was dressed differently in a pink confetti-dotted party dress. The gift box packaged with the doll included a child-size, heart-shaped necklace.

New International Barbie dolls in 1984 included the Irish Barbie doll (#7517) and the Swiss Barbie doll (#7541).

1985
Mattel, Inc., says. . .

"Innovation means applying new ideas to concepts that have proven to be successful, a practice that has kept Barbie at the front of the fashion doll market for more than 27 years.

"Times change and so does the Barbie doll. Her ability to keep up-to-date is a key to her continuing success. Girls today can become anything they want to be, from a glamorous personality to astronaut to rock star, just like Barbie. Joining Barbie in her musical group are The Rockers, Diva, Dee Dee, Dana and Derek."

(Source: 1985 Annual Report)

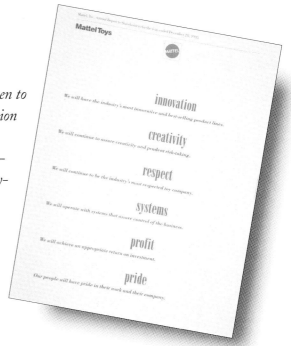

Thanks to Kitty Black-Perkins, the Barbie doll returned to the workplace in 1985 in the guise of one of the most important dolls to emerge in the 1980s: the Day-to-Night Barbie doll (#7929). This doll also came in both Black (#7945) and Hispanic (#7944) versions. She was outfitted in a pink suit with white lapels and wore a hat. Her accessories included a pink attaché case, shoulder bag, Chanel-inspired pink and white spectator pumps, a calculator, business cards, financial newspaper, a credit card, and jewelry. Girls playing at going to work helped to shape the Day-to-Night Barbie doll via focus group research. Her pink daytime

1985 ◆

◆ Rudi Gernreich, the fashion designer who introduced the topless bathing suit for women in the 1960s, died of cancer at the age of 62. Among his many innovative designs, he was also associated with the miniskirt, knit tank suits, colored stockings, the see-through blouse and unisex outfits.

◆ In a bold move, the Coca-Cola Company announces that it is abandoning its old formula and that Coke is now the "Real Thing." By July, complaints from cola lovers pressure the company to return to the original version, now named Coca-Cola Classic.

◆ Nancy Reagan and Raisa Gorbachev, wife of Soviet leader Mikhail S. Gorbachev, meet for the first time in Geneva, Switzerland. The first ladies, who shared an interest in fashion, met at Maison de Saussure, the 18th-century chateau that was home to the Reagans during their Geneva visit.

suit transformed into evening wear by reversing the skirt and removing the jacket. This marked the beginning of the "We Girls Can Do Anything" theme.

A treat for fans of haute couture fashion was BillyBoy*'s design of a new Barbie doll, the likes of which hadn't been seen since Barbie first hit the market in 1959. Le Nouveau Theatre de la Mode (#6279) Barbie doll exemplified the early era of Barbie doll fashions with a streamlined, tailored fashion that represents the essence of *Contemporary Barbie*. Le Nouveau Theatre de la Mode was developed in concert with BillyBoy*'s wish to commemorate Barbie's 25th anniversary through a special fashion show titled, "The New Theatre of Fashion." (For more insight into the marvels of BillyBoy*, refer to Chapter 7, Pure Couture).

These career dolls, designed by Kitty Black-Perkins, were dressed in tailored suits and came packaged with a nighttime ensemble just in case. Left to right: **Day to Night**–*Black,* **Day to Night**–*Blonde,* **Day to Night**–*Hispanic.*

MALIBU CHRISTIE wearing "SEARS REGULATION OLYMPIC OUTFIT," 1976

Well-educated, Barbie symbolizes women today.

smashing!" and "There's a new rock show on TV!"

As Barbie became more and more a definite personality through her packaging, fan magazine and small booklets which accompanied the doll, new characters appeared to befriend her. These dolls complemented actual cultural tendencies. They were CHRISTIE, who was black, CASEY, Francie's friend, STACY, Barbie's British friend and TWIGGY, London's Top Teen Model, the first doll modeled from a real fashion star.

In 1969, after only one year's absence, Ken was back with a completely new look. A huskier body, pinker skin, a handsome new face, and he could talk, too. He had new friends, such as BRAD. And by 1973, Ken had long hair and was called "Mod Hair Ken."

The 1970's opened with the most poseable doll ever—New Dramatic Living Barbie, who represented all the new tendencies of movement of the contemporary teenager. She could pose to dance, jump

and exercise. Live Action Dolls in 1971, could simulate dance and sold with their own stage, could perform live rock shows. In 1972, Talking Busy Barbie had hands that could hold, which was followed by the 1972 Walk Lively Dolls and the 1975 Free Moving Dolls, all representing actual interests of the moment.

The 1977 "Superstar Barbie" represented another evolution in the Barbie personality. Now she is an active "Superstar." The last part of the 70's until now, Barbie has lead a life of fashion, sports and fun. The 1985 Barbie represented a woman with many possibilities. Day-to-Night Barbie is an active business woman by day and a glamorous woman by night. She has a computer, as well as a calculator, a credit card, a business card, and international daily newspapers and magazines, all in an attaché case. She wears a pink suit that turns into a frothy evening dress. The idea of this most recent evolution of Barbie is, "We girls can do ANYTHING, right Barbie?" and that seems to say it all. Today's active woman is pos-

The BillyBoy* booklet that accompanied Le Nouveau Theatre de la Mode *featured a short history of the Barbie doll to 1985, along with many photos of fashions designed for the Barbie doll by BillyBoy*'s legendary couture designer friends.*

The first porcelain doll was introduced for the 1985/86 toy seasons. Known as Blue Rhapsody (#1708), it was made from the Superstar Barbie face mold. This was a milestone, notwithstanding the fact that many collectors "dissed" the doll: It was still the first Barbie doll made strictly for the adult market.

The only new International doll introduced in 1985 was the Japanese Barbie doll (#9481), which used the 1981 Oriental face mold.

The lead glamour doll was Peaches 'n Cream Barbie (#7926). Her peach-toned gown included the change-around ruffled stole successful in previous versions of glamour Barbie dolls. The doll included a "date spinner" which could be dialed to select a date (date themes included going to the theatre, attending the ballet performance or concert, going to a party, and other typically-teenage activities). This doll also came in Black Peaches 'n Cream Barbie doll version (#9516).

Complementing Barbie doll's career looks were fashion playsets such as the Vet Fun Fashion Playset (#9267) and the Travel Fashion Playset (#9264). In addition, the Barbie Home & Office structure was introduced in 1985. This portable case featured an office on one side and a bedroom on the other. The office included a fold-out desk, chair, computer and telephone.

Dreamtime Barbie (#9180) came packaged with a pink stuffed bear named B.B.—the first bear ever included with a Barbie doll.

This year, Barbie also received her first designer wardrobe from Oscar de la Renta. The designer created four gowns for Barbie, including a red satin dress with gold lamé flounce, a black and gold lamé dinner suit, a pink brocade ball gown, and a fuchsia and gold satin ensemble. "Barbie is the ideal customer," said de la Renta. "She looks like a perfect size 6, and she keeps her figure. She's the all-American girl." De la Renta's name would subsequently appear on six more gowns in 1986.

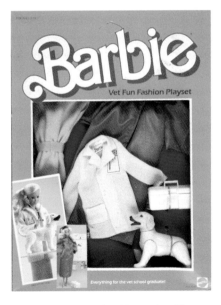

Barbie served the health needs of her legions of pets and horses when she became a veterinarian with this Vet Fun Fashion Playset in 1985.

UNICEF Barbie
*promotes global
goodwill.*

Chapter 3

CONTEMPORARY BARBIE®
SNAPSHOTS: 1986-1990

1986
Mattel, Inc., says. . .

"Our traditional continuing brands will always be an important factor in Mattel's success. Barbie, celebrating her 28th year, continues to set sales records and remains the worldwide standard in the fashion doll segment despite renewed competition.

"The breadth and depth of our product line have greatly improved for 1987. We expect to expand our leadership in the fashion doll market through our established Barbie brand and two new lines introduced in 1987—Spectra, fashion dolls from outer space, and Hot Looks, soft poseable larger dolls with an international fashion model theme.

"The Barbie doll, created in 1959, remains a legend. Having withstood the test of time, she continues to set sales records and remains the standard by which other fashion dolls are measured. More than 300 million dolls in the Barbie family have been sold since her debut. In 1986, Barbie emerged with a brand new look—a star in her own rock band. With her four rock-and-roll superstar friends, Barbie and the Rockers proved to be one of Mattel's most successful product line extensions.

"Mattel introduced the Spectra collection of fashion dolls from outer space early in 1987. Each of these 11.5" dolls has a shiny body and sparkly hair, is fully poseable, and comes dressed in a lacy fashion outfit. Space-age accessories combining beauty and fantasy provide hours of fun fashion play."

(Source: 1986 Annual Report)

1986

◆ Perry Ellis, top U.S. fashion designer who founded the "slouch look" in fashion, died at the age of 46, reportedly due to viral encephalitis. He was a participant in Billy Boy*'s 1985 Barbie fashion show, *Le Nouveau Theatre de la Mode.*

◆ The space shuttle Challenger explodes immediately after take-off from Cape Canaveral, killing all seven astronauts, including Christa McAuliffe, a schoolteacher who was the first private citizen picked to go into space.

The 1986 Mattel Toys catalog began with this introduction:
"This year, Barbie is more exciting than ever! She's doing more things,
going more places, taking on new challenges. One minute she's a glamorous movie star, the next she's a rock star. . . and then, she's an astronaut blasting
off into space! And whatever she does and wherever she goes, Barbie always looks
beautiful and elegant."

The lead glamour doll in 1986 was Magic Moves Barbie (#2126). By means of
a switch, this doll moved one or both arms through her hair. Her dramatic outfit

Magic Moves Barbie could
"magically" brush her hair.

Astronaut Barbie came in both Black and Caucasian variations.

was a glittery body suit and belt, long skirt, and fur-trimmed cape that could be fashioned as either a coat or a skirt. Also marketed was the Black Magic Moves Barbie (#2127).

The first career doll of the 1980s that wasn't a ballerina or a generic suited doll was Astronaut Barbie (#2449). This was not the Barbie doll's first venture into space—Barbie had been clad as an astronaut as far back as 1965, a full 20 years before anyone heard of Sally Ride. Designed by Carol Spencer, the 1986 version astronaut "is venturing beyond the world of fashion and glamour to exciting space exploration. She's dressed for first class travel in a glittery space suit that can change to a sparkly skirt and tights." Her accessories included a space helmet,

Greek Barbie *poses amidst classical urns.*

computer, flagpole, and two space maps that could be punched out of the package. The doll was also available as Black Astronaut Barbie (#1207). Additional Astro Fashions were offered for separate sale.

Sears celebrated its 100th anniversary in business in 1986 with the Celebration Barbie doll (#2998).

Also that year, the second porcelain Barbie doll—named Enchanted Evening—was issued.

The International dolls of 1986 included the Greek Barbie doll (#2997) and the Peruvian Barbie doll (#2995).

Dream Glow Barbie dolls came in Caucasian (right), Black (below) and Hispanic variations. The costumes glowed in the dark.

One of the first special effects Barbie dolls of the 1980s was Dream Glow Barbie (#2250). This doll was outfitted in a pink ruffled tiered gown with parasol—both adorned with stars that glowed in the dark. The ensemble also included glow-in-the-dark shoes. Fans of Dream Glow Barbie could also buy additional Dream Glow fashions. The Dream Glow Bed and Dream Glow Vanity completed the Dream Glow experience. The doll was also available as Black Dream Barbie (#2242).

This Barbie World of Fashion booklet illustrated **Dream Glow Barbie** *wearing various Dream Glow fashions. Note that even Ken's costume glowed!*

In addition to her demanding job as astronaut, Barbie doll had another career in 1986. She was the lead singer in a rock group, Barbie and the Rockers (#1140). Her eyelids were painted in neon purple and pink, and she was outfitted in a pink-and-silver lurex costume. Her ethnic colleagues in the band included Dee Dee, Dana, redheaded Diva, and Derek, the male member in this otherwise all-female rock group. In 1986, Rocker Barbie faced new competition in the fashion doll marketplace from Jem, Hasbro's "truly outrageous" 12-inch blonde punk goddess. Among several simultaneous vocations, Jem headed a rock group called "The Holograms" [See Sidebar]. It is interesting to note that the new face mold for Diva was also used for the first Native American Barbie doll (#1753) seven years later, in 1993.

*Barbie was an active rock and roller throughout the 1980s. This **Dancing Action** doll was the second Rocker Barbie issued.*

BARBIE VS. JEM — ROCK WARS

The Barbie doll's first serious competitor in some years emerged in 1986. Her name was Jem, and she had a rock band called the Holograms. Jem's manufacturer, Hasbro, Inc., invited little girls to enter a contest by dialing 1-800-ROCKGEM and singing the Jem theme song ("Jem is truly outrageous, truly, truly, truly outrageous . . ."). So many girls called that the phone company had to install extra lines.

By 1986, MTV, the music cable television channel, had grown enormously popular. Rock videos introduced little girls to a whole new way of thinking about fashion: Eight-year-olds were asking their moms if they could dye their hair pink and cut holes in their sweatshirts and do a lot of other things that Barbie didn't do. It occurred to people at Hasbro that there might be a market for a fashion doll that looked less like Barbie and more like the people on MTV.

Hasbro created an entire history for their creation: Jem. By day she was Jerrica Benton, co-owner of Star Light Music Company and benefactor of Starlight House, a shelter for homeless girls. By night, she was rendered Jem, through the magic of "Synergy," a super-holographic computer that filtered power through her Jem Star earrings. As Jem, she was "a truly outrageous rock singing sensation," according to her own press.

Just as Rocker Barbie had a back-up band that included Dee Dee, Dana, Diva and Derek, Jem had the help of her little sister, Kimber, and friends Aja and Shana. Together, they were known as "Jem and the Holograms." Adventures unfolded as Jerrica competed for control of Star Light Music against evil co-owner Eric Raymond; while Jem and the Holograms came up against the mischievous "bad-girl" rock band, "The Misfits."

By 1986, Mattel got more explicit with an adult-targeted marketing strategy and created a new division called Timeless Creations. The idea was to manufacture a line of higher quality collector dolls for the discriminating collector. These would include the Porcelain Series, the Bob Mackie Collection and others. The sales channels for some of these dolls focused on direct-to-consumer marketing, such as advertisements in mass market magazines (e.g., *Sunday Parade*) as well as specialty doll publications (e.g., *Doll Collector, Barbie Bazaar*).

Tropical Barbie, notable for her exceptionally long hair, appeared in 1986 with a special friend, Tropical Miko (#2056), whose face mold is that of a beautiful Pacific Islander. Tropical Barbie also came in a Black Tropical Barbie version (#1022).

Gift Giving Barbie (#1922) was 1986's version of the Happy Birthday Barbie doll. Wearing a purple and pink ruffled dress, she came with three little boxes and matching stickers that could be used for gift wrapping. In addition, a pink child-sized charm and ribbon were included in the package.

Factoid

Fifty-four dolls have been designated as Barbie and Ken's family and friends.

FROM JEM TO TEACHER BARBIE IN A DECADE

When Mattel got wind of an attempt by arch rival Hasbro to launch a new rock-and-roll doll called "Jem and the Holograms," Ms. Barad's boss, then executive vice president Judy Shackelford, put her in charge of developing the counter-strike: "Rocker Barbie." Ms. Barad and her team managed to produce the doll in just four months in 1986, one-third of the normal development time. It immediately trounced Hasbro's version.

Top management took notice. Mattel had initiated a market segmentation strategy, but it was limited to three different dolls a year, maximum. Jill Barad took the concept to a new level. An executive who worked with her at the time said, "She understood kids, girls, retail, and American fashion, and could spot the right advertising approach."

Even as President of the company, Ms. Barad took a hands-on approach to Barbie. When Mattel was considering a new schoolteacher version of the doll in 1994, Ms. Barad saw that something was missing: Barbie had glasses, chalk and a blackboard, but, "I thought, 'where are the students?'" Ms. Barad says. She proposed adding a talking feature to the doll and packaging her with two student dolls with desks of their own. The additions meant increasing the price from $12.99 to more than $20. But she was right again. More than four million Teacher Barbie dolls were sold in two years.

SOURCE: *The Wall Street Journal,* 5 March 1997, pA-1

1987
Mattel, Inc., says. . .

*"We're pleased with Mattel's 1988 product line which features innovative
breakthroughs in our major toy categories. With Perfume Pretty
Barbie, Mattel continues to strengthen its well-established fashion
doll line. Barbie remains the highest volume brand in the industry, due in no small part to our ability to reintroduce the product
line year-after-year to fit the current life-styles of girls.*

*"Mattel created the fashion doll toy category 29 years ago
with the introduction of the Barbie doll. Today, the World of
Barbie is a collection of dolls, fashions and accessories to delight
little girls everywhere. Additions to the line this year include
Perfume Pretty Barbie doll, and California Dream Barbie
Surf 'N Shop playset and Beach Taxi vehicle."*

(Source: 1987 Annual Report)

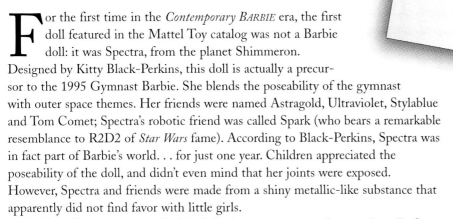

For the first time in the *Contemporary BARBIE* era, the first
doll featured in the Mattel Toy catalog was not a Barbie
doll: it was Spectra, from the planet Shimmeron.
Designed by Kitty Black-Perkins, this doll is actually a precursor to the 1995 Gymnast Barbie. She blends the poseability of the gymnast
with outer space themes. Her friends were named Astragold, Ultraviolet, Stylablue
and Tom Comet; Spectra's robotic friend was called Spark (who bears a remarkable
resemblance to R2D2 of *Star Wars* fame). According to Black-Perkins, Spectra was
in fact part of Barbie's world. . . for just one year. Children appreciated the
poseability of the doll, and didn't even mind that her joints were exposed.
However, Spectra and friends were made from a shiny metallic-like substance that
apparently did not find favor with little girls.

In Mattel's 1987 catalog, Barbie dolls do not appear until page 69, well after
Popples, Color Clicks, Lady Lovelylocks and the Pixietails, The Heart Family,
Princess of Power, and Baby Heather. The positioning of the Barbie and family
dolls so far into the catalog suggests that Mattel did not prioritize the Barbie

1987 ●

◆ Nancy Lopez is inducted
into the Ladies Professional
Golf Association Hall of
Fame when she wins her
35th career victory. Her first
tournament win came in
1977.

◆ The Supreme Court rules (7-
0) that women must be admitted to Rotary Clubs, hitherto all
male. On July 4, Lions Club
International votes to admit
women and on July 7 Kiwanis
International followed suit.

◆ Mary R. Stout, a former U.S. Army
nurse, becomes the first woman to
head a national veterans' organization: the Vietnam Veterans of America.
At the time she was elected, the organization had 35,000 members, only
about 300 of whom were women.

◆ Aretha
Franklin is the
first woman to
be inducted
into the Rock
and Roll Hall of
Fame.

FROM OUTER SPACE ALIENS TO GYMNAST BARBIE

Kitty Black-Perkins related this interesting piece of Barbie doll design history: "In 1990, we did a doll called Spectra. She was not a part of Barbie's world, but a little outer space doll with friends. She was a resurgence of the poseable dolls, Young Sweethearts, that we previously did. If you look at Spectra, she has poseable knees and elbows. The difference is the vacuum metal on the body. The poseable knees and elbows concerned us, and we wondered whether it would bother kids. With our Barbie doll, we have always been so particular about how she looks. When we did research we found out that kids wanted Barbie to do the things that they could do. So with that in mind, we wanted to give her things to do that would emphasize her new movement. The kids really do think that Gymnast Barbie can do the same things that they can do. She was launched worldwide and she's doing great! Based on her success, we will probably design a poseable doll every year from now on."

SOURCE: Author's interview with Kitty Black-Perkins, August 1995.

Spectra, from the planet Shimmeron, was an early precursor to Gymnast Barbie.

brand that year. It was, in fact, a difficult year for Mattel and the company underwent a full-scale reorganization. It was also, according to Mattel's annual report, "one of [the] worst years in [the toy industry's] history" overall.

The lead glamour doll in 1987 was Jewel Secrets Barbie (#1737). This doll came with a 24-page storybook, describing the tale of Barbie and the Jewel Secrets. The skirt of her pink-and-silver shimmery gown was transformed into a little girl's purse. Under the floor-length skirt, Barbie wore a miniskirt with a changeable ruffle. Her choker-style necklace was adorned with "gems" that

Jewel Secrets Barbie *poses with and without her long bag-skirt.*

changed colors at the touch of a dial. The doll also was available as Black Jewel Secrets Barbie (#1756).

BillyBoy* designed his second and final Barbie doll this year. The Feelin' Groovy (#3421) doll, subtitled "Glamour-a-Go-Go," was very *au courant*, including a tailored fuchsia and black costume and black aviator-style sunglasses.

The American Beauties collection kicked off with Mardi Gras Barbie (#4930) in 1987.

Funtime Barbie (#1738 blonde wearing blue outfit, #3718 blonde wearing pink outfit, #3717 blonde wearing lavender outfit, #1739 Black wearing pink outfit) came with her own digital watch. Her outfit was a two-piece short set with a clock motif on the top. She also came with pastel-colored sun glasses.

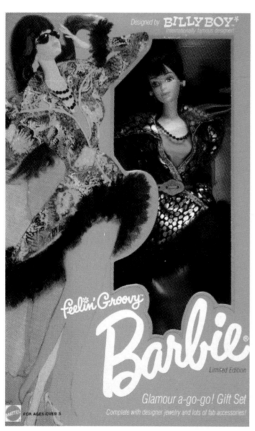
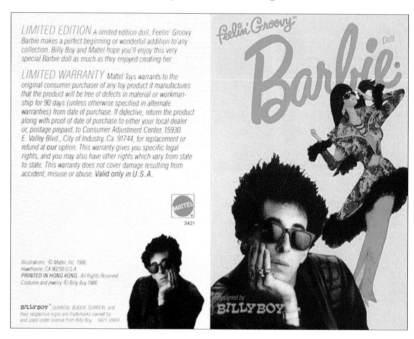

This booklet (top left) came packaged with the **Feelin' Groovy Barbie** doll and featured a photo of BillyBoy* on the front and back covers. The inside of the Feelin' Groovy Barbie booklet (left) described the mystical origins of BillyBoy* along with his credo, "Life is fabulous." Feelin' Groovy Barbie was designed to reflect that attitude.

The Barbie doll continued rockin' out as a Rocker, but in the form of a hyperactive Dance Action Rocker (#3654). When the doll's waist was tilted, her arms moved up and down, "just like they're really dancin'!" Ken doll (looking much like the actor Richard Dean Anderson of MacGyver fame) joined Derek as the second male in the band. The dolls came packaged with a cassette of their "hit" songs.

Wal-Mart celebrated the company's 25th anniversary with the Pink Jubilee Barbie doll (#4589). She was dressed in a long pink gown with an adjustable pink feather boa and silver accessories.

In 1987, the International dolls included the German Barbie doll (#3188) and the Icelandic Barbie doll (#3189).

1988
Mattel, Inc., says. . .

(On the cover: 1959 Barbie in Solo in the Spotlight and 1989 SuperStar Barbie)

"It was the best year ever for Barbie. Fresh new advertising drove consumers to the stores, where U.S. sales were up by more than 30 percent.

"A 30-year success, she's known worldwide as the most popular doll of all time. More than 500 million Barbie dolls have been produced to date, and 90 percent of all girls age 3 to 11 in the U.S. own at least one.

"Retailers were skeptical in 1959, but consumers left no doubt. . .they loved Barbie. The fashion doll category was created overnight, and she has dominated it since. First there were fashions, then friends, careers, and accessories. She's a new doll every year, and yet she's always glamorous and fun—she's always Barbie. Imagination is the key, the imagination of little girls. They can role-play and rehearse their fantasies and their futures. Even in a world of high-tech and fast pace, it's imagination that makes little girls grow. In 1989, there are more than 250 individual Barbie packages, including 32 different dolls, 153 fashions and 43 accessories. The attention to detail that distinguished the original concept continues to set Barbie apart today. From sculpting and face paint to hair styling, jewelry and wardrobe, she sets the standard."

(Source: 1988 Annual Report)

The biggest news this year actually happened at year's end: The introduction of the 1988 Holiday Barbie doll. First in the series, the doll was fairly limited in number. They quickly disappeared from the toy store shelves. (For more on the background of Happy Holidays Barbie, see sidebar in Chapter 1, *Contemporary BARBIE* History).

*On anyone's list, this **1988 Happy Holidays Barbie** doll is among the treasures issued in the* Contemporary Barbie *era. By Christmas of 1995, offers as high as $750 for this doll were seen on the Internet.*

In Mattel Toys' 1988 catalog, the Barbie doll is brought back to page 1 in a full-head photograph of Perfume Pretty Barbie. Perfume Pretty was designed by Cynthia Young, who received a Doll of the Year award for the doll. Young reminisced: "The very first doll that I designed after joining Mattel was Perfume Pretty. That was our lead glamour doll of the year. She was ultra feminine, a little girl's dream." Young recalled that the doll came with a "real Barbie fragrance," actually designed by a Paris-based parfumier. Once the parfumier mixed the ultimate fragrance, the entire Mattel design team was given full-sized flaçons of perfume. Perfume Pretty also came in a Black version (#4552). The Black doll uses what collectors refer to as the "New Black" face mold first used in the Christie doll of 1988.

No one-hit-wonder pop phenomenon, the Barbie doll succeeded for a third year in a row in the rock star incarnation of Barbie and the Sensations (#4931). Retro fever was hitting the fashion world with Yves St. Laurent's flower power loose floral shirts for evening wear and Jean-Paul Gaultier's adoption of thick-soled Doc Martens shoes. This doll and her all-girl group went retro with '50s-style fashions, including saddle shoes, white ruffled bobby sox, and short skirts with net petticoats (except for Bopsy, who wore pedal pushers). In addition, the dolls wore glasses in a shape reminiscent of the Barbie doll's first pair of "cat's-eye" glasses from 1959. Sensations Barbie's colleagues in the band included Belinda (a Black doll) and Becky (an Asian doll). Like Rocker Barbie, Sensations Barbie came packaged with a cassette tape of the group's hit songs.

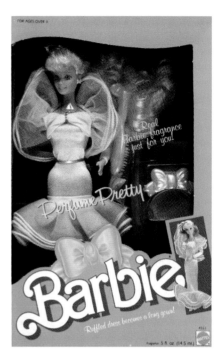

Perfume Pretty Barbie, *designed by Cynthia Young, was packaged with specially-designed perfume created especially for the doll and its customers.*

Do Ken & Barbie Share a Closet?

"Carina Guillot and her 12-year-old daughter, Jocelyn, stepped into a Tampa, Fla., toy store and picked out a 'My First Ken' doll. It was wearing a purple tank top and lace apron over a turquoise and purple skirt.

"'Oh, my God,' said Guillot, 'Now we have a cross-dressed Ken.'

"Clerks checked this one out, as you can imagine, but could find no tampering with the package.

"Reporters at the scene went straight to the miniature transvestite's birthplace—Mattel Inc.—where spokeswoman Donna Gibbs gave them the strangest look and said, 'I'd guess it slipped through.'

"Then she offered to replace the doll. 'Nothing doing,' answered Guillot: 'This is like a real collector's item.'"

SOURCE: San Jose *Mercury News,* July 23, 1990

1988 ◆

◆ The word "Tomboy" is obsolete, according to a Penn State University professor who reported that 82% of young women participate in sports.

◆ After nine years in power, Margaret Thatcher becomes Britain's longest continuously serving prime minister of the twentieth century.

◆ There are now 10,513 McDonald's restaurants world-wide, but Pepsi's combined restaurants (Pizza Hut, Taco Bell and Kentucky Fried Chicken) total 17,373.

◆ America's last Playboy Club, in Lansing, Michigan, closes. The first Playboy club opened in Chicago in 1960, and there were once 22 such establishments throughout the country.

Doctor Barbie (#3850) emerged in 1988. She carried a kit of 20 medical supplies including a stethoscope, blood pressure gauge, doctor's bag, water pitcher, tumbler and tray for the hospital bedside, and other pieces. Consistent with the Barbie doll's previous careers of the 1980s, Doctor Barbie came outfitted with both a doctor's white coat along with a party dress for evening glamour. No Black Doctor Barbie was issued this year, but Nurse Whitney (undoubtedly Doctor Barbie's right hand in surgery) was Black.

Animal Lovin' Barbie was based on the prevailing themes of environmentalism and animal rights. Barbie came packaged with a panda bear. Zizi Zebra and Ginger Giraffe (each with long, brushable hair) and friends could be purchased separately. In classic Barbie style, Animal Lovin' Barbie wore a leopard-print ensemble accented with golden lurex thread, perfect for those glamorous anthropological outings!

Factoid

During the summer of 1988, the premiere issue of Barbie Bazaar *magazine is published.*

*Echoing environmental and pro-animal rights sentiments, **Animal Lovin' Barbie** was outfitted in a glitzy safari outfit (note the pink high topped hiking boots) and came packaged with her panda bear friend.*

In 1988, the International dolls included the Canadian Barbie doll (#4928), wearing an authentic uniform of the Canadian Mounted Police, and, the Korean Barbie doll (#4929). The Korean doll used the 1981 Oriental face mold.

California Barbie doll (#4439) came with a Beach Boys' record written especially for the doll. Under her colorful clothes, Barbie wore a swimsuit and she came packaged with a comic book, record, sun visor, sunglasses, camera and other accessories.

***Canadian Barbie** (above), was dressed as a Royal Canadian Mounted Police woman.*
***California Barbie** (above left) was accompanied by tunes from the Beach Boys which were included in the package. Note the innovative packaging with the two beach chairs and palm tree at the bottom.*

1989
Mattel, Inc., says. . .

"Highlights from the more than 800 toys in the company's 1990 product line demonstrate the innovation and play value which consumers expect from Mattel. A new line each year generates excitement, and produces demand. Western Fun is the theme for a new Barbie line which captures the popular fashion style of the American Southwest. Longtime friend Ken and new friend Nia are outfitted in boots, suede, and big-buckle belts. An Ice Cream Fun set makes real ice cream, and a doll in a gold-sequined gown by designer Bob Mackie is the first in a new Barbie collector series. . . .

"We have a significant number of enduring consumer franchises at Mattel which have sold well over time. These core products provide stability in what can be a volatile industry.

"At the top of the list, of course, is Barbie. Sales for Barbie products have increased $160 million in two years, from $430 million in 1987 to $590 million in 1989—impressive growth for a consumer franchise in its 29th and 30th year."

(Source: 1989 Annual Report)

The year 1989 was a pivotal one for Barbie collecting. It ushered in Barbie's 30th anniversary—an occasion celebrated in grand style with a Thirtieth Anniversary Pink Jubilee party for Barbie at Lincoln Center in New York City in February. Some 1,200 special guests and members of the press were invited by way of a special silver tray with an engraved invitation. The Pink Jubilee doll was packaged in a plain white box with the Barbie/Mattel logo on the face and wrapped with a large pink ribbon. Each doll was numbered, and only 1,200 were ever made. The doll wore a

1989 •

◆ The Berlin Wall is opened, and for the next few days hundreds of thousands of East Germans stream into West Berlin. This is taken as evidence that the long Cold War is finally over.

◆ Giorgio di Sant'Angelo, fashion designer noted for avant-garde accessories and clothing styles, died at the age of 56 of lung cancer. He created innovative fashions in the 1960s that included gypsy and Native American styles.

◆ For the first time, compact discs surpass the sales of vinyl albums.

◆ The richest man in the U.S., according to *Forbes* magazine, was Sam Moore Walton, founder of Wal-Mart stores. Walton is said to be worth $8,700,000,000.

Barbie's 30th anniversary magazine featured this comprehensive Barbie family tree.

rose-colored gown with a tulle overskirt spangled in silver stars. A pink feather boa and lavish earrings completed the look. One reporter commented that, "No one else in the crowd—which included toy manufacturers, collectors and Barbie fans— looked nearly as ravishing."

Mattel also helped the mass of Barbie collectors celebrate the doll's 30th anniversary. A nostalgic licensing program was launched, and many companies

THE BARBIE LIBERATION ORGANIZATION

In 1989, the Barbie Liberation Organization (BLO), an amorphous group of activists and self-proclaimed media intervention superstars, switched the voice boxes in 300 Talking Barbie dolls and Talking G.I. Joe dolls during the Christmas season. The goal of the action was to reveal and correct the problem of gender-based stereotyping in children's toys. The corrected G.I. Joe doll said

things like, "I love school! Don't you?" and "Let's sing with the band tonight." The liberated Barbie doll said, "Dead men tell no lies." The mainstream media latched onto the scheme and a legend was born.

SOURCE: *Brillo, Cleaning Up The Web*, Issue #1: Armed and Dangerous—Hacking Barbie with the Barbie Liberation Organization.

UNICEF Barbie—done in Black, Asian, Caucasian, and Hispanic variations— appeals to the universal character of all children. This was the first Barbie doll to be offered in four ethnic versions.

were granted permission to use the nostalgic image on products. Clay Art made a Barbie mask, picture frame and mug; Leaverly Greetings made greeting cards; American Postcard Company created full color Barbie doll postcards. Life size Barbie doll mannequins were known to welcome customers into department stores where Barbie doll pendants, watches and t-shirts were being sold.

Barbie also went political in 1989. The UNICEF Barbie doll was offered in a record four variations, all called "Barbie." UNICEF Barbie doll was manufactured as Asian (#4774), Black (#4770), Caucasian/blonde (#1920), and Hispanic (#4782).

FAO Schwarz offered its first customized doll in the form of Golden Greetings Barbie (#7734). The chain's entré into Barbie's world would be followed annually by many more, and equally successful, customized Barbie dolls.

The 1989 International dolls included the Mexican Barbie doll (#1917) and the Russian Barbie doll (#1916)—the latter doll reflecting the softening of Cold War era tensions.

The American Beauties collection issued its second and final in the series, the Army Barbie doll (#3966).

***American Beauties Army Barbie**
(left) was the last in the series. The
first **Russian Barbie** doll (right) was
issued when "Russia" was still a
synonym for the entire Soviet
Union.*

HOT DATE: BARBIE AND G.I. JOE

"Anniversaries honor an American love affair. When the first generation of Barbie doll consumers was playing with Barbie, they were also playing with Tressy and boys were playing with G.I. Joe. The 1970s were not the best of times for Barbie and G.I. Joe; too many people burning bras and draft cards. Barbie's sales dropped. Mattel learned that parents of that era wanted more creative, less commercial toys, like paint sets or clay. Hasbro, manufacturers of G.I. Joe, took him off the market completely in 1978. They said he was being 'furloughed' because of the rising price of oil, a major component of plastic. But the real problem may have been the still-fresh memory of soldiers coming home in body bags. War toys weren't fun.

"But by 1989, all that changed. Barbie and G.I. Joe were back on the list of all-time toy best sellers. Barbie turned 30 in February 1989, and Mattel went all-out with a black-tie birthday bash at Lincoln Center in New York. The invitations were shocking-pink paper affixed to a silver platter."

SOURCE: *Newsweek*, February 20 1989, p 59

1989 ◆ ◆ ◆ ◆ ◆ ◆ ◆ ◆ ◆ ◆ ◆ ◆ ◆ ◆ ◆ ◆ ◆

◆ Rap's big breakthrough comes in January with the debut of "Yo! MTV Raps" on MTV. A rap star, Fresh Prince, gets his own TV sit-com ("The Fresh Prince of Bel-Air"); and a rap duo, Kid 'N' Play, stars in movies such as *House Party* and its sequel, *Class Act*. Rap finally entered advertising jingles for everything from family cars to refrigerated crescent roll dough.

◆ There is a moment, early one morning this year, when the time is 1:23:45-6/7/89.

1990
Mattel, Inc., says. . .

"Barbie is the preeminent brand of the toy industry, and one of the most universally recognized consumer products in the world today. Ongoing changes keep Barbie in step with the latest trends. In 1990, for instance, the doll hosted an international Children's Summit where children from 28 countries discussed issues relevant to them. Their deliberations identified world peace as a principal concern, and Mattel donated funds to this cause.

"Worldwide, Barbie gross revenues in the product's 31st year reached $740 million, up from $600 million in 1989, $485 million in 1988 and $430 million in 1987. This growth of more than 70 percent in three years demonstrates the success of our efforts to further expand a toy franchise that is second to none.

"Mattel today has marketing organizations in 23 countries around the world. . . . Eastern Europe presents a new growth opportunity. New Mattel offices were opened in Berlin, Budapest and Prague during 1990, and Mattel was the first toy company to advertise when the barriers fell.

"There are 71 million children from birth through age 10 in Europe, versus 40 million in the United States.

"At the company's principal Barbie manufacturing plant in Kuala Lumpur, for instance, Barbie dolls are produced on an automated production line which integrates assembly, hair rooting, grooming, sewing and packaging."

(Source: 1990 Annual Report)

1990 •

◆ Halston, top American fashion designer in the 1970s, died of AIDS at the age of 57. He became famous as the milliner who created the pillbox-style hat worn by former first lady Jacqueline Kennedy for her husband's inauguration in 1961.

◆ The 1990 Census reports that the population of the U.S. in 1990 is 249,632,692 —a 10.2% increase over 1980.

◆ Between 1980 and 1990, women's earnings increased from 64 cents per male dollar to 72 cents per male dollar. However, the narrowing of the female-male earnings ratio is in part accountable to a drop in male earnings during the period.

◆ For the first time ever, the top five positions in the U.S. singles record chart are held by female artists. The hitmakers include Madonna, Heart, Sinead O'Connor, Wilson Phillips, and Janet Jackson.

By 1990, Barbie dolls were commanding increasing shelf space at retail stores, particularly in giant retailers such as Toys 'R Us, Kmart and Wal-Mart Stores. As important, Barbie began to make a big splash in a new pond. Friendship "Freudenschafts" Barbie (#5506) made her debut in East Berlin, Budapest and emerging Central European markets. Priced at around $5, she did not contribute much to Mattel's bottom line, but she did help make the point to the industry that Mattel was committed to overseas expansion in new markets.

Back on home turf, Dance Magic Barbie (#4836) was the lead glamour doll in this anniversary year. Her ball gown could be detached to reveal a ballerina tutu, or it could be attached in the back for a salsa train, capitalizing on the dance trend of the moment. Her lip color changed from pink to rose with ice water,

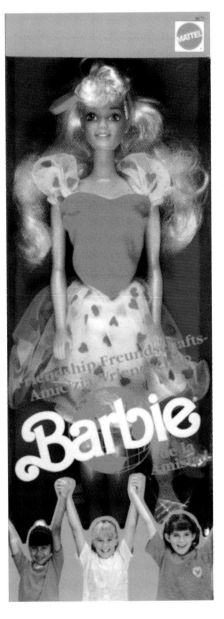

*These two **Freudenschafts Barbie** dolls were developed for the global market. They commemorated the fall of the Berlin Wall. At left is Berlin Wall #1 (1990) with friendship heart theme. Berlin Wall #2 (1991) is at right.*

BARBIE BEATS BRINKLEY

People magazine reported that models Christie Brinkley, Beverly Johnson and Cheryl Tiegs approached Matchbox Toys to create a line of dolls called the Real Model Collection. "I'd been approached many times about becoming a doll," Brinkley said, but she had always turned down the offer.

The dolls were unveiled at the 1990 annual toy fair in New York City. The dolls were Barbie-doll-sized, priced at $13.99 each, and had available additional outfits, a mini-photo studio and a 35-inch limousine complete with a whirlpool bath.

To help create vinyl doll models of the real-life personalities, Matchbox enlisted the advice of Joyce Christopher, who crafted the original Barbie doll.

Cheryl Tiegs is reported to have said: "It's strange having something look so much like you."

SOURCE: *People,* Feb 12, 1990 v33 n6 p116(2)

and changed back with warm water. The doll was also available as Black Dance Magic Barbie (#7080) version.

Flight Time Barbie doll (#9584) had flight wings. Serving her first stint as a pilot, the Barbie doll could also double as a flight attendant by changing her tie into a scarf. Her third costume variation was a ruffly skirt for parties. The package included doll-sized luggage and a child-size set of airline wings. Also available were Black Flight Time Barbie (#9916) and Hispanic Flight Time Barbie (#2066).

Summit Barbie doll, like the 1989 UNICEF Barbie doll, was featured in four variations. They included the Asian (#7029), Black (#7028), Caucasian-blonde (#7027) and Hispanic (#7030). Mattel designed the Summit Barbie doll as part of the Barbie Children's Summit, which brought 40 youngsters from 28 countries together to discuss the most important issues facing the world's children.

The Wet 'n Wild Barbie doll (#4103) had a special effect swimsuit that changed color in icy water. All 1990 dolls had extra-long hair. There was no Black Wet 'n Wild Barbie doll; the Black Christie Wet 'n Wild doll was #4121.

A popular doll with young girls—Ice Capades™ Barbie doll (#7365)—came adorned in lace skating skirt, glittery leotard and headdress, and ice skates. The doll's costume was transformed into human-size proportions by the Ice Capades touring company and was featured in road performances throughout the country.

1990 was yet another year of rock stardom for Barbie doll and friends. In 1990, Barbie and the Beat hit the top of the charts. Beat Barbie (#2751) came with a leather-look outfit, guitar and cassette tape with Beat music. Her clothes glowed in the dark, depending on the amount of light used. Midge and Christie joined Barbie doll in the Beat trio.

Barbie doll cruised the skies in 1961 as an American Airlines flight attendant. Now, here she is piloting the plane as **Flight Time Barbie***.*

1990 ◆

◆ Following a heated controversy, the Professional Golfers Association announces that it will not hold tournaments at clubs that have exclusionary policies based on race or sex.

◆ Margaret Thatcher, the longest-serving British prime minister of the 20th century, announces her resignation. She had been elected prime minister in May 1979. Her term in office—more than 11 years and 29 weeks—was the fifth-longest consecutive term in British history and the seventh longest overall.

SUMMIT BARBIE

In late November 1990, Mattel invited 40 children from 28 countries as far away as the Philippines, South Africa and the Soviet Union to the first Barbie Summit. Held in New York's Waldorf-Astoria Hotel, the conference featured tots as young as 6 years old discussing world hunger, degradation of the environment, and war and peace issues.

Televised advertising for the event—based on the theme "Together we can do it"—was launched November 9, 1990, in both 30- and 60-second versions tied in with Barbie Summit Month promotions. Mattel contributed a percentage of the profits from every Barbie doll sold in November 1990 to charity, with the minimum contribution set at $500,000.

Throughout the month of November, ballots were available at toy stores throughout the U.S. for children to express their opinion on what they felt was the most pressing issue facing the world. The ballots were tallied, and the results were reported to children attending the November 19 Barbie Summit.

Mattel's idea for creating the Barbie Summit and the accompanying television ad campaign was an indirect result of the fall of the Berlin Wall. Mattel's management team was impressed with photos of Anika Polzin, a six-year-old whose first goal after crossing into West Germany was to buy a Barbie doll. Polzin was invited to the Barbie Summit as an honorary delegate.

The other 40 delegates—including the eight-member delegation from the U.S.—were selected by the editors of Scholastic Inc., a New York based educational publishing company. The firm judged original artwork entries depicting a better world which were submitted by first- through fourth-grade students worldwide.

All delegations to the Summit rode on a float in the 1990 Macy's Thanksgiving Day parade.

Mattel hosted a children's summit in 1990 to air issues relevant to children from around the world. This was clearly one way of many that Mattel could "give back" to its global community.

Dance Club Barbie doll (#3509) was said to be a dancer on the latest TV dance show, á la "Soul Train." This Barbie doll and her Dance Club compatriots (Ken, Kayla and Devon) each came packaged with their own audio cassettes. The Hot Dancin'™ Set (#4841) was offered separately and it included a VHS videotape, dance lessons on doing "The BARBIE" dance, and a guest appearance by Paula Abdul. A special Child World limited edition of Dance Club Barbie (#4917) included a blue cassette player with a strap and working karaoke-type microphone. An audio cassette included in the package featured "Barbie" singing "Doin' the Barbie," "Our Game," and "Dreamin'."

Continuing the Great Shape aerobics theme established in 1984, the Barbie and the All Stars (#9099) Barbie doll of 1990 came ready to work out in exercise gear. The doll carried an exercise bag for sports gear, along with an appropriate post-exercise party fashion. All Stars fashions, sold separately, provided various sporting attire including tennis, weight-training, skateboarding and skiing.

Dance Club Barbie *from 1990 was packaged with an audio cassette.*

FINALLY, BARBIE DOLL ADS GO ETHNIC

"For more than 30 years, Mattel's Barbie has been one of the best-selling dolls in the country. There are Hispanic Barbies, Black Barbies, Asian Barbies and, of course, White Barbies. Yet the only doll featured in its print and TV ads is a fair-skinned, blue-eyed lass who tools around in a fancy sports car and changes her designer clothes faster than you can say Oscar de la Renta.

"Starting Fall, 1990, Barbie ads went ethnic. Mattel announced it would launch an ad campaign for the Black and Hispanic versions of the popular doll. With an eye toward capitalizing on ethnic spending power, Mattel featured multicultural Barbies in such outlets as *Essence* magazine and on 'Pepe Plata,' a children's show. It also included Barbie's ethnic sisters in some network spots.

"Why the slowness in integrating Barbie's dollhouse? Whatever the reason, the company can no longer ignore ethnic markets. Hispanics buy about $170 billion worth of goods each year, and Blacks spend even more."

SOURCE: *Newsweek,* August 13, 1990

FAO Schwarz honored Barbie as the Statue of Liberty with the doll **Liberty Belle.**

What can you say about a doll designed by the guy who outfitted Cher, Carol Burnett, and countless Broadway casts? You say, "Bob Mackie," you think, "glitz and glamour," and you count the Bob Mackie Gold Barbie doll among your all-time favorites!

Chapter 4

CONTEMPORARY BARBIE®
SNAPSHOTS: 1991-PRESENT

1991
Mattel, Inc., says. . .

"1991 turned out to be the best year in the history of our company. Our belief that the Barbie doll was an undermarketed brand with tremendous growth potential has proven to be correct. We've nearly doubled our Barbie sales volume to $840 million in four short years.

"Barbie products reached $840 million in Mattel sales volume during 1991, nearly doubling the $430 million in sales that this principal core brand generated just four years ago in 1987. More than 50 million doll units were produced in 1991, ranging from low-cost dolls starting at about $6 each to holiday and birthday dolls retailing for about $30 and collector dolls selling for more than $200. Fashions and accessories also contribute to the success of this 33-year-old brand franchise, as do new "Barbie for Girls" consumer products including everything from shoes and clothing to linens, backpacks and furniture. A cosmetics and work-out videotape take Barbie to new dimensions, and in 1992 the world's favorite doll will even speak.

"A 1991 Mattel/McDonald's Happy Meal promotion was a great success. More than 45 million Barbie and Hot Wheels premiums were distributed in three weeks, along with coupons for dollars off on Mattel products. . . ."

(Source: 1991 Annual Report)

1991

◆ Almost 66% of married women are working or looking for work this year, as compared with 46% in 1973.

◆ The first world championship of women's soccer is won in Guangzhou, China, by the U.S., which defeats Norway, 2-1.

◆ Jack Ryan, an inventor who worked for Raytheon Co. and for Mattel Inc., died. He designed the best-selling Barbie doll, as well as the Chatty Cathy doll and Hot Wheels toy cars, and was at one time married to actress Zsa Zsa Gabor.

Bob
Mackie 1990

This year signified a major transition in Mattel's Barbie doll marketing strategy: Several key lines were introduced that were explicitly targeted to adult collectors, emphasizing John Amerman's belief that the doll was previously "undermarketed."

The most significant event in 1990/91 Barbie doll history was the introduction of Bob Mackie Designer Barbie® dolls—the first vinyl collection of Barbie dolls explicitly designed for the adult collector. By late 1991, three glamorous Mackie designs were introduced: the Gold Barbie doll (#5405), the Platinum Barbie doll (#2703) and the Black Barbie doll (#2704), which was also known to collectors as Starlight Splendor. Janet Goldblatt, veteran Barbie doll designer, worked directly with Mackie in 1990 to help bring his series to market. While Mattel had introduced porcelain Barbie dolls in the latter 1980s, the Bob Mackie Barbie dolls ushered in a truly new level of Barbie doll glamour. They continue to be among the most highly prized dolls on the secondary market. (See Chapter 5, Pure Couture, for a further discussion of Mackie and his importance in the world of *Contemporary BARBIE*).

The second crucial Barbie collecting event in 1991 was the introduction of the Barbie Porcelain Treasures™ Collection. These limited edition dolls reproduced classic Barbie dolls "from over three decades of Barbie fashion leadership." The first doll in the series was Gay Parisienne Barbie (#9973). Based on a very rare outfit from the introduction of Barbie in 1959, the doll was an exact replica of the original, complete with satin lined "fur" stole and bubble skirt hem. Even the gold velveteen clutch purse was lined in silk. Her light blue lingerie replicated a 1959 undergarment set with 1991 additions of garters and seamed stockings. The entire Porcelain Treasures line came with certificates of authenticity. A porcelain 30th Anniversary Ken doll (#1110) was simultaneously introduced, wearing the 1961 Tuxedo ensemble. His 1991 additions included striped boxer shorts, undershirt, and knee socks complete with garters.

The Swan Lake Barbie doll (#1648) was the first in a series of Barbie prima ballerina dolls that some collectors call the Music Box series. Designed after the Swan Queen from Tchaikovsky's ballet, the doll wore a white shimmery tutu, tights, and feather headdress, and her arms are newly sculpted to hold a graceful ballet pose. She came in a display case with the look of etched glass and stood on a rotating music box that plays ballet music. Her hair was done in elaborate braids gathered up into the headdress, which was accented by tiny pearls.

The second in the Bob Mackie series, the **Platinum Barbie** (left) doll, was a successful followup to the initial **Gold Mackie**. Her pearlized white sequins sparkle with a silvery glow.

Every Bob Mackie Barbie doll comes packaged with a copy of Mr. Mackie's sketch of the doll. Many collectors frame these sketches and exhibit them behind the dolls. Shown are sketches for Mackie's **Gold** (facing page) and **Platinum Barbie** (below) dolls.

Air Force Barbie (right) was packaged with her flight bag and official uniform from the flying Thunderbirds. *Stars 'n Stripes Navy Barbie* (above, left to right) came in both Black and Caucasian versions. Note the packaging variations.

The year 1991 also ushered in two important new career dolls: the Navy Barbie doll (#9693 and #9694 in the Black version) and Air Force Barbie doll (#3360). Navy Barbie doll was outfitted in a replica of the official new uniform worn by enlisted women in the U.S. Navy, including a white jumper blouse with authentic insignia, t-shirt, skirt, tie, hat and high heel shoes. She also came with uniform pants, flat shoes and a nautical map. Air Force Barbie doll was similarly authentically dressed in a one-piece flight suit and the official A-2 flight jacket issued to front line Air Force pilots and crew. A blue flight cap and scarf completed the ensemble.

The lead glamour doll, Costume Ball Barbie (#7123), wore a costume that changed from a pink tiered ruffled gown into a butterfly with shimmering wings or fantasy flower. In addition, the Barbie doll skirt doubled as a child-size mask. She was also available as Black Costume Ball Barbie (#7134).

Hawaiian Fun Barbie doll (#5940) was a typical bathing suit Barbie doll with long blonde hair, a hula skirt and sunglasses. The doll was packaged with a child-size "friendship bracelet" filled with fruit-scented fragrance for girls to wear. The significance of this doll is that her Hawaiian Ice Party Playset™ was used to make shaved ice confections flavored with Kool-Aid® Brand Tropical Punch unsweetened Soft Drink Mix. A packet of Kool-Aid Tropical Punch mix was included with the set. This was Barbie doll's first alliance with Kool-Aid, which would be repeated in 1994 in the form of the Wacky Warehouse Kool-Aid Barbie doll premium.

The Ice Capades Barbie (#9847) was reprised in 1991. This year, the doll included a transformable purple and glitter costume, along with ice skates.

All American Barbie (#9423) came outfitted in a denim skirt and vest with American flag motif, along with two pairs of Reebok® Hi-Tops. Barbie doll's companions in the line included Christie, Ken, Teresa and Kira, and all of their denim outfits were also studded with metallic stars.

Another important fashion tie-in of 1991 was with Benetton's United Colors of Benetton™ label. Benetton Barbie doll (#9404) wore brilliantly-colored and patterned clothing in the style of the Italian casual fashion line. Additional Benetton outfits were sold separately. The use of the Benetton brand helped to further build the global Barbie brand as Benetton shops are found in select retail districts and in shopping malls around the world.

*Lead glamour doll, **Costume Ball Barbie's** outfit was changeable, and her skirt doubled as a child-sized mask.*

*The **All American Barbie** doll Christie (far left), came appropriately packaged with an American flag and wearing the All American fabric: denim. The **United Colors of Benetton Barbie** (left), the first issue, came fully accessorized with colorful hat, slouchy hobo bag, leg warmers and belt.*

VOLLEY OF THE DOLLS

"**I**ndignantly claiming that she has been cloned, Barbie starts a heavyweight bout with Miss America. Miss America is a line of dolls developed by Kenner Products under license from the Miss America Organization. Mattel believed that Miss America's head is too similar to Barbie's copyrighted cranium. In March 1991, Mattel complained to the U.S. Customs Service, and shipments of Miss America (who is manufactured in China) were intercepted. "We detained Miss America," says a Customs spokeswoman "pending a decision on whether she infringed on [Mattel's] copyright." In fact, Customs blocked the entry of three of the five Miss America models. Raquel and Justine, who had a different head shape, were allowed in. The other detainees—Devon (a blonde dance major),

COMPARING BARBIE DOLL TO MISS AMERICA DOLL		
	Barbie	*Miss America*
Height	11.5"	11.5"
Weight	5 oz.	5.5 oz.
Chest	5.5"	5.5"
Waist	2.75"	2.75"
Reach	3.5"	3.5"

Tonya (a Black aspiring veterinarian) and Blair (an Olympic gymnast in training) sat in a government warehouse. Kenner was found guilty by Customs officials."

SOURCE: *People*, 36:95, September 9, 1991

Nigerian Barbie (right), was dressed in a gold topped dress with animal print skirt. *Czechoslovakian Barbie* (far right) is a favorite among adult collectors of the International Barbie dolls. She signalled the opening of eastern European markets. The doll might better have been named "Czech Republic" Barbie, but forecasting border changes is not an easy business for anyone, even Barbie!

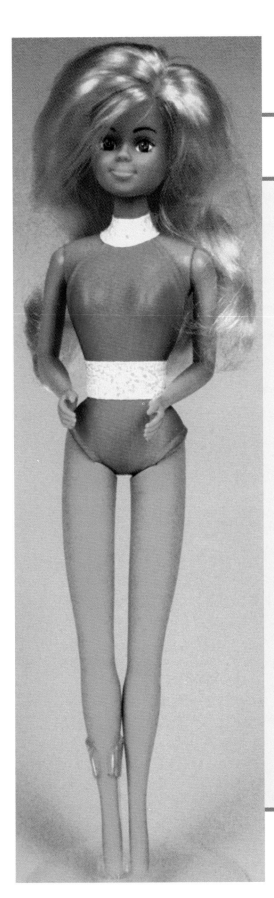

1991 DOLL WARS: HAPPY TO BE ME, MISS AMERICA AND PETRA POSE NO COMPETITION

Several dolls were introduced this year under the banner of political correctness, but ended up posing no lasting competitive threat to the Barbie doll. Happy to Be Me, a red-headed doll with a so-called more "realistic" figure was promoted to bash Barbie as a terrible role model for girls. The news about Happy generated headlines the world over lauding Happy as a doll that would help young girls accept their less-than-ideal bodies.

The doll, in fact, had a sold-out launch in Minneapolis. The Barbie-hating prophecy was fulfilled when thousands of Happys sold out in Byerly's supermarkets in the Twin Cities over Thanksgiving. Forecasters thought Happy would rival the Cabbage Patch Kids phenomenon.

It simply didn't happen!

Then Kenner introduced the Miss America Fashion Doll Collection, an officially-licensed line of nine beauty pageant dolls and accessories. The 11-inch, Barbie-doll-sized creations had flexible bodies (like Barbie doll), painted faces (like Barbie doll), combable hair (ditto), authentic Miss America insignia, and evening gowns or talent outfits that stripped down to a swimsuit. The dolls also came with a cassette tape featuring Bert Parks singing, "Here She Comes, Miss America."

As a competitive response to the Kenner doll, Mattel's American Beauty Queen Barbie was introduced. The Barbie version wore a gown that transformed to a bathing suit and then to a ballerina costume.

Finally came Petra, an 11-inch Swedish doll, popular in Europe, that entered the U.S. market. To introduce the doll into the U.S., Lundby of Sweden—which markets the Petra dolls—had produced a 30-second television commercial that opened with a little girl, Petra in hand, telling a friend: "She came from Europe to play with your Barbie doll. I hope they'll be good friends." Mattel sought a restraining order to prohibit Lundby of Sweden from airing the commercial.

U.S. District Judge David Kenyon issued a restraining order barring Lundby from airing the ad.

Petra was one of Barbie's most formidable competitors in European markets.

In 1991, Mattel changed the name of the International doll series to the Dolls of the World (DOW) series. The new DOW dolls this year were the Brazilian Barbie doll (#9094), Czechoslovakian Barbie doll (#7330), Malaysian Barbie doll (#7329) and the Nigerian Barbie doll (#7376). Second editions of the Internationals were offered in the DOW line, including the Eskimo Barbie doll (#9844) (a second edition of the 1982 doll), the Parisian Barbie doll (#9843) first introduced in 1980, and the Scottish Barbie doll (#9845) which was first introduced in 1981. The Malaysian doll used the 1981 Oriental face mold.

In 1991, Janet Goldblatt designed Mermaid Barbie and received Mattel's Creative Excellence Award for Bathtime Barbie, creating a new foam-fashions-in-the-bathtub play pattern.

This year, the Barbie doll was packaged with computer software for the first time. The Earring Magic/Radio Shack Barbie doll (#25-1992, Radio Shack stock number) included a software pack with the Barbie Design Studio program and a manual from Hi Tech Expressions.

*Darryl Hannah was perhaps Janet Goldblatt's model for the **Mermaid Barbie** doll.*

1991 · · · · · · · · · · · · · · · · ·

◆ "Baseball caps are the new t-shirts," the *New York Times* announces, billing them as going from "home plate to fashion plate."

◆ *Beauty and the Beast*, a Disney Studios animated film featuring the voice of Angela Lansbury and the music of Howard Ashman and Alan Menken, becomes the first animated movie to be nominated for an Oscar for Best Picture.

1992
Mattel, Inc., says. . .

(Hollywood Hair Barbie shares the cover of the annual report with the Genie from Disney's *Aladdin*, "Big Bones" from the Hot Wheels "Attack Pack" line and "Baby Walk 'n Roll").

"With revenues that approached $1 billion in 1992, the 34-year-strong Barbie doll is the leading product of the toy industry, having grown almost $500 million over the past four years. She is a big sister and a role model to girls around the world, and through her, girls play out their fantasies.

"Fashions, cars, houses and playsets all have contributed to the growth of Barbie. 'Barbie for Girls' products ranging from girls' clothing and shoes to skates, backpacks, cosmetics and furniture also take Barbie beyond the doll. The Barbie doll itself, however, remains the core of our business, and the average American girl, three to ten years old, now owns eight.

"The key is to make Barbie fresh and new every year, to develop multiple doll segments based on established play patterns, and to drive sales through effective advertising, promotion and merchandising."

(Source: 1992 Annual Report)

Direct mail emerged in the 1990s as a key marketing distribution channel for a broad range of consumer and commercial markets. So Mattel, in tune with leading-edge marketing strategies, initiated direct mail sales of the Barbie doll in 1992 with the Crystal Rhapsody Barbie, the first in the Presidential Porcelain Collection. (See sidebar, How Life Imitates Art in Barbie's World)

In 1992 Mattel also opened a Barbie boutique in New York City toy store FAO Schwarz and a toy shop at Disneyland. The latter move gave Mattel outlets for its products at all three Disney theme parks, which attract some 50 million visitors each year.

1992

◆ Four women are elected to the Senate, bringing the total to six, the most ever. Among the newly elected is the first Black female Senator.

◆ Donna Redel is elected the first woman chairperson of the New York Commodity Exchange. The 39-year-old Redel was an executive vice president of the Redel Trading Company.

◆ By August of this year, Mattel had completely automated its trade transactions for goods entering the U.S. West Coast. Mattel earned the distinction of being the largest shipper to go paperless.

◆ Martina Navratilova wins her 158th tennis title—surpassing every other player, male or female. She took her first championship in Czechoslovakia in 1973.

*Some collectors' favorite Mackie— **Neptune Fantasy Barbie**—poses on a Delaunay-inspired background.*

The Classique Collection's Benefit Ball Barbie, designed by veteran Barbie doll designer Carol Spencer, excited collectors. With her "foil" effect turquoise gown, and red hair, the doll continues to be a favorite with collectors as the first in an exciting series aimed at adult collectors.

Bob Mackie had major hits with two magnificent, highly detailed dolls: Empress Bride (#4247) and Neptune Fantasy (#4248). These have had significant staying power on the secondary market with collectors.

Featured on the evening news in 1992 was the introduction of the Teen Talk™ Barbie doll (#5745). The news wasn't so much the doll itself: it was what the doll "said" when her voice chip was activated by a push of the button in the doll's back. Each doll featured four so-called "fun phrases," randomly selected from approximately 270 sayings. One of the 270 sayings was, "Math class is tough!" This caused a furor among women's special interest groups ranging from the American Association of University Women (who attacked the math comment in a report on how schools shortchange girls) to radical feminist organizations. Mattel offered to make exchanges for the so-called offensive doll. It is not known how many of the dolls were actually returned.

Collectors who yearn to collect rare variations of Barbie dolls should be challenged by this fact: Teen Talk dolls were packaged wearing a range of different fashions, with different hair colors in straight and curly styles. According to Mattel, based on the scores of different sayings and voice chips, the number of Teen Talk Barbie doll variations mathematically computes to over 6,400 dolls. Another collector reality is that of the (reportedly) 350,000 talking Barbie dolls produced, only about one percent—or about 3,500—of the dolls contain the sound chip with the controversial phrase. The doll also was packaged as Black Teen Talk Barbie doll (#1612).

Barbie not only talked in 1992—she also took on a new appearance. New facial sculpting gave Barbie several different looks. Among the new face molds were the "New Smile," found in Teen Talk Barbie, Rappin' Rockin' Barbie, and Snap 'N Play Barbie; "The Neptune," found in Bob Mackie's Neptune Fantasy Barbie (#4248), Barbie as Scarlett in red, and other Mackie dolls; and, the "New Hispanic" face mold used for the Teresa doll and the second issue of the Italian Barbie doll (#2256).

Barbie was also tied in to the United Colors of Benetton brand in 1992 with the Benetton Shopping Barbie, which was packaged with a (cut-out) Benetton logo shopping bag.

United Colors of Benetton Shopping Barbie, *the second Benetton Barbie, was dressed in brightly colored clothes typical of the United Colors of Benetton style.*

HONEY, THEY BLEW UP BARBIE!

"Mattel has just created My Size Barbie, a three-foot mannequin. Touted as, 'a girl's best friend' and, 'the first Barbie little girls can actually share clothes with!' the $100 My Size, which makes her debut this fall, comes with a maillot, a tutu and a long skirt made from glittery elastic that will stretch to fit a normal three-foot kid.

"Bob Mackie has made two limited edition Barbie's: The $250 Empress Bride wears an antebellum tulle skirt, a beaded tiara and a floor-length veil that could double as My Size Barbie's hankie. Neptune's Fantasy Barbie is a miniature Vegas diva. For $170, she comes wrapped in green sequins and a teal velvet cloak whose spiked collar frames her head like a claw. She could be the headline act at a Lilliputian Tropicana."

SOURCE: *Newsweek,* July 27, 1992, 120:42

Crystal Rhapsody *porcelain Barbie, designed by Cynthia Young, was done with Swarovski crystals and inspired by Botticelli's* Birth of Venus.

HOW LIFE IMITATES ART IN BARBIE'S WORLD

Cynthia Young, Barbie doll designer, tells a wonderful story about how the design for the Crystal Rhapsody Barbie doll evolved. Overall, the doll was inspired by the beauty of Swarovski® crystals. Jill Barad challenged Barbie doll designers to create a gown for Barbie using the radiant crystals. The gown's silver bodice shimmered with the reflected light of 75 Swarovski crystal rhinestones, combining multi-colored aurora borealis crystals and clear silver crystals. The bodice flowed into a straight skirt of black silk velvet. Framing the entire gown was pearly white, Fortuny pleated satin.

But where did the idea for this pleated design come from? Young relates: "The doll's white satin Fortuny pleated skirt fanned out behind her with a black velvet silhouette. The inspiration for this came from a painting by Botticelli, the *Birth of Venus*. I was trying to think of a theme for a new doll, and I have an art book at home on which the *Birth of Venus* is on the cover. I just happened to look at the image and thought, 'the shell that Venus is coming out of, you could move it behind her and that could become her skirt. . .'." Now, that's life imitating art!

Continuing on the thread of designers receiving clues for Barbie designs from great art, Young recalled another such flash of inspiration. "Super Power Barbie, released in 1995 as Flying Hero Barbie, was inspired in a similar way. Debby Meyer, one of the designers with whom I work on my team, had an inspiration that came from *The Creation of Adam* by Michelangelo. You can see on the doll's costume that there are lights. These are touch-sensitive. We did not use these in production. Instead, we translated this into a toy with lights that sparkle and shine on the back of the cape. . . ."

And you thought the Sistine Chapel was a complicated project!

The Creation of Adam, *by Michelangelo (top);* Birth of Venus *by Botticelli (bottom).*

*FAO Schwarz's customized Barbie dolls changed in tone with this **Madison Avenue Barbie** doll in 1992. Prior to 1992 the FAO Schwarz dolls were all dressed in long glitzy gowns. This tailored day suit became a rave with collectors. The outfit came complete with fuchsia undergarments as well as an FAO Schwarz shopping bag.*

Customized Barbie dolls for retail stores made a particular impact on collectors in 1992. The FAO Schwarz Madison Avenue Barbie doll (#1539) was a collector favorite. Designed by Ann Driskill, whose fashion designs often reflect the kind of tailoring present in the earliest Barbie doll costumes, Madison Avenue Barbie was clad in a fuchsia and lime green suit with all of the important accouterments for a Manhattan shopping trip.

Another customized doll for a retail outlet—the Toys 'R Us Barbie for President doll—came in both Caucasian and Black versions (#3722 and #3940, respectively). While Barbie doll had been involved with political causes before (such as the UNICEF and Summit Barbie dolls), this was the first time in her career that she had made a run for the White House. Did Geraldine Ferraro's Vice Presidential nomination in 1988 influence Barbie doll designers? Perhaps so. . . .

*In 1992, George Bush, William Clinton and Ross Perot were greeted by a fourth major candidate: Barbie. There were two box variations for the **Barbie for President** doll: The initial box was printed with the presidential seal across the top (above), and the second box was decorated with stars (left).*

It was a case of art imitating life once again when the Stars and Stripes Army Barbie doll (#1234 Caucasian, #5618 Black, also available in gift sets with Ken) appeared quickly on toy store shelves in 1992. Dubbed by collectors "Desert Storm Barbie," this doll wore the uniform of a soldier serving in the Gulf War, complete with beret and camouflage fatigues. The doll's box also refers to the event as "Rendezvous with Destiny."

Rappin' Rockin' Barbie Doll (#3248) and her friends, Christie and Teresa, were based on the hip music trend that went mainstream by 1992. Barbie doll and friends each came with a boom box that played a rap beat sound. When played together, they sounded like a rap group. They came outfitted in hip-hop costumes and each wore a long gold chain, a style popular with rap artists of the time.

Capitalizing on the trend in music,
Rappin' Rockin' Barbie *and friends
came packaged with boom boxes. Their
black and neon colored outfits and caps
reflected the street styles of the time.*

Real rap beat Boom Box™!

rappin' rockin'

Barbie®

yo!

Dance with Barbie to a jammin' beat!

*The Stars and Stripes series offered **Army Barbie** and she quickly became known as "Desert Storm Barbie."*

Another trend doll—Rollerblade™ Barbie doll (#2214)—took a cue from the "hottest skating trend sweeping the nation," Mattel wrote. This doll straddles trend and licensed dolls, as Barbie wore skates with the Rollerblade trademark advertising the product. Each doll came with an officially licensed set of Rollerblade skates. Different from people-sized Rollerblades, Barbie's Rollerblade skates flickered and flashed as they rolled.

The lead glamour doll in 1992 was Sparkle Eyes Barbie (#2482) which had blue "rhinestone" eyes that sparkle. The Black Sparkle Eyes Barbie doll (#5950) came

Rollerblade Barbie (below) tied in with the brand-named in-line skates. Barbie's skates had the special effect of flickering when they rolled. An ophthalmologist's dream patient, glamour doll *Sparkle Eyes Barbie* (right) had "rhinestone" implanted eyes.

Totally Hair Barbie was packaged with Dep styling gel.

• Dep® Styling Gel!
• Ultra long hair!
• 5 hair accessories!
• Super styling booklet!

ALCOHOL FREE

Dep

HAIR & BODY

STYLING GEL

NET WT. 1 OZ (28g)

TOTALLY HAIR BARBIE: A $100 MILLION SUCCESS

Totally Hair Barbie is the most successful Barbie doll segment ever, generating $100 million in worldwide sales during 1992.

The Totally Hair Barbie doll makes the most of a popular play feature, with hair so long it reaches her toes. Styling gel comes packed with the doll for added fun, and for the first time in 20 years this Barbie is available with a choice of blonde or brunette hair. To maintain the momentum of Totally Hair Barbie, a Hollywood Hair doll has been introduced for 1993. The new doll again has special extra-long hair, but this time with the added unique feature of a hair mist that turns her blonde hair to pink, in patterns or all over.

SOURCE: 1992 Mattel Annual Report

1992

◆ Judit Polgar, the youngest person ever to earn the rank of chess grandmaster, celebrates her 16th birthday. She achieved this ranking the previous December. There were only 401 active grandmasters in the world at the time.

◆ In an advance for women in professional sports, Manon Rheaume becomes the first woman to play in one of the four major professional sports (baseball, football, basketball, and ice hockey) when she appears as goal tender for the Tampa Bay Lightning in an exhibition ice hockey game.

◆ Anita Colby, the first "super model" and beauty writer, died at 77.

with green rhinestone eyes. Like most glamour dolls of previous years, Barbie's pink costume transformed into several looks: a floor-length ball gown, a silvery mini dress, and a dress with a pink sparkle train.

Totally Hair Barbie doll (#1112) came with the longest Barbie hair ever at ten inches, reaching her ankles. She wore a Pucci-style knit dress, her hair was tied back in a pink scarf, and she came packaged with a tube of Dep® Styling Gel. Totally Hair Barbie doll also came in a Black version (#5948) and a Brunette version (#1117).

The 1992 Dolls of the World included the English (#4973), Jamaican (#4647) and the Spanish (#4963) Barbie dolls.

English Barbie (left) was one of the Dolls of the World offered in 1992. This was the second British Barbie, following up the Royal Barbie International of 1980, the first year the Internationals were offered. Jamaican Barbie (center) had a multi-print cotton ensemble which caused some discussion amongst collectors who questioned whether the outfit was consistent with the International Barbie doll image of earlier years. This same year a second Spanish Barbie doll (right) followed the first issued in 1983.

sculpting gave Barbie several different looks. Among the new face molds were the "New Smile," found in Teen Talk Barbie, Rappin' Rockin' Barbie, and Snap 'N Play Barbie; "The Neptune," found in Bob Mackie's Neptune Fantasy Barbie (#4248), Barbie as Scarlett in red, and other Mackie dolls; and, the "New Hispanic" face mold used for the Teresa doll and the second issue of the Italian Barbie doll (#2256).

Barbie was also tied in to the United Colors of Benetton brand in 1992 with the Benetton Shopping Barbie, which was packaged with a (cut-out) Benetton logo shopping bag.

Customized Barbie dolls for retail stores made a particular impact on collectors in 1992. The FAO Schwarz Madison Avenue Barbie doll (#1539) was a collector favorite. Designed by Ann Driskill, whose fashion designs often reflect the kind of tailoring present in the earliest Barbie doll costumes, Madison Avenue Barbie was clad in a fuchsia and lime green suit with all of the important accouterments for a Manhattan shopping trip.

Another customized doll for a retail outlet—the Toys 'R Us Barbie for President doll—came in both Caucasian and Black versions (#3722 and #3940, respectively). While Barbie doll had been involved with political causes before (such as the UNICEF and Summit Barbie dolls), this was the first time in her career that she had made a run for the White House. Did Geraldine Ferraro's Vice Presidential nomination in 1988 influence Barbie doll designers? Perhaps so. . . .

It was a case of art imitating life once again when the Stars and Stripes Army Barbie doll (#1234 Caucasian, #5618 Black, also available in gift sets with Ken) appeared quickly on toy store shelves in 1992. Dubbed by collectors "Desert Storm Barbie," this doll wore the uniform of a soldier serving in the Gulf War, complete with beret and camouflage fatigues. The doll's box also refers to the event as "Rendezvous with Destiny."

Rappin' Rockin' Barbie Doll (#3248) and her friends, Christie and Teresa, were based on the hip music trend that went mainstream by 1992. Barbie doll and friends each came with a boom box that played a rap beat sound. When played

1993 ❖

◆ Mattel agrees to buy rival Fisher-Price Inc. in a stock swap worth about $1.1 billion. The merged company would rival Hasbro Inc. as the world's largest toy company.

◆ Julie Krone wins the 125th running of the Belmont Stakes, riding Colonial Affair—a 13-1 longshot—in the third leg of the U.S. Triple Crown. She thus becomes the first woman to win a U.S. Triple Crown race.

◆ Comic book hero Superman dies at the hands of the villain Doomsday in Superman No. 75. Later this year, the super-hero's editors find a way to bring him back to life.

◆ Honoring the memories of eleven million people killed systematically during the Nazi Holocaust (1933-1945), the United States Holocaust Memorial Museum opens in Washington, DC.

Masquerade Ball Barbie, *by Bob Mackie, haughtily poses with mask in hand.*

*Charleston, anyone? It's the Roaring '20s, and **Flapper Barbie** dances atop a fur stole as Rudy Vallee croons a tune.*

Bob Mackie had a huge hit with Masquerade Ball Barbie doll (#10803). The doll is dressed in a harlequin-pattern gown constructed with black and multicolored bugle beads. Some dolls are known to have the Mackie fragrance infused in the doll; in addition, some dolls were packed with small flaçons of Mackie eau de toilette.

Mattel introduced the Great Era series with the Flapper Barbie doll (#4063) and the Gibson Girl Barbie doll (#3702). These dolls, aimed at the adult collector market, are recreations of important fashion eras.

The Australian Barbie doll (#3626) and the Italian Barbie doll (#2256) joined the Dolls of the World series in 1993. The Italian was a second edition after the first Italian Barbie doll introduced in 1980. This doll used the New Hispanic face mold, first found on the Teresa doll in 1992.

Sea Holiday Barbie (above) was dressed for a cruise and packaged for the international market.

The first doll in the Great Eras Series was the Gibson Girl Barbie (right).

1994
Mattel, Inc., says. . .

(Cover: Celebrating 50 years)

"The production of Barbie and other fashion dolls involves more detail than is readily apparent. The painting of the face, for instance, involves an average of 15 steps, and the doll's body is assembled from as many as 25 different parts. No one comes remotely close to the quantity of 90 million fashion dolls Mattel produces in a year, nor can any company match the high quality and low cost Mattel achieves in this category.

"The proceeds from the sale of the Dr. Barbie doll, combined with grants from the Mattel Foundation, resulted in a $2 million initiative supporting children's preventive health care facilities at federally-funded Head Start preschool locations."

(Source: 1994 Annual Report)

Mattel celebrated 35 years of the Barbie doll in grand style this year. The company issued a new line of Nostalgic Barbie dolls, kicking things off with a reproduction of the first Barbie doll (#11590 blonde and #11782 brunette). Donned in her zebra-striped swimsuit and sold with a reproduction box which replicated the original doll's packaging, the doll became

Mattel launched its successful Nostalgic Barbie line in 1994, with the 35th Anniversary Barbie dolls. Brunettes (left) were rumored to be in shorter supply than blondes (right). This giftset (center), only available in blonde to the mass market, was very limited. The package included reproductions of two of the most highly prized vintage outfits in Barbie's fashion history: Roman Holiday and Easter Parade.

*The **Gold Jubilee Barbie** continues to be a secondary market treasure due to its very limited production.*

an instant hit with collectors. In particular, the blonde doll packaged as a gift set (#11591) with two of the most rare costumes from 1960—Roman Holiday and Easter Parade—was very difficult to find.

The Barbie doll PR machine never worked as hard as when it cranked up to celebrate the doll's 35th anniversary. To mark the occasion, Mattel sponsored a bi-coastal celebration that brought out the stars. In the Los Angeles community of Compton, Jill Barad presented a $250,000 donation to actress Demi Moore on behalf of the Charles Drew Head Start Medical Clinic. Barad presented an additional check for $250,000 to actor/director Henry Winkler, founding president of the Children's Action Network, to support the organization's National Immunization Campaign. These contributions were part of Mattel's $1 million year-long campaign to support health care initiatives funded by the sales of the new Dr. Barbie doll and other Barbie products. On the day of these presentations, Ruth Handler appeared at FAO Schwarz in New York City, for a doll signing event. Handler, the Barbie doll's unofficial "mother," also published her biography this year. *Dream Doll* (Longmeadow Press) told the story of Handler, who, along with her husband, Elliot, and their partner, Harold Mattson, co-founded Mattel in 1944 as a plastics toy company. The book traces the life of this business powerhouse who was born Ruth Mosko in 1917, the daughter of Jewish-Polish immigrants living in Denver.

In honor of Barbie's 35th anniversary, Mattel released the brilliant Gold Jubilee Barbie doll (#12009), a limited and numbered edition of 5,000. There were an additional 2,000 units sold on the international market, and 200

1994 ·

◆ After many years away from the concert stage, Barbra Streisand mounts an international concert tour. The tour plays to sell-out audiences.

◆ Jacqueline Kennedy Onassis, 64, widow of U.S. President John F. Kennedy, died of cancer. Her clothing and hair styles were emulated by millions of women and the Barbie doll.

◆ South Africa holds its first universal suffrage elections. African National Congress President Nelson Mandela on May 2 proclaimed victory, declaring black South Africans "free at last."

◆ Israel and Jordan sign a peace treaty, formally ending 46 years of war and mistrust.

dolls were produced for Mattel employees. The doll was made with Mattel's best "collector grade vinyl," described by Mattel as "porcelain vinyl." The doll was an immediate success with collectors. Its initial retail price of $295 was eclipsed, within weeks of the initial release, by a secondary market price as high as $1,000.

Dr. Barbie, in Black and Caucasian versions (#11814 and #11160, respectively), was released this year. As a symbol of Mattel's initiative to raise funds for children without access to health care, Dr. Barbie was a pediatrician. She was packaged with two newborn patients of different races (babies came as Black, Caucasian and Hispanic versions, which varied randomly by package). Dr. Barbie's magic stethoscope produced a heartbeat sound when pressed to the chest of her blanket-wrapped baby patient. Accessories included a doctor bag, pacifier, rattle, baby bottle, reflex instrument, and ear checker—details which were reminiscent of the Barbie doll's richly-accessorized medical costumes of the 1960's, such as Registered Nurse (#991) or Candy Striper Volunteer (#889).

Dr. Barbie, a pediatrician, came complete with patient and "working" stethoscope (left). The brunette variation of the 1994 doctor (right) was exclusively available at the Barbie Festival sponsored by Mattel in Orlando.

The Scarlett and Rhett dolls from Gone with the Wind *were welcomed by collectors.* **Barbie as Scarlett** *dressed in her black and white honeymoon dress was a favorite among many collectors.*

One of 1994's greatest Barbie doll hits was the introduction of the Hollywood Legends Series, kicked off by the ultimate Hollywood Legend: Scarlett O'Hara of *Gone with the Wind* fame. There have been many versions of Scarlett dolls through the years including, but not limited to, Cissettes, Alexanders, and Franklin Heirlooms, among others. However, none to date have been as authentically and meticulously detailed as Barbie as Scarlett. Mattel offered four versions of Barbie as Scarlett O'Hara: Scarlett in her white and green barbecue dress (#12997); Scarlett in green velvet drapery dress with braided gold and green belt (#12045); Scarlett in red velveteen gown with beads and feather accents (#12815); and, Scarlett in her black and white honeymoon dress from her marriage to Rhett Butler (#13524). Speaking of Rhett, the Ken doll was also dressed as Scarlett's groom in black tuxedo and cape (#12741). Arguably the most remarkable aspect of these dolls is the authentic costume detail, in which every feature faithfully reflects the original movie costumes designed by Walter Plunkett.

The film's story line was even depicted on Barbie boxes such as the green barbeque dress box (left). The dolls also appeal to collectors of Hollywood and movie memorabilia, as well as Civil War junkies.

Attention to detail was no more apparent than in this iconic dress (left) from GWTW, allegedly sewn in desperation from the drapes that hung in Tara. Remember when Scarlett in red velvet (center) looked askance as she wore this dress? Ken, as Rhett (right), looked dashing in his morning suit, complete with top hat.

Customized Barbie dolls were hot in 1994. One of the most important designer dolls in *Contemporary BARBIE* doll history was Bloomingdale's Savvy Shopper Barbie designed by Nicole Miller. According to Bloomingdale's management, the doll could not be kept on the shelf. The doll is dressed in a quintessential Nicole Miller outfit: black velvet short cocktail dress with a black silk overcoat bearing a colorful tiny print typical of Miller. Miller also designed a series of people-sized silk accessories to celebrate the 35th anniversary of the Barbie doll. (For more on Nicole Miller, see Chapter 5, Pure Couture).

Another favorite customized doll was the Hallmark Victorian Elegance Barbie doll (#12579), first in a series of Hallmark-commissioned Barbie dolls. Hallmark had successfully launched its first Barbie doll Christmas ornament in 1993 with a miniature replica of that year's Happy Holidays Barbie doll, along with a Nostalgic #1 Barbie doll ornament. 1994's introduction of Hallmark's first actual Barbie doll has led the company to commission additional holiday Barbie dolls.

Barbie's successful career as an Astronaut was repeated this year in a celebration of the Apollo mission's 25th anniversary. Astronaut Barbie doll (#12149 Caucasian, and #12150 Black) came dressed in astro gear, including space helmet and a flag to plant on the moon. Was that, "One small step for womankind. . . ?"

FLO-JO'S INTO BARBIE

"Long before 'the fastest woman alive' won five Olympic medals, married gold-medalist Al Joyner, co-chaired the President's Council on Physical Fitness and Sports or ran her own business, Florence Griffith was a little girl who played with Barbie dolls in the L.A. projects.

"'I had 10 brothers and sisters, and my parents divorced when I was six,' says Flo-Jo, now 34. 'My sisters and I would pretend that Barbie and Ken were Mom and Dad. We'd put the dolls together, hoping our parents would get back together too.'

"They didn't. But Flo-Jo's childhood games led to an enduring passion for sewing and fashion. 'We couldn't afford Barbie clothes, so my mother taught me to make them. That was such a joyful time for me—doing something creative that we both loved.'

"She still designs for Barbie, but now with her daughter, four-year-old Mary (dubbed Mo-Jo by the press). 'We have close to a thousand dolls between us, and she always begs to sew for them.'

"Flo-Jo also makes garments for far bigger bodies. She has designed the Indiana Pacers' uniforms and women's athletic clothing sold in Japan. But her dream is to design uniforms for a U.S. Olympic team."

SOURCE: *Life,* August 1994, page 79

New Dolls of the World included Chinese Barbie (#11180), Dutch Barbie (#11104), Kenyan Barbie (#11181), and the second Native American Barbie doll (#11609). Kenyan Barbie used the new Nichelle face mold first employed in 1991 (and used extensively in Mattel's Shani line of dolls). The Kenyan figure was the first Barbie doll to have flocked hair (à la the earliest Ken dolls). Mattel also packaged the Chinese, Dutch and Kenyan Barbie dolls together in a Dolls of the World Giftset (#12043).

Dutch Barbie *(above) from Dolls of the World in 1994, reminded vintage Barbie collectors of the Barbie in Holland outfit offered in 1963 as part of the Travel Costume Series (#0823). The second African Barbie doll (top right),* ***Kenyan Barbie,*** *used the beautiful Nichelle face mold (from the Shani line) and had close-cropped hair.* ***Chinese Barbie*** *(bottom right) was the first issue Chinese Barbie doll.*

1994 saw new innovations in marketing the Barbie doll. The cable television shopping channel, QVC, began to sell Barbie dolls that year. (The Home Shopping Network had successfully sold Barbie dolls, as well.) Dolls featured on QVC's hour-long Barbie doll program often sell out within the hour. The new distribution channel of home shopping for Barbie dolls expanded Mattel's access to new potential collectors; at the time of this writing, QVC was available in over 50 million U.S. homes.

A second emerging growth area impacting Barbie doll collectors was the entire field of licensing. Shady Character signed a license with Mattel in 1994 to manufacture men's and women's pajamas and lounge wear under the Nostalgic Barbie label. Their varied selection included six designs from the 1959 to 1964 Barbie period, such as knit and woven boxer shorts, nightshirts and other lounge wear categories. These were available through the QVC channel, at FAO Schwarz stores, and through a variety of other retail outlets. (For more on the subject, see Chapter 6, Custom Made).

CYNTHIA YOUNG REMEMBERS SOLO IN THE SPOTLIGHT. . .

Cynthia Young

Both Cynthia and I are among the earliest generation of Barbie doll collectors. I asked her about her favorite vintage Barbie doll memory. She responded instantly with this nostalgic, sweet story: "As a child, my favorite Barbie doll was Solo in the Spotlight. I remember one night when my parents went out for the evening. They left my sister and me with our grandmother. When they picked us up at 10 p.m., we were asleep and so we thought it was the middle of the night. After they woke us up, our parents gave each one of us a Barbie doll case, with the doll packed inside wearing Solo in the Spotlight, and all these Barbie doll clothes hung up on their little hangers in the case. We were still half asleep! This gift was not for any occasion. When I woke up in my own bed, the doll case, doll and costumes were on a table in my bedroom. I thought it was a beautiful dream. . . ."

This nostalgic memory is what drives many adult collectors to open themselves up to the Barbie doll. . .déja vù all over again!

SOURCE: Author's interview with Cynthia Young, August 1995.

1995
Mattel, Inc., says...

"It was another year of record performance, and the most encouraging news is that we believe the best is yet to come!... 1995 was Mattel's seventh consecutive year of record sales and record earnings.... In addition to introducing great new products and line extensions for every brand, Mattel is entering the interactive world in 1996. What we are doing is leveraging our time-tested brands and characters through new means of play. As an example, girls can design fashions for Barbie on their home computer, then print out the patterns on actual fabric using their own PC's printer.... We produced over 100 million fashion dolls in 1995, up from 80 million the prior year.... The continuing growth for Barbie will require additional investment, and we plan to have another fashion doll plant operational by the second half of 1997....

"With a number one share in most every major global market, Barbie penetration continues to grow.... Most of the 100 dolls in each year's product line are designed for little girls, but the adult collector market also provides excellent opportunity for Mattel. There are 83 million women in the world today who grew up with the Barbie doll, and every one of them is a potential collector. Special edition dolls, infomercials, and magazine advertising have contributed to a doubling of the Barbie adult collector business in each of the last three years, for annual sales of more than $175 million in 1995."

(Source: 1995 Annual Report)

1995

◆ Shannon Faulkner makes history by becoming the first woman to enroll in the Citadel—a Charleston, SC, military school with a 152-year history of single-gender education. She drops out after one week.

◆ The University of Connecticut men's and women's basketball teams are both ranked number one in their respective AP polls, marking a first in NCAA history. The women's team reached the top of the polls on January 17, one day after beating Tennessee, 77-66.

◆ Mega media deals abound: Walt Disney Company buys Capital Cities/ABC; Westinghouse makes a bid for CBS; and Seagrams acquires MCA.

◆ Kate Mulgrew is the first actress to play a regular role as captain of a Federation Starship. She is Kathryn Janeway on TV's sci-fi drama "Star Trek: Voyager."

Based on Mattel's 1994 success with the kickoff of the Nostalgic line of Barbie dolls, the company introduced Solo in the Spotlight® Barbie doll (#13534) with a blonde ponytail—a reproduction of the iconic fashion sold between 1960 and 1964. The doll also came in a brunette version (#13820). Solo in the Spotlight had been one of the best-selling outfits from the vintage era. Busy Gal (#13675) reproduced a brunette Barbie doll in one of the most popular fashions from the early 1960s: Barbie doll as fashion designer, including period-perfect red suit and a portfolio of fashion sketches.

*The third Nostalgic Barbie doll was **Busy Gal.** She wore the vintage costume of the same name, which was the outfit of an early 1960s fashion designer. The doll was packaged with fashion portfolio and drawings, and had black glasses akin to the ones worn by Edith Head.*

*Mattel brought out its second in the Nostalgic series of Barbie dolls in 1995. **Solo in the Spotlight** wore one of the most popular outfits from Barbie's vintage era. She came in blonde and brunette variations.*

The porcelain doll celebrating Mattel's 50th anniversary wore a red and gold Fortuny pleated gown.

The eagerly awaited Christian Dior Barbie doll (#13168) from the Designer series was a favorite among many collectors. The doll wore the first replica from the couture house of Dior. A design by Gianfranco Ferré, the doll wore a two-piece beaded, brocade costume, studded with gold beads on a rich tapestry background. Her hair, coiffed by Alexandre of Laurent, was up in (appropriately enough) a French twist, reminiscent of Catherine Deneuve. Perhaps, that's because this doll used the popular 1987 SuperStar face mold, and Deneuve is one of cinema's global superstars.

In 1995, customized dolls proliferated in both volume and scope. Of particular note were the Bloomingdale's Donna Karan Barbie doll, issued in both blonde and brunette versions; and the Wessco International Travel Barbie doll. Both dolls, which were designed by Ann Driskill's group, reflect a tailored suited look.

The Hollywood Legends Series presented its second and third releases in the form of Barbie as Dorothy in the *Wizard of Oz* (#12701) and Barbie as Maria in *The Sound of Music* (#13676). The Maria doll used the 1977 SuperStar face mold.

Mattel Toys celebrated 50 years of business in 1995. The company commemorated the golden anniversary with a special porcelain doll: the 50th Anniversary Barbie doll (#14479). The blonde doll wore a red velvet gown with a gold pleated metallic fabric in Fortuny pleats at the bottom. Fifty red roses, each accented with a sequin and bead, adorned her neckline, shawl and hairpiece. The doll wore a gold tone bracelet with the Mattel logo on one side and "50 Years" on the other.

Bob Mackie offered yet another stunning example of his sequin-and-bead artistry: Goddess of the Sun. The doll's costume and headdress are reminiscent of Mackie's very popular Neptune Fantasy, but instead of teal blue, the ensemble is gold. "Sunrays" of sequins and gold fan behind her torso, and rich gold beading is worked in a vertical design on the skirt of the floor-length gown.

Popular culture has always influenced Barbie doll marketers and designers. For the first time, the Barbie doll was matched with a television program. The popularity of the television show "Baywatch" married nicely with the popularity of the Barbie doll and resulted in the Baywatch™ Barbie doll (#13199). The doll's dolphin friend made realistic sounds and helped to present an ecological message. In addition, Baywatch Barbie can be viewed as a career doll since she performs the role of lifeguard. Furthermore, based on the popularity of the show's star, David Hasselhoff (especially in Europe, and particularly Germany), Baywatch Barbie and friends could be seen as global dolls. While Mattel claimed that the doll bore no likeness to any of the show's cast members, many believed that she strongly resembled Pamela Anderson Lee, the blonde lead actress in the cast. Mattel also put together a variety of cross-promotional deals for girl's apparel, swimwear and accessories.

Mattel paired Barbie with the popular "Baywatch" television series. Many observers believe that the doll was modeled after Pamela Anderson Lee (but perhaps Pamela Anderson Lee has modeled herself after Barbie?).

Teacher Barbie doll (#13914) and Black Teacher Barbie doll (#13915) added an important career to Barbie doll's resumé. The doll was packaged with a boy and girl student in a classroom with a real chalkboard, bell, clock and pencil sharpener. In 1995, Mattel also marketed the Caring Careers™ Fashion Giftset, which added the jobs of firefighter, teacher and veterinarian to Barbie's 35 years of work experience.

Mattel packaged three career outfits in the Caring Careers set (below): firefighter, teacher and veterinarian. **Teacher Barbie** *(right), initially praised, encountered some problems in the children's market since the doll was not wearing underwear (as is the case with nearly all Barbie dolls!).*

THE RENAISSANCE OF DOROTHY

Abbe Littleton recalled the story of her early designs for the Barbie doll. "When I first came to Mattel in 1983, my supervisors told me to design what I wanted. I thought Barbie should be a movie star. Through being a movie star, she could play characters that allowed her to be a mermaid, a Fifties girl, or Marilyn Monroe. I finally sketched Barbie as Dorothy from the *Wizard of Oz*. That was in late 1983.

"Eleven years later, my boss said, 'We're thinking of testing a *Wizard of Oz* theme for Barbie.' I pulled out my old doll and doctored her up. I put a Little Debbie head on the body and turned her hair into braids. We tested the prototype and all of the adults loved it. She really looked like Dorothy.

"Then we took her and adapted the doll to Barbie's style: we added white eyelet fabric and gave her a fuller dress. She came out very sweet looking."

SOURCE: Author's Interview with Abbe Littleton, November 1995

Mattel kicked off two new collector's series for children. The American Stories Collection dolls reflected American historical periods and included Colonial Barbie (#12578), Pilgrim Barbie (#12577) and Pioneer Barbie (#12680). The Children's Collector Series featured the Rapunzel Barbie doll with her down-to-the-floor hair (#13016).

The American Stories Collection kicked off in 1995 with these three dolls: ***Colonial*** *(far left),* ***Pilgrim,*** *and* ***Pioneer Barbie,*** *which appealed to both younger and adult collectors.*

1995

◆ POG collecting becomes the rage among elementary-school-aged boys and girls, a reincarnation from their past lives as milk-bottle caps.

◆ Internet surfing goes mainstream with a product offering called, "Internet in a Box."

◆ Donna Karan celebrates 10 years in the fashion biz.

◆ Radio call-in talk shows create a new form of electronic populism.

◆ Susan Molinari (R-NY) is the first congresswoman to wear trousers on the Congressional House floor, and the first woman elected to the House Leadership Committee.

The year 1995 brought the **Polynesian Barbie** doll (left) to the Dolls of the World series. She was clad in "grass" skirt and came complete with lei. The **German Barbie** doll (center) from the Dolls of the World Series of 1995 was the second issue German, following the first offered in 1987. Instead of wearing white tights, her legs were painted white. Mattel offered the second **Irish Barbie** doll (right)—the first was available in 1984. She was very popular with collectors, and had the red hair of a typical Irish "Colleen."

"BARBIE ELEVATED TO DOLL ROYALTY"

"It is not clear what the Emperor Franz Josef would have made of it. His descendants, Austria's illustrious Habsburg clan, are marketing Barbie dolls to make ends meet.

"At a ceremony in the marble palace of the Habsburgs' imperial villa last week, doll collectors were invited to pay £3,000 (about US$4,500) for the "Archduchess Barbie," one of a rare and regal set of Barbie dolls produced in collaboration with Archduke Markus von Habsburg-Lothringen and the American toy company Mattel.

"The archduke makes no bones about welcoming a plastic doll into the family; proceeds from the sales of the 12in *(sic)* Barbies bedecked in silk and tiaras will go towards restoring the Kaiservilla, the Habsburg summer residence at Bad Ischl, a retreat favoured by Emperor Franz Josef at the turn of the century. The income from opening the building to the public has so far proved a

disappointment, but the 10 Barbie dolls on offer were snapped up in an instant. . . .

"Mattel made a limited edition of Habsburg Barbie [dolls] modelled on Empress Sissy, wife of the Emperor Franz Josef. The venture has been so successful that the Archduke is contemplating giving permission for a Barbie version of Franz Josef himself.

"'Although the price of £3,000 per model was high, I thought there would be enough people in Austria who would want to buy it, and there were,' said the Archduke. 'I think we could have sold another 10 at the same price.'

"It could be the start of a regal Barbie explosion. Mattel is now considering approaching royal families throughout Europe."

SOURCE: *The London Sunday Times,* 30 July 1995

New Dolls of the World included the German Barbie doll (#12698) first introduced in 1987; Irish Barbie doll (#12998), first introduced in 1984; Polynesian Barbie doll (#12700); and the third Native American doll (#12699).

Since the introduction of Teen Talk Barbie in 1992, kids and collectors alike anticipated the arrival of another contemporary talking Barbie. It came in the form of 1995's Super Talk Barbie doll (Caucasian and Black versions, #12290 and #12379, respectively). Of the Super Talk costume that she designed, Cynthia Young said: "I tried to do something that was trendy and denim, stylish and fitted. I liked to blend denim and gold, to achieve an effect of 'opposites'."

Thanks to new technology not available for the 1992 Teen Talk, Super Talk has 100,000 phrases available to her. But based on Mattel's lessons from Teen Talk's "math class is tough" remark, the company carefully screened every single phrase for Super Talk. John Amerman, Mattel CEO, was quoted in a 1994 *Los Angeles* Magazine profile titled "King Barbie," as saying that, in this age of political correctness, "we're bound to screw up on at least one of them!"

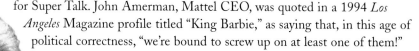

BARBIE DOES THE BOULEVARD MONTPARNASSE

In 1995, the Barbie doll made a very big impression in the City of Lights. At the Musée Grévin, Jill Barad, Mattel President and Chief Operating Officer, unveiled a replica of Barbie wearing the same design as a House of Christian Dior gown that appears in the museum, a French waxworks in Paris.

By sharing the stage at the Musée Grévin with waxen impressions of Bill Clinton, first feline Socks, Boris Yeltsin and Madonna, Barbie's role as an American cultural icon was confirmed. (For more on Ferré and the House of Dior, see Chapter 7, Pure Couture).

1996
Mattel, Inc., says...

"Our global power brands of Barbie, Fisher-Price, Disney and Hot Wheels grew 10 percent worldwide. . . . Looking ahead to 1997 and beyond. . . our mandate for the future, which is to Simplify and Focus—Build and Grow. . . . We will now dedicate ourselves to building the six core categories where we are now the #1 market share leader. The first category is Fashion Dolls. We are the undisputed leader here based on our Barbie business, which now accounts for $1.7 billion in annual sales. . . . Core brands increased 10%, mainly due to greater demand for BARBIE and BARBIE-related products, which increased 20% primarily due to strength in dolls and fashions, especially in the United States."

(Source: 1996 Annual Report)

According to *Playthings* magazine's 14th Annual Best Seller Survey, the Barbie doll beat out stiff competition in 1996 for the second year in a row. Rivals such as Baby Go Bye Bye, longtime favorite Batman, newly resurrected Star Wars, upstart Beanie Babies, and video game kings Sega and Nintendo, could not unseat the Barbie doll's top position as the most popular toy of the year. According to the Toy Manufacturers Association, total doll sales rose 12.1 percent between 1995 and 1996, with the Barbie doll taking the mass share of the market.

In 1996, Mattel expanded the Barbie doll line in volume and segmentation of dolls to produce the largest number of dolls named "Barbie" in its 37 year history. That year, the Barbie doll scaled the depths of the ocean (as Ocean Friends Barbie) to the heights of outer space (as Star Trek Barbie). Career-wise, Barbie was a veterinarian, a ballerina and an Olympic gymnast, as well as a chef, policewoman, and business executive (in the Cool Career outfit set).

1996

◆ Shannon Lucid becomes the first U.S. astronaut to spend six months in space. Lucid, a 53-year-old biochemist, pilot, and junk food addict, stayed aboard the Russian space station Mir with two cosmonauts for 188 days.

◆ Amy Van Dyken is the first female swimmer to win four gold medals at one Olympics.

◆ Sherry Lansing is the first woman studio boss to get a star on Hollywood Boulevard. Lansing, the first female President of Production at Twentieth Century Fox, left in 1983 to produce her own films. In 1992, she moved to Paramount, becoming the first woman to chair that studio.

◆ Alice Rivlin is the first woman appointed Vice Chair of the Federal Reserve Board.

*Robert Best designed this first set, **Star Trek Barbie and Ken**, in the Pop Culture Series.*

The largest number ever of collectible (i.e., targeted-to-adult) Barbie dolls was available: more than 30 such dolls made their debut, including Barbie as Eliza Doolittle in *My Fair Lady* (heavily promoted through the Twiggy-hosted television infomercial) and Pink Splendor Barbie. The latter caused quite a stir among collectors due to its astronomical initial retail price of $900. This price marked a new high in primary market issues of Barbie dolls. While this massive pink confection-of-a-doll was elegantly designed by the talented and prolific Cynthia Young (designer of the 1996 Classique Starlight Dreams Barbie doll), and was constructed with seemingly yards of pink fabric and 24-karat gold thread, many questioned its price point vis-a-vis its value-for-money.

"Beam me up, Ken!" Barbie ordered. Star Trek Barbie and Ken were greatly anticipated by collectors in 1996. The set was packaged with a photographic cardboard scene of the Starship Enterprise bridge. Barbie and Ken were clad in first-generation Federation garb—she as an engineering officer in red, he in gold as a commanding officer. Doll-sized phasers, communicators, and tricorders were included in the dolls' package.

The influence of couture on Barbie dolls was extensive, represented by dolls associated with the designs of Nicole Miller (Macy's City Shopper), Calvin Klein (Bloomingdale's), and the perennially popular Bob Mackie, with Goddess of the Moon.

While he designed Star Trek Barbie and Ken, Robert Best's real design coup for 1996 was the Barbie Collectibles doll, Portrait in Taffeta. This original, in brown taffeta, had golden upswept hair and was one of the finest, most unique dolls ever brought to market in the contemporary era. Best made his mark on many adult collectors who now call themselves "Robert Best collectors."

The number of department store and other consumer branded exclusive dolls was never greater in the Barbie doll's history. Exclusives were requested by Avon, Bloomingdale's, FAO Schwarz, Hallmark, Hills, JC Penney, Macy's, Sears, Service Merchandise, Spiegel, Target, Toys 'R Us, Wal-Mart, Wessco, and Wholesale Clubs.

Several nostalgic Barbie dolls were issued in 1996. An American Girl style Barbie doll dressed in Poodle Parade (a vintage outfit #1643 that sells on the secondary market for about $500 mint and complete) was packaged with the hard-to-find reproduction tote bag decorated with faux needlepoint poodle. While the face mold and hair styling on this doll was questioned by some critical vintage collectors, the reproduction outfit was most welcome. Nostalgic Enchanted Evening, presented in blonde and brunette ponytails, wore the desirable vintage reproduction pink satin gown trimmed in faux white mink (#983). Third in the Nostalgic series was the celebration of the 30th

*The 1996 Nostalgic **Poodle Parade Barbie** wore a reproduction of the very rare outfit from the early 1960s.*

1996 ◆

◆ Pamela Davis is the first woman to pitch in a minor-league baseball game. She pitched one inning for the Jacksonville Suns, the Detroit Tigers AA team: no runs, one hit, one strikeout.

◆ The U.S. Women's Softball Team is the first team to win the event's Olympic gold medal. It was the first time the game was played in the Olympics.

◆ Ossie Clark, 54, icon of '60s design who defined "mod," dies. His shop, Quorum, was at the epicenter of the 1960s fashion explosion.

BARBIE DOES MANHATTAN!

Barbie doll has been a part of the art scene since her inception in 1959. She was a fashion designer in 1962, complete with portfolio and sketches, wearing Busy Gal (#981)—the basis for Mattel's Nostalgic doll issued in 1995. In 1965, she became an art aficionado in her Modern Art (#1625) ensemble. That outfit featured a celery green chiffon dress with sheer flowers, gloves, her signature mules, and an impressionistic painting in the style of Monet.

Contrast that earliest artsy confection with her contemporary incarnations featured in "Art, Design, and Barbie: The Evolution of a Cultural Icon," an exhibit displayed at the Liberty Art Gallery between December 1995 and February 1996 in New York City. The exhibit was divided into three sections: The Ancestry of Barbie, which presented a short, global history of dolls; Barbie's History, with fourteen dioramas featuring Barbie doll's themes through her 36 years; and Barbie: Fantasies and Realities, which presented the original modern artists' works.

The Ancestry of Barbie exhibited the continuum of dolls through the ages: from an African fertility doll to the American Shirley Temple doll. Dolls were shown representing agents of magic, symbols of a girl's rite of passage, and value-role models. Other featured dolls included a Hopi wolf kachina, nineteenth-century paper dolls, Chinese, Japanese and Kuwaiti dolls, and the Bild Lilli that originally inspired Ruth Handler, the so-called "mother" of Barbie.

"Like all toys," the exhibition notes stated, "dolls represent the cultural beliefs of the society that produced her," so, the exhibit continued with dioramas that detailed the history of Barbie. This section of the exhibit included a series of large black-and-white photographs that reflected the historical life and times of the era.

The third and most challenging section of the exhibit—Barbie: Fantasies and Realities—presented works by some 50 European and American modern and contemporary artists and architects interpreting the Barbie doll's image through their unique styles. The entire *oeuvre* ranged from the sublime to the ridiculous; my favorites included the following:

- Chuck Jones' "Bugs Barbie," spotlighting Bugs Bunny with a blonde wig flirting with a very amorous Elmer Fudd-with-shotgun.

- "Colossus of Barbie," by architect extraordinaire Robert A.M. Stern, with Ken and Barbie as sand sphinxes-cum-pyramids, with tiny Barbie and Ken figures on their heads; similar Barbie and Ken figures played beach games on the sand below them.

- Heike Muehlhaus's 1993 work "Barbieburg Gate" ("Barbieburgerton") hearkened to the lowering of the Berlin Wall, the incursion of capitalism in Eastern Europe, and had a Barbie doll as an icon in the Brandenburg Gate.

- Andreas Baier's homage to Edward Hopper, entitled "Nighthounds"—a photo that featured the famous Nighthawks' image with a Barbie flavor. The Barbie doll's long-haired pooch, in giant size, peered through the glass window of the diner, with pink light streaming through the roof of the building.

- "Guess Who's Coming for Sushi," Barry Sturgill's classic photograph of Barbie dolls dressed in kimonos (such as the Barbie in Japan outfit from the early 1960s), with Godzilla hovering above the dolls and the Tokyo skyline, clutching a toy train in his monster paws.

- Emilio Ambasz's "Barbie Knoll," an architectural rendering and model subtitled, "The ecological embodiment of the Barbie doll." This work featured a blueprint scheme of Barbie Knoll, alongside an actual scale model of the Knoll. A key feature of the Knoll is a hillside with Barbie doll's body curvature.

- The piece de resistance might have been "Nude Barbie Descending a Staircase," a send-off of Marcel Duchamp's seminal work for the New York Armory Show, by Marian Jones.

The exhibit was sponsored by Mattel Inc., American Express, Merrill Lynch, and Olympia & York. While on view in New York, proceeds from the exhibit benefited the four children's museums of New York: The Brooklyn Children's Museum, Children's Museum of Manhattan, Children's Museum of the Arts (SoHo), and the Staten Island Children's Museum.

SOURCE: Notes from a Friend of the Barbie Doll, *Toy Trader* magazine, February 1996

anniversary of Francie, "Barbie's MODern cousin," in the form of a reproduction doll dressed in the original swimsuit design and packaged with the vintage outfit Gad Abouts (#1250).

The Barbie Millicent Roberts collection was anticipated by many collectors as the answer to a wish for the proverbial good old days of high quality dolls and facial molds, detailed costumes and accessories, and excruciating attention to detail. The Barbie Millicent Roberts Giftset included a blonde doll in a pink and black Chanel-styled suit, along with pink lingerie. The giftset, a limited release, was very difficult to find. Two outfits were also issued separate from the doll: Goin' to the Game and Picnic in the Park.

In 1996, the Olympic games were held in Atlanta. Gymnast Barbie was there along with Kerri Strug, Shannon Dougherty and Dominique Dawes. Gymnast Barbie was blonde, brunette, and African-American, and even had red hair for a few of the events (in a special Toys 'R Us version).

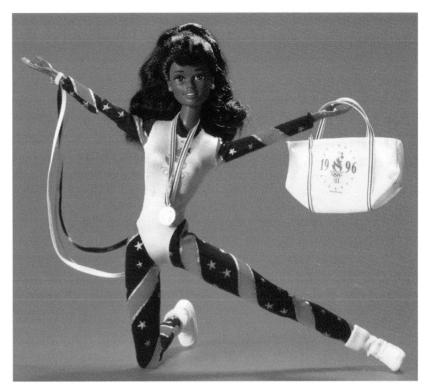

*A fully-articulated **Gymnast Barbie** was issued to commemmorate the Olympics in 1996.*

Denim-clad Barbie dolls proliferated the collector list this year. They included GAP Barbie, Calvin Klein Barbie for Bloomingdale's, JC Penney's exclusive Arizona Jeans Barbie, a Chuck E. Cheese Barbie doll, Style Barbie, and a series of denim outfits sold with the Lee jeans label.

A welcome addition to the Barbie doll line was the introduction of the Fashion Avenue line of clothing for the Barbie doll and friends. This line brought back the flavor of vintage tailored fashions, from denim to dressy. These were as much a hit with adult collectors as they were with children. All came packaged with accessories, and some even included the hard-to-find hosiery and miniature accessories that adult collectors really appreciate.

Big news for adult collectors was the kick-off of the Official Barbie Collectors Club by Mattel, the company's first venture into the club scene since the early 1960s. Interested joiners called Mattel at 1-800-524-TOYS, and for $7.50 they could receive a packet of Collector Information. The packet included a letter from Ruth Handler, a Barbie trivia sheet, a family tree with Barbie's family and friends, and a black and white 8 x 10 glossy of Barbie in Enchanted Evening attire.

*Very regal indeed, this doll from 1996 was modeled after **Empress Sissy** of Austria.*

*The very limited edition **Billions of Dreams Barbie** dazzled collectors in 1997.*

1997

According to Reuters, doll sales in 1996 rose a strong 8.6 percent, with continuing recognition going to Barbie. This year, the world's largest toy maker introduced 125 new Barbie dolls, ranging from a basic bathing suit model at $6 to the limited edition Billions of Dreams Barbie (retailing at $300). Engineers worked overtime with the Barbie doll this year, as two of the new dolls—Hula Hair Barbie and Bubbling Mermaid Barbie—had hair that changed color when wet. More movement was introduced into the Barbie doll's body with Workin' Out Barbie, which went beyond the previous year's ultra-flexible Gymnast doll. And, Barbie added yet another career to her long resume: dentist. Mattel's market research revealed that a good number of young girls were identifying dentistry as a future career path. Characteristic of the cross-branding approach that increasingly marks contemporary toys, Dentist Barbie was packaged with a doll-sized tube of Crest toothpaste (tartar control, of course).

This was the year that Mattel responded to collectors in several ways: in the quality of dolls (better face molds, makeup, clothing, accessories, details); the number of dolls (more limited, more exclusive distribution); and price points (lower overall). A tour of 1997 Toy Fair revealed that collectors' critiques were being heard by the Barbie doll development teams at Mattel.

One of the great surprises of 1997 was the outstanding Grand Premiere Barbie doll, inaugurating the new Official Barbie Doll Collector's Club. It was available only to "charter members" of the Club as a "Members Choice First Edition." The doll was a striking, pale-faced blonde with upswept hair, dressed in a high-style gown with a pink silk shantung skirt over a black velvet sculpted-to-the-body gown. Black faux maribou accented the neckline of the gown. The Official Barbie Collectors Club was launched and, by phoning Mattel at 1-800-431-TOYS and paying $39.99, joiners received a welcome kit with a membership card, binder, membership pin, and an opportunity to purchase the members-only doll.

The Billions of Dreams Barbie doll celebrated the billionth (!) production unit of Barbie since 1959. Mattel, in its promotion for the doll, also pointed out that the name of the doll represents "the billions of dreams that Barbie doll has inspired along the way." This limited edition doll was dressed in a long ice-blue gown decorated with Swarovski crystals, first seen in the Crystal Splendor doll in 1992. The most expensive doll of the year, collectors didn't suffer the same level of sticker shock associated with the $900 price tag of 1996's Pink Splendor: This time around, the price was about $300.

Sad to say, this was the last year for the Great Eras Collection. But, the series ended with great drama: the two dolls that finished this collection were among the

Factoid

Barbie has a menagerie of 35 pets, including 16 dogs, 12 horses, 4 cats, a parrot, a chimp, a panda, a lion cub, a seahorse, a giraffe, and a zebra.

1997

◆ On January 1, Jill Elikann Barad took the helm as President and Chief Executive Officer at Mattel, Inc.

◆ Ruth Handler, co-founder of Mattel and the "mother" of the Barbie doll, was inducted as a Laureate to The National Business Hall of Fame, sponsored by *Forbes Magazine* and Junior Achievement.

◆ The Women's National Basketball Association (WNBA) was established for professional female players.

best in the series. The Chinese Empress was a gorgeous, richly detailed doll wearing a mandarin-collar jacket with long sleeves that cover Barbie doll's fingertips—a tradition in Mandarin culture. The French Lady Barbie was inspired by the Napoleonic era, and wore a resplendent gown with a fitted waistline and skirt with golden metallic braid, with accents of fleurs-de-lis.

Mattel reproduced Wedding Day Barbie in the Nostalgic Series in both blonde and titian (redhead) versions. This very-hard-to-find vintage outfit is generally found only with its delicate illusion netting usually torn. A second reproduction was Fashion Luncheon, worn by an American Girl style Barbie doll (original vintage #1656). Finally, Francie collectors were treated to a third reproduction: an African-American Wild Bunch Francie doll (modeled after the original fashion #1766).

Who is the greatest Hollywood Legend of them all? Can you say "Norma Jean?" The 1997 Hollywood Legends series found Barbie as Marilyn Monroe in a series of three dolls that were must-haves for crossover collectors. Barbie was adorned in three iconic costumes: the white halter dress from *The Seven Year Itch* (in that memorable subway-vent scene); and two outfits from *Gentlemen Prefer Blondes*—the pink strapless number (remember Madonna in the "Material Girl" video?) and the red gown worn by Marilyn in the "Little Rock" musical number.

Following up the 1996 Star Trek Barbie and Ken set was the second in the Pop Culture series: Barbie Loves Elvis. The Elvis doll's face mold was one of the best lookalikes ever created in dolldom. Barbie wore, of course, a typical '50s outfit—poodle skirt, bobby socks, and saddle shoes. The Nostalgic face mold was used on

Nostalgic reproduction **Wedding Day Barbie** *doll wore a hard-to-find outfit with delicate netting.*

Harley-Davidson Barbie *(below right) was a major image change for the doll.*

this Barbie doll. Elvis was packaged with a "chrome" microphone, and wore a gold lame jacket and black shirt and pants. This is the young Elvis that most of us choose to remember.

One of the most interesting licensed exclusives to come out of the Barbie doll's world was Harley-Davidson Barbie, a cross-brand match made in Harley Heaven. The doll pushed the image to represent "today's free-spirited woman," according to Mattel's Web site. She was dressed in black faux leather with silvery studs from head to toe (as it were, from cap to boots). Always a promoter of healthy living, the doll was packaged with a helmet which Barbie no doubt wears every time she hops aboard her motorcycle.

*Here's the **Barbie doll as Marilyn Monroe**, wearing the strapless pink gown from* Gentlemen Prefer Blondes *also worn by Madonna in her "Material Girl" video (left). Barbie doll as Marilyn Monroe poses over a subway vent in her famous white halter dress (center) from* The Seven Year Itch. *Barbie doll poses in a musical number as Marilyn Monroe from* Gentlemen Prefer Blondes *(right).*

ROBERT BEST IS A GIRL'S BEST FRIEND

Robert Best designed the 1997 series of dolls featuring Barbie as Marilyn Monroe. "I have always been a huge Marilyn Monroe fan. To prepare ourselves for designing the Barbie doll as Marilyn Monroe, our team went through every book and publicity photo. I must have watched *Gentlemen Prefer Blondes* one hundred times; I can practically recite all of the script's words in my sleep!

"I really try to be accurate when I'm working on a project where I'm duplicating a costume. The most important things are to be both authentic and accurate. This is important both for the public figure on which I'm basing the doll as well as for the collector."

So how did Mr. Best select the three designs for Barbie as Marilyn? "I wanted to deliver on several levels: glamour, recognizability, and an overall 'wow!' factor. The white pleated dress (from the famous subway scene in *The Seven Year Itch*) is an indelible icon of the twentieth century. The pink strapless gown (worn by Marilyn as Lorelei Lee during the

song, "Diamonds are a Girls Best Friend" in *Gentlemen Prefer Blondes*) was a perfect marriage of this glamorous movie star and the Barbie doll. . . . When you watch that number, it's so cotton candy, it's so beautiful, she's glowing and radiant, the song is tongue-in-cheek funny. And a broader audience might relate to it through the Madonna connection (in which Madonna wore a replica gown in her "Material Girl" video). The red dress, also from *Gentlemen Prefer Blondes*, was ultra-glamorous, a great color, and a new look for Barbie with its plunging neckline. Plus, the showgirl aspect of the gown was really fun.

"Mostly, we remember Marilyn for her face and her figure. She's not someone like Audrey Hepburn or Jackie Kennedy who are known for their great wardrobes and sense of chic. But when you think about Marilyn, it's these glamorous gowns we remember."

SOURCE: Author's interview with Robert Best, August 1997

A rare beauty in brown, **Portrait in Taffeta Barbie** *doll was designed by Robert Best.*

Designer news was hot in 1997. Store exclusives included Barbie dolls from Anne Klein for Macy's, and Ralph Lauren for Bloomingdale's. The Anne Klein doll was smartly dressed for a day at the office in a post dress-for-success mode. Her accessories included details such as the Anne Klein "lion" logo on a belt buckle and name logo on her black purse.

Another prominent American designer, Ralph Lauren, lent his name to a designer Barbie doll for Bloomingdale's. The Ralph Lauren doll was reminiscent of the designer's classic, quintessential American style, with a double-breasted navy woolen blazer, embroidered Ralph Lauren crest, and gold buttons. She also wore a long "camelhair" overcoat and grey "flannel" trousers, and carried a plaid satchel. The Ralph Lauren doll was originally designed as a Barbie-and-Ken set, but was ultimately sold as a single Barbie doll at the request of the designer himself.

The Runway Collection was inaugurated with Byron Lars' first in a series of dolls by this talented African-American fashion designer. In The Limelight Barbie doll sashayed down the catwalk in a couture-inspired lime green and fur-trimmed high-style ensemble.

Yet more high-style news was made by Mattel's design wunderkind, Robert Best. His second design for Barbie Collectibles was Serenade in Satin, a spectacular follow-up to the previous year's Portrait in Taffeta.

A growing corporate partner with Mattel, Avon's exclusive dolls have become a staple part of the latest contemporary Barbie doll tableau. In 1997, Avon sponsored a very limited doll to celebrate the first Avon representative, Mrs. P.F.E. Albee, born in 1835. Thematically, she fit well with the Hallmark Victorian-styled dolls.

Mattel surprised many at Toy Fair with the first in a series of Barbie dolls inspired by famous artists. Water Lily Barbie doll, inspired by the paintings of Claude Monet, wore a dress reminiscent of his lush Impressionist masterpieces. The floor-length gown was marked by a huge skirt in blue and green tones, studded with sheer pink waterlilies.

Mattel unveiled the first in the Artist series, here with Barbie inspired by Monet's series of waterlily paintings.

*Nostalgic reproduction **Evening Enchantment Barbie** doll wore the vintage outfit from 1960.*

Brava! to Ann Driskill for this year's incredible Classique design: Romantic Interlude. The doll wore a tailored gown of black velvet, nipped in at the waist, with a white satin underskirt and cuffs, studded with rhinestone buttons. But perhaps the best feature of this doll was her short hair. This doll was based on a design that Driskill had done for an auction staged at the first Barbie Festival, sponsored by Mattel in 1994.

In a new Designer series came Janet Goldblatt's interpretation of a Bill Blass Barbie. The doll was absolutely true to the original Blass couture design—on the cutting edge of fashion with a dramatic, colorful gown in yellow, fuchsia, and black and white. Her short hair with pink streaks added to the unique look of this doll, which was targeted to adult couture doll collector tastes.

The second Christian Dior Barbie, following the initial 1995-96 doll, celebrated the 50th anniversary of the designer and his "New Look." Appropriate, then, that this doll wore the typical New Look silhouette: cinched-in waist, calf-length skirt in black wool crepe with knife-pleating, and a great straw hat. This '40s-design delight was a nominee for the 1997 Dolls' Award of Excellence sponsored by *Dolls* magazine.

Bob Mackie continued his delightfully fantastic series of Barbie with the tenth doll, in the guise of Madame du Barbie. This clever design was based on an eighteenth-century royal dress in France. Think of a character out of *Les Liaisons Dangereux (Dangerous Liaisons)* and you get the picture. The width of her dress was reminiscent of Empress Bride Barbie; the hair was like a white/blonde version of the Empress Sissy; and the beading was typical Mackie glitz—this time, in pale, pale blue brocade.

University Barbie was yet another new conceptual addition to the Barbie doll line, straddling collector ages. Barbie was dressed as a varsity cheerleader for one of 18 universities, including: Auburn, Clemson, Duke, Georgetown, North Carolina

SHARE A SMILE BECKY

In May 1997, Mattel and Toys 'R Us unveiled Share a Smile Becky, the first 11½-inch fashion doll to come with her own bright pink and lavendar wheelchair. In addition, checks for $10,000 were presented to the National Parent Network on Disabilities (NPND) and The National Lekotek Center.

Mattel worked closely with Toys 'R Us and NPND to develop the newest member of the Barbie doll world. NPND provides a presence and national voice for parents of children, youth, and adults with special needs. NPND shares information and resources in order to promote and support the power of parents to influence and affect policy issues concerning needs of people with disabilities and their families. Becky will be on the cover of the "Toys 'R Us Annual Differently-Abled Catalog,"

which is produced by Toys 'R Us in conjunction with the National Lekotek Center, which leads the way for accessible play for children with disabilities and their families through a nationwide nonprofit network of play-centered programs.

Share a Smile Becky is Barbie doll's friend with a disability and was created so the Barbie doll world will reflect the richness and diversity of the real world. The Becky doll's bright pink and lavendar wheelchair was realistically designed, with iridescent mylar around the wheels and a backpack that fits on the back of the wheelchair. Becky was available exclusively at Toys 'R Us stores and comes with a reply card to join WOW—Winners on Wheels—a fun boys and girls club for kids who use wheelchairs.

"TAKE BACK YOUR MINK," MATTEL DECREES!

In recent years, collectors have been warmly wrapping their Barbie dolls in tiny mink coats dyed red, tourmaline, even pink, and sold for $200 or so at furriers across the country.

But to the delight of animal-rights advocates and the dismay of furriers, Mattel, Inc. has been trying to put a halt to this fashion statement. Mattel sent out letters in the winter of 1997 threatening legal action against businesses that use the Barbie doll or invoke her name to sell doll furs, which are often designed to fit the doll's statuesque 11½-inch frame, and come with her tucked inside.

Mattel's main concern is that the coats violate its trademark, said Lisa McKendall, Director of Marketing Communications. But Mattel is also worried about the Barbie doll's image. "We would not have Barbie wear real fur—she's a friend to animals," Ms. McKendall said.

While Mattel did offer mink stoles for Barbie in the 1960s ($7 to $10 then, $1,000 today on the collectors' circuit), a 1989 promotional publication, *The Barbie 30th Anniversary Magazine*, included a resume for Barbie that listed her current occupation as "animal rights volunteer."

People for the Ethical Treatment of Animals (PETA) established an alliance of sorts with Mattel, informing the company whenever it hears about a furrier selling Barbie doll coats. "Mattel knows real fur is a turnoff—even the Cruella De Vil doll wears fake fur," said Daniel L. Mathews, the group's Director of Campaigns, referring to the furloving villain of the movie "101 Dalmatians."

SOURCE: *The New York Times*, 23 February 1997, p44

In 1997, the Barbie Millicent Roberts collection included these accessories, the Signature Series, looking remarkably like a famous upscale French collection. (From the Final Touches Assortment).

Designed by Ann Driskill, **Romantic Interlude Barbie** *was the first Classique doll with short hair.*

State, Oklahoma State, Penn State, University of Arizona, University of Florida, University of Georgia, University of Illinois, University of Miami, University of Michigan (my alma mater), University of Nebraska, University of Tennessee, University of Texas, University of Virginia, and University of Wisconsin. According to Mattel, this was the first phase of this doll and many more university tie-ins will be planned.

The American Stories series, targeted to young collectors, continued with Patriot Barbie, dressed in a blue and red military jacket with gold rope trim, and holding a liberty bell. She could be an historical "sister" to the FAO Schwarz Barbie as George Washington, which was also issued this year.

Dolls of the World had four dolls issued in 1997. Russian Barbie, a timely release, was in a detailed costume richly trimmed in braid. French Barbie was dressed as a Can Can dancer in black, white and fuchsia, the colors and style of outfit worn by the original Parisian Barbie doll in 1980 when this important collector series began. Arctic Barbie, nose-kissin'-cousin to 1982's Eskimo Barbie (but now more politically correct in name), was a beautiful doll with Kira face sculpting. The outfit was pure Inuit: mukluks and fleece pants, topped by a hood with faux white fur. Finally, Puerto Rican Barbie was dressed in a floor-length traditional costume, not unlike the original Hispanic Barbie.

The first doll in the new Classic Ballet series collection was Barbie as the Sugar Plum Fairy. This collection will feature dolls from classic ballets. The third doll in the Children's Collector series was Barbie as Cinderella. She was similar to last year's Cinderella doll produced by Mattel.

Main line dolls for younger collectors can be attractive to many adult collectors who like to acquire dolls primarily targeted to young people. Mattel's market research indicates that many young girls want to be dentists, so the 1997 career doll was Dentist Barbie, packaged complete with a dental chair, little Kelly-sized patient, dental instruments, and a miniature tube of Crest (another licensed product tie-in). Dentist Barbie "spoke" two phrases to her little patient: "Let's brush" and "Great checkup!"

Workin' Out Barbie was the latest in a long line of exercising Barbie dolls that started with Great Shapes Barbie in the 1980s, but this time the doll could really aerobicize because she was more limber than ever, equipped with suction cups on her exercise shoes. Like the workout dolls from the 1980s, she came packed with a cassette that played workout music.

BARBIE LOVES ELVIS; BARBIE COLLECTORS LOVE ABBE

As related by Abbe Littleton:

"The inspiration for the Barbie Loves Elvis giftset came from a piece of fabric. I was shopping for fabric for my Classique doll design, Midnight Gala (released in 1995). I found a piece of fabric that had all these Elvis icons all over it. My mother-in-law is a big Elvis fan; she's always talking about Graceland! I was more of a Beatles than an Elvis fan back in the 1960s.

"I thought it would be great if Barbie were an Elvis fan. I envisioned that, in the doll's packaging, we could include some fan paraphernalia. I first designed the doll in a 1990s context. She had short hair. She was hip and cute, with the current Barbie face sculpting.

"One day in 1993, I came to my office and picked up a voicemail message from marketing. I was told that there would be a meeting with someone named 'Priscilla.' I just assumed there was this new marketing person named 'Priscilla.' I showed up to the meeting, and asked who Priscilla was, and my boss said, 'Priscilla Presley.' All I could think was, 'What am I going to wear!'

"When Priscilla walked into the boardroom at Mattel headquarters, she was stunning. I gave my presentation and she got excited, too. This turned into a brainstorm-ing session. We had no idea that the release of the dolls would coincide with the anniversary of his death.

"We conducted research to help my designs to be accute. We visited Graceland in Memphis to get a real feel for Elvis Presley. When we returned to Mattel headquarters, I realized that if you really wanted to be taken back in time, we had to do research on the 1950s. I decided on a poodle skirt for the Barbie doll. I couldn't find all the fabrics I needed. So I brought one of my own pink sweaters into the design studio and we cut it into pieces to use for Barbie's sweater design. We ended up using Sweater Girl (#976) as a guide that would be accurate for the 1950s timeframe. We experimented with different kinds of heads, and tried everything. The one that worked best was the Nostalgic head.

"Speaking of heads, we knew that Elvis's head and hair had to be perfect. We decided to sculpt the front curl in his hair because it had to be just-so. Our sculptor, Jussuf Abbo, did a fabulous job on the doll."

"During the design process and through my research, I became a fan of Elvis," Abbe confessed. Now Abbe and her mother-in-law are both fans of The King!

SOURCE: Author's interview with Abbe Littleton, August 1997

The second in the Winter Princess series, Evergreen Princess, was issued in 1994.

Chapter 5

CONTEMPORARY THEMES

One of the most impressive aspects of *Contemporary BARBIE®* is the doll's continual evolution of personalities and activities. By design since Barbie doll's inception, the doll changes with the individual who is playing with it. In 1997 alone, over 100 new issue dolls named "Barbie" were available on the (relatively) mass market. Given that large volume, collectors can shape their collections based on themes of dolls. While some collectors choose to acquire examples from every category available, others choose to focus their collections on a particular theme.

The major themes that *Contemporary BARBIE* reflects include:

career	hair play
bridal	holiday
special effects	glamour
athletic	"foodie"
global	beach/sun worshipping
trend	shopping

◆ CAREER BARBIE

In the contemporary era, Barbie has had careers from A to Z, from Astronaut (in 1985 and 1994) to zookeeper (as Animal Lovin' Barbie in 1989). She has had at least 100 careers since her birth. The careers span a broad range from the sciences (such as doctor) to politics (such as running for President and attending international political events for UNICEF and the Children's Summit), to the arts and athletics (as fashion designer and skater for the Ice Capades and the Olympics, respectively). Barbie has been an airline hostess for American Airlines, Braniff (now defunct), Pan Am (also defunct), and Singapore Airlines. And, in a 1984 issue of *Barbie* magazine featuring Day-to-Night Barbie on the cover, Barbie became the star of her own cooking show, the "Glamorous Gourmet."

The Barbie doll has also been designed as a professional shopper for several prominent merchants, including Bloomingdale's (twice), FAO Schwarz (twice), Meijer's and Spiegel, as well as for Benetton.

Over the years, the career-oriented Barbie doll has appeared both as a woman of color and as Caucasian. The 1984 seminal Day-to-Night Barbie doll, who Kitty Black-Perkins designed as a career "every woman," came in Black, Caucasian and Hispanic versions. By 1989 and 1990, respectively, the UNICEF and Summit dolls came in Asian, Black, Caucasian and Hispanic versions.

*An early example of a career doll in the contemporary period, **Doctor Barbie** came equipped with her medical bag and, prepared for a quick change, an evening dress.*

Barbie became a dentist for the first time in 1997.

Contemporary BARBIE AS CAREER WOMAN

Astronaut	1985	Navy Officer	1991
Day-to-Night Barbie	1985	Army Officer (Desert Storm)	1992
Rocker	1986	Presidential candidate	1992
Tennis Star	1986	Air Force Thunderbirds	1993
Olympic Skater	1987	Police Officer	1993
Rocker (Dancin' Action)	1987	Rockette	1993
Ballerina	1988	Astronaut (25th Apollo)	1994
Doctor	1988	Dr. Barbie	1994
Environmentalist, zookeeper	1988	Silver Screen (movie star)	1994
Sensations rock star	1988	Circus Star	1995
SuperStar Movie Star	1988	Dr. Barbie	1995
Tennis Star	1988	Firefighter	1995
Army Officer (American Beauties)	1989	International Traveler	1995
Aerobics Instructor	1990	Teacher	1995
Air Force	1990	Chef	1996
The Beat (rock star)	1990	Olympic Gymnast	1996
Flight Time (pilot)	1990	Pet doctor/veterinarian	1996
Ice Capades (pro skater)	1990	Space explorer (Star Trek)	1996
Summit (diplomat)	1990	Dentist	1997
UNICEF (diplomat)	1990	Paleontologist	1997 (TRU exclusive)
Marine Corps Officer	1991		

The 1988 glamour doll, **SuperStar Barbie,** was a movie star who came complete with a changeable ensemble.

In 1995, Barbie took on one of the most challenging careers in her history: fire fighting. Both Caucasian (top) and Black (above) Barbie dolls were **Fire Fighters,** and came complete with faithful dalmations at their sides.

Part of the Stars 'n Stripes series, **Marine Corps Barbie** *(right) wore her dress uniform in 1991. Is it Cagney or Lacey? No, it's Barbie doll (left) as the Toys 'R Us* **Police Officer Barbie** *in 1993.*

IT'S A BIRD! IT'S A PLANE! IT'S BARBIE!

One small step for Barbie, one giant step for toykind: The National Air and Space Museum veers from its very boy-oriented, hardware-heavy image with the opening of an exhibit called "Flight Time Barbie: Dolls From the Popular Culture Collection of the National Air and Space Museum." Exhibit Curator Mary Henderson dreamed up the museum's fantastically popular (more than 900,000 visitors) exhibit.

In the small, two-case exhibit (with explicatory text printed on a hot-pink panel), we trace the Barbie doll's aviation career trajectory from her humble beginnings as a ponytailed circa-1961 stewardess (they weren't called "flight attendants" then) serving on pilot Ken doll's flight in the fold-out Friend Ship playkit, to 1992's Operation Desert Storm Barbie, and 1994's Astronaut Barbie.

"You understand that once a Barbie enters the museum, it's not a toy, it's an artifact," says Henderson, smiling. Many of the artifacts were donated by Mattel, but the exhibit includes a few things from the bottom of Henderson's 13-year-old daughter's toybox.

A pair of Air Force Barbie dolls exchange a high-five in the '90s airport playset, which includes a pink aircraft (complete with in-flight meals and an unheard-of-amount of leg room), pink ticket counter, pink passenger lounge, and pink gift shop.

In the last section of the exhibit, we meet Air Force Barbie in her leather bomber jacket and fatigues (no heels; a short black boot) and astronaut Barbie holding a silver mesh bag filled with glow-in-the-dark moon rocks—ready, as always, to accessorize, no matter what solar system she finds herself in.

SOURCE: *The Washington Post*, 6 June 1996, pT05

Shopping Barbie dolls are popular
among collectors, and this doll was no
exception. In 1995, Spiegel quickly sold
out of this **Shopping Chic** doll following
the publication of its prototype photograph in Miller's.

◆ Barbie the Bride

Collecting bride dolls is a favorite theme for many doll collectors, Barbie-focused or otherwise. Both young and older collectors appreciate the beautiful detail applied to Barbie bride dolls—the highly-prized Bob Mackie Empress Bride doll providing one notable example. In the *Contemporary Barbie* doll era, the Barbie doll has come packaged solo and with entire wedding parties (such as Wedding Day for Midge in 1991). In addition, many bridal fashions have been packaged separately for Barbie.

Dream Bride Barbie, 1991, was typical of bridal Barbie dolls. She came complete with a Barbara Bush-style double-strand pearl choker reminiscent of the earliest Barbie bridal outfits.

BARBIE BRIDE THEME DOLLS IN THE CONTEMPORARY ERA

Romantic Wedding Barbie 1987
Wedding Fantasy Barbie . . . . 1989 (Caucasian and Black)
Wedding Party Barbie . . . . 1989 (Porcelain reproduction)
Dream Bride Barbie 1991
Wedding Day for Midge (Barbie doll) 1991
Bob Mackie Empress Bride 1992
Romantic Bride Barbie . . . . 1993 (Caucasian and Black)
Wholesale Clubs-Wedding Fantasy Gift Set 1993
TRU-Dream Wedding Barbie . . . . 1993 (Caucasian and Black)
My Size Barbie Bride . . . . 1994 (Caucasian and Black)
Star Lily Bride . . . . 1994 (Porcelain)
Wal-Mart Country Bride . . . . 1995 (Caucasian, Black and Hispanic)
Wedding Party Barbie . . . . 1995 (Caucasian and Black)
Rose Bride (Wholesale Club) 1996
Wedding Flower Collection-Romantic Rose Bride 1996
Wedding Day Barbie . . . . .1997 (Blonde and Redhead)
Dream Bride (Service Merchandise) 1997

Here comes The Bride. . . . Both Bob Mackie Barbie doll collectors and bride doll collectors highly prize the
Empress Bride *doll from Mr. Mackie. Among some Mackie collectors, this doll far surpasses all others of his designs.*

◆ SPECIAL EFFECTS BARBIE

Barbie first bent her legs in 1965, twisted and turned in 1967, and "spoke" in 1968 (in both English and Spanish). Since then, the *Contemporary BARBIE* era has seen Barbie dolls with amazing features, physical and otherwise. These features are especially exciting for young girls, and Mattel designers and engineers work hard to develop new and interesting features to add even greater dimension to the doll and longevity to the child's play cycle with it. Special effects encompass a variety of forms and features including lights, color, "disappearing acts" or "visual hide and seek," movement (á la Dance Action, Dance Moves, and Gymnast), hair play features and innovative materials (e.g., Bedtime Barbie). Some special effects dolls serve dual-duty: the Angel Lights Barbie, issued in 1992, serves as both a light-up doll and a holiday doll (it can be used as a Christmas tree topper).

*The **Locket Surprise** dolls, although not a huge hit among collectors, employed a new design that allowed the doll's chest cavity to be opened for storing small items.*
***Twinkle Lights Barbie** incorporated fiber optic technology to glow in the dark.*

Contemporary BARBIE special effects dolls released to date

Year	Doll	Special Effect
1980	Beauty Secrets Barbie	Doll's arms moved by pressing her back
1981	Western Barbie	"Winks" with a press of her back
1981	Magic Curl Barbie	Curly hair would "uncurl" with spray of Magic Mist
1986	Magic Moves Barbie	Doll moves arms with touch of switch
1986	Dream Glow Barbie	Gown and parasol glow in the dark
1987	Dancin' Action Rocker Barbie	Arms move when waist tilts
1990	Dance Magic Barbie	Doll "dances"; icy water changes lip color
1990	Wet 'N Wild Barbie	Beachwear changes color in icy water
1991	Bath Magic Barbie	"Magical beads" become sponge fashion accessories when dropped into water
1991	Lights & Lace Barbie	"Jeweled" belt lights up
1992	Rappin' Rockin' Barbie	Boom boxes play rap rhythms
1992	Rollerblade Barbie	Skates flicker and flash as they roll
1992	Teen Talk Barbie	Doll "talks" (four sayings)
1993	Angel Lights Barbie	Fiber optics light; can be used as tree topper
1993	Locket Surprise Barbie	Doll's heart-shaped chest cavity opens
1993	Secret Hearts Barbie	Pattern in fabric can be temporarily "erased"
1993	Twinkle Lights Barbie	Fiber optics light up in the dark
1994	Bedtime Barbie	Innovative "cuddly" material
1994	Bicycling Barbie	Doll's legs bend to operate bicycle
1994	Dance 'n Twirl Barbie	Doll dances in response to music
1994	Gymnast Barbie	Doll bends in infinite ways
1995	Hot Skatin' Barbie	Poseable/bendable doll "skates"
1995	Super Power Barbie	"Magical power shield" lights when touched
1995	Supertalk Barbie	Doll "talks" (100,000 sayings)
1996	Bubbling Mermaid	Doll blows bubble via specially engineered "mermaid" body sculpting
1996	Foam and Color	Doll's hair can be colored with special foam tint
1997	Hula Hair Barbie	Doll's removable hula shirt is made from fabric with golden holographic designs
1997	Talk with Me Barbie	Doll "talks" via programmable CD-ROM
1997	Movin' Groovin'	Doll magically "walks" by itself

In 1994, **Bedtime Barbie** was manufactured with a cuddly fabric that allowed her to be safely taken to bed by youngsters.

◆ ATHLETIC BARBIE

Major themes for Barbie doll designers since 1959 have been sports, fitness and athletics. Collectors of vintage Barbie doll clothing highly treasure several such outfits, including "Tennis, Anyone," "Ski Queen," "Icebreaker" and "Ballerina," all marketed in the early 1960s. The athlete theme has thus resonated with collectors through the entire history of the Barbie doll.

In the *Contemporary BARBIE* era, the doll was featured as "Our U.S. Olympic Favorite!" Gold Medal Barbie in 1976 (similar versions were made for the Australian, Canadian, and Italian markets). Once again, Barbie will be an Olympian in 1996 to commemorate the Games in Atlanta.

But between the 1976 Olympian and the present day, the Barbie doll has partaken in nearly every sport available. . .with the exception of bungee jumping! She has rollerskated, in-line skated, hot skated, gymnasticated, bicycled, aerobicized, golfed, baseballed and skied. . .to name just a few.

*This **Hot Skatin' Barbie** doll (top) used a jointed body so Barbie could perform ice skating and in-line skating. This 1995 **Equestrienne Barbie** doll (above) was released for the international market, but was available through select U.S. retail channels. Her riding jacket is reminiscent of Versace print designs.*

***Ski Fun Barbie** hit the slopes in 1991*

Athletic dolls are highly popular, especially with younger collectors who wish to see the doll "do what I do," according to Black-Perkins. An example of this phenomenon was 1994's fantastically popular Barbie Gymnast doll—one of Mattel's most successful dolls to date in capturing the interests of younger collectors (see sidebar in Chapter 3 for insights into the evolution of the Gymnast Barbie doll).

Barbie took up aerobics in the early 1980s. The phenomenal rise of aerobics as a new fitness regime began in 1971 when Jacki Sorensen, a dancer from Malibu, led the first aerobics dance class of six students in a church basement. By the time the Barbie doll donned her Great Shapes spandex gear in the early 1980s, aerobics had become a whole culture unto itself.

*Mattel debuted **University Barbie** in 1997 in three versions for 18 universities.*

Contemporary Barbie doll athletes

Rollerskating	1980
Ballerina	1983
Great Shapes	1983
Tennis Star	1986
Olympic Skating	1987
Tennis Star Gift Set	1988
All Stars (Aerobics)	1990
Ice Capades	1990
Ice Capades (2nd edition)	1991
Ski Fun	1991
Target Baseball	1993
Target Golf Date	1993
Bicycling	1994
Gymnast	1994
Hot Skatin'	1995
Winter Sports (International)	1995
Equestrienne Gift Set (International)	1995
In-Line Skater	1996
Olympic Gymnast	1996
Twirling Ballerina	1996
Wal-Mart Skating Star	1996
University Barbie	1997
Workin' Out	1997

Golf Date Barbie (left) and *Baseball Barbie* (right) were customized dolls sponsored by Target. They carry out the Barbie-as-athlete theme which has been popular since Barbie first appeared in Ice Breaker and Tennis Anyone outfits in 1960.

The greatest impact of aerobics, other than on circulatory systems and ideal body types, has been on fashion. The outfits people wear for aerobic dance classes once would have been taboo in public: too sloppy, or in some cases too revealing. But the new, hyper-oxygenated sense of leisure wear, favored now by lots of fashion-conscious people who might not ever dream of actually exercising, says it's fine to go almost anywhere dressed for the gym. Since 1982, when Jane Fonda urged viewers to "go for the burn," on her workout tape—one of the best-selling videotapes in history—it has become common to see women and men in malls, restaurants, and on trains and planes wearing exercise suits and Lycra capri leggings as tight and close-fitting as skin. So, quite naturally, both aerobics and the miracle fabrics of Spandex and Lycra have impacted Barbie doll fashions.

◆ GLOBAL BARBIE

This category of collectors bridges both the young and adult collecting segments. Global Barbie doll collectors tend to collect in one of two ways: Either they go for all of the International/Dolls of the World dolls, or they purchase those dolls representing nations the collector has visited or finds particularly intriguing. Many collectors also acquire Barbie and family dolls available on the international market. Popular editions include the dolls marketed in the Philippines, India, and throughout Europe (these dolls manufactured for the market outside of the U.S. are not detailed in this book; some are described in books listed in the bibliography). Holiday dolls available on the international market have attracted the growing interest of American collectors as well.

For global Barbie doll collectors, the magic year and product development story began in 1980 with the introduction of the Barbie International Collection. Between 1980 and 1984, 11 International dolls were available in the series. In 1985, the name of the line-up was changed to the "Dolls of the World Collection" (DOW), but many collectors still use the short-cut nickname, "Internationals."

At least two new International/DOW Barbie dolls have been made every year since 1980, with the exception of 1985. When the line's name changed that year, the only new doll was the Japanese Barbie.

Collectors often ask about the process used in determining which countries will be represented by DOW dolls in a particular year. Because there have been three DOW dolls produced annually in the latter part of the *Contemporary BARBIE* era, Mattel identifies at least one nation or region in which they have a production plant, subsidiary, or large or emerging collector population. Another of the

This booklet introduced Barbie to children around the world. The Dolls of the World have become one of the most sought after collections in the contemporary era.

three dolls might be a second edition of a previously-released International doll. A third doll will normally be from a country not previously released. In the case of the 1995 Dolls of the World, both the German and the Irish Barbie dolls were second editions; the "new" addition to the series was the Polynesian doll. A fourth doll considered to be part of the DOW line in 1995 was the third Native American Barbie doll.

So, Mattel. . .where are the Polish, French-Canadian, Welsh, Danish, and Hungarian Barbie dolls?

The 25 most prevalent ancestry groups in the United States

1. German
2. Irish
3. English
4. African-American
5. Italian
6. American
7. Mexican
8. French
9. Polish
10. American Indian
11. Dutch
12. Scotch-Irish
13. Scottish
14. Swedish
15. Norwegian
16. Russian
17. French-Canadian
18. Welsh
19. Spanish
20. Puerto Rican
21. Slovak
22. White (other ancestry not listed)
23. Danish
24. Hungarian
25. Chinese

SOURCE: U.S. Bureau of the Census 1990 data,

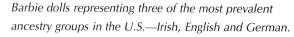

Barbie dolls representing three of the most prevalent ancestry groups in the U.S.—Irish, English and German.

International/Dolls of the World by Year and Mattel Stock Number

1980   *Parisian* (#1600), *Royal* (British, #1601), *Italian* (#1602)

1981   *Oriental* (#3262), *Scottish* (#3263)

1982   *Eskimo* (#3898), *India* (#3897)

1983   *Spanish* (#4031), *Swedish* (#4032)

1984   *Irish* (#7517), *Swiss* (#7541)

1985   *Japanese* (#9481)

1986   *Peruvian* (#2995), *Greek* (#2997)

1987   *German* (#3188), *Icelandic* (#3189)

1988   *Canadian* (#4928), *Korean* (#4929)

1989   *Russian* (#1916), *Mexican* (#1917)

1990   *Nigerian* (#7376), *Brazilian* (#9094)

1991   *Czechoslovakian* (#7330), *Malaysian* (#7329), *Scottish* (reissue, #9845), *Parisian* (reissue, #9843), *Eskimo* (reissue, #9844)

1992   *English* (reissue, #4973), *Spanish* (reissue, #4963), *Jamaican* (#4647)

1993   *Italian* (#2256), *Native American 1* (#1753), *Australian* (#3626)

1994   *Chinese* (#11180), *Kenyan* (#11181), *Dutch* (#11104), *Native American 2* (#11609)

1995   *Native American 3* (#12699), *Polynesian* (#12700), *Irish* (reissue, #12998), *German* (reissue, #12698)

1996   *Norwegian* (#14450), *Japanese* (reissue, #14163) *Oshogatsu* (#14024), *Mexican* (reissue, #14449), *Indian* (reissue, #14451), *African, Native American 4* (#15304)

1997   *French* (second issue, #16499), *Puerto Rican* (#16754), *Russian* (second issue, #16500), *Arctic* (second issue, #16495)

Top row, left to right: **Mexican Barbie** joined the line of Dolls of the World in 1996. The fourth **Native American Barbie** doll was issued in 1996. Looking like a lovely Nanook of the North, **Arctic Barbie** joined the Dolls of the World series in 1997.

Bottom row, left to right: **Ghanaian Barbie** was the second African doll in the Dolls of the World series. **French Barbie** doll was the second doll "from France," following the first issued in 1980 at the debut of the Dolls of the World series. Marking the break-up of the Soviet Union, this **Russian Barbie** doll is dressed in an authentic, detailed costume.

◆ BARBIE DOLL AS TREND-SETTER

The Barbie doll, by definition and design, often takes a cue from leading-edge trends in the worlds of fashion, music and athletics. These dolls are especially attractive to younger collectors because they often reflect a fad or activity in which young people are involved. The production lead-times on these dolls are as much as one-half shorter, meaning that from the inception of the design through production, the time-to-market may be one year instead of the usual two.

The following sampling of trendy Barbie dolls reflects fads prevalent at the time of their release:

- Western fashion and music influences have been omnipresent since the advent of the Western Barbie doll in 1981 (#1757) through 1995's Wal-Mart Country Bride (#13614) Barbie doll in pink gingham wedding dress.
- POG Fun Barbie doll (#13239), a Toys 'R Us exclusive in 1994, capitalized on the POG collecting trend that emerged in 1993.
- Sunflower Barbie (#13488) of 1994 echoed the fashion trend of big yellow Van Gogh-inspired sunflowers in clothing, jewelry and interior decorating.
- Troll Barbie (#10257) borrowed the popular collectible gnome theme and translated it to Barbie doll's printed stretch pants, plastic earrings, and attachable troll hair ornaments.
- Rock music has provided the inspiration for several Barbie dolls in the 1980s. In 1988, Barbie and the Sensations (Barbie doll #4931) hearkened back to the Doo-Wop music of the 1950s (note Barbie's short circle skirts, sunglasses and ponytail). In 1986, Barbie and the Rockers (Barbie doll #1140 and #3055, second edition) were dressed in neon-colored spandex club outfits. And, in 1992, Rappin' Rockin' Barbie (#3248), reflected the street music innovated in urban areas of the country. These are far cries from the days when Barbie doll sang at the microphone, sultry and sophisticated, as Solo in the Spotlight (1960-64, #982)!

*Wal-Mart offered **Country Bride Barbie** as its annual customized doll of 1995 in Caucasian, Black and Hispanic ethnic variations.*

*The limited edition **Pog Fun Barbie** (far left) played off on a current fad: pog collecting. **Sunflower Barbie** (center) combed the fashion magazines and found the sunflower motif popular in 1994. **Troll Barbie** (left) capitalized on the resurgence of the troll fad of the 1960s.*

Rocker Barbie (right) and **Barbie of the Sensations** (far right) harmonize to the strains of their role models—pop divas like Vanessa Williams and Debbie Gibson. In 1995, **Dance Moves Barbie** (above) was a flashy disco diva, complete with microphone. Karaoke Disco, anyone?

◆ BARBIE AS HAIR PLAY DOLL

Barbie doll designers have incorporated hair play features in the dolls since the 1970s, when focus groups revealed that hair play was a key dimension in play value associated with Barbie dolls. It is fair to say that most "main line" Barbie dolls, which are targeted to girls under 10 years of age, are hair play dolls (note that most dolls—even the adult-targeted Bob Mackie collector dolls—are packed with small plastic hair brushes). While hair play dolls are not meant to

In 1993, **Hollywood Hair Barbie** broke the record for the longest-haired Barbie doll of all time. Needless to say, this quintessential hair play doll was very popular with young girls.

be adult-oriented collector dolls, some collectors acquire the dolls because they appreciate a particular face mold, hair style, or face painting colors, and they use them as mannequins for dressing up (I also know a hairdresser who owns every one of these dolls!).

actoid

Totally Hair Barbie was the most successful Barbie doll in Mattel's history with over 10 million dolls sold worldwide in 1992.

This **Paint 'n Dazzle** activity doll came packaged with fabric paints that could be used to decorate Barbie's denim outfit.

Supermarkets and drugstore chains offered the **Schooltime Fun** doll in 1995. Befitting the school theme, she carried a backpack and wore flat shoes.

In 1990, **Cool Looks Barbie** appealed to young girls and wore an orange, pink and black outfit that reflected the fad fashions of the time.

Hair play dolls in the *Contemporary BARBIE* doll era

Beauty Secrets Barbie	.1980
Pretty Changes Barbie	.1980
Golden Dream Barbie	.1981
Magic Curl Barbie	.1982
Twirly Curls Barbie	.1983
Super Hair Barbie	.1987
Perfume Pretty Barbie	.1988
Style Magic Barbie	.1989
Totally Hair Barbie	.1992
Hollywood Hair Barbie	.1993
Troll Hair Barbie	.1993
Glitter Hair Barbie	.1994
Cut 'N Style Barbie	.1995
Sparkle Beach	.1996
Splash 'n Color	.1996
Hula Hair	.1997

◆ HOLIDAY BARBIE

The Happy Holidays series, introduced in 1988, was not originally conceived as a series, but as a market test or pilot project. It was the first vinyl Barbie doll ever produced in the at-the-time stratospheric $20 price range, and she was glorious in her new display packaging. The doll was scarce. As Joe Blitman stated in his appearance in the Barbie-as-Scarlett infomercial with Leeza Gibbons, "Mattel didn't know what it had" in terms of sales potential. Only

TRANSFORMING DESIGNS

Sometimes designs beget new designs. Kitty Black-Perkins created a unique Barbie doll for an AIDS benefit in Los Angeles in the late 1980s. The one-of-a-kind doll wore a black velvet gown with diamond-like crystals sewn all over it, and the gown lit up. Jill Barad appreciated this doll so much that two mass market versions of it were inspired and manufactured: the 1991 green velvet Happy Holidays (facing page) Barbie doll and the 1993 Angel Lights Barbie.

In 1994, this doll, the seventh in the Happy Holidays series, took the collector market by storm and shot up in value almost instantly. The fur-trimmed gown was an obvious attraction.

Clockwise from top: *The **1989 Happy Holidays Barbie** wore a fresh white dress trimmed with fur. The fuchsia-colored gown of **1990 Happy Holidays Barbie** was a surprise color for the holiday season. The rich dark green velvet of the **1991 Happy Holidays** gown continues to be a favorite of many Barbie collectors. Among the more glamorous gowns, the **1992 Happy Holidays** version glistened with silver and glass beads. The **1993 Happy Holidays Barbie** doll brightly glowed in her red tulle gown.*
(Dolls for these photos loaned by Sandi Holder of the Barbie Attic).

300,000 units of the doll were produced, and they were sold in a retail-minute. (See the sidebar story about the Happy Holidays Barbie doll in Chapter 1, *Contemporary BARBIE* History).

There are a range of holiday-oriented Barbie dolls suited to every budget. The Happy Holidays Barbie dolls retailed for $30 beginning in 1988, and usually begin at $35 as current releases.

In addition to this line, however, Mattel manufactures a line of more main-line holiday dolls for supermarkets including: Holiday Hostess in 1993, Holiday Dreams in 1994, and Caroling Fun Barbie in 1995. Wholesale or warehouse clubs, such as BJ's Wholesale Club, Pace and Sam's Club, offer a line of holiday dolls that began with Winter Royale in 1993, continued with the popular Season's Greetings in 1994, and most recently featured the Winter's Eve Barbie in 1995—a doll that quickly disappeared from wholesale club shelves.

Mattel also offers the Winter Theme series of Barbie dolls. These have included: Winter Princess in 1993, Evergreen Princess in 1994, Peppermint Princess in 1995, Jewel Princess in 1996, and Midnight Princess in 1997.

Many collectors, both young and older, enjoy displaying these dolls at Christmastime because their design, colors and fabrications complement the red, green and gold themes of the holiday.

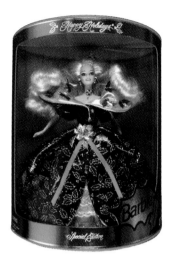

*By Christmastime the Caucasian version of the **1995 Happy Holidays** doll was impossible to find and the Black version was very hard to find. Mattel announced a voucher campaign to give those who missed out a second chance to obtain the doll. . .around Easter 1996!*

*The third in the Winter Princess series, **Peppermint Princess,** was available for the 1995 holiday season.*

*The **1996 Happy Holidays** doll was quickly seized by collectors due to its desirable fur- and brocade-trimmed costume.*

The brunette **1997 Happy Holidays Barbie doll** wore a red and gold costume with unique ribbon detail at the back and shoulders.

The last in the Winter Princess Series, **Midnight Princess** (below right) wore a gown with a richly-decorated bodice and collar.

Hallmark has offered ornaments in the form of miniature Barbie dolls (below right) since 1994.

A Limited Time Offer for BARBIE Doll Collectors!

Available exclusively to members of the 1996 Hallmark Keepsake Ornament Collector's Club

Note: The Club Edition Ornament featuring BARBIE™ shown above, is available as an optional purchase once you join the 1996 Keepsake Ornaments Collector's Club. Actual size of ornament: 3 5/16" H x 3 1/4" W

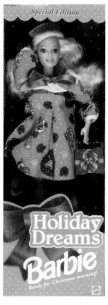

Top row, left to right: *Wholesale clubs scored a major hit with this **Season's Greetings** doll released for the 1994 holiday season. Her red velvet fitted jacket and red and green tapestry skirt scored high with adult collectors. A supermarket special from 1994, the **Holiday Dreams** doll was festive in her holiday-inspired sleepwear, nightcap and wrapped "gift." Wholesale clubs offered **Winter's Eve** in 1995, following up 1994's spectacularly popular Seasons Greetings. These dolls were whisked off store shelves and quickly increased in value. In 1993, **Holiday Hostess** was offered by supermarkets and drugstore chains.*

*Warehouse clubs distributed **Winter Fantasy** in 1996, becoming one of the most popular holiday dolls.*

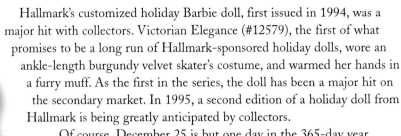

Hallmark's customized holiday Barbie doll, first issued in 1994, was a major hit with collectors. Victorian Elegance (#12579), the first of what promises to be a long run of Hallmark-sponsored holiday dolls, wore an ankle-length burgundy velvet skater's costume, and warmed her hands in a furry muff. As the first in the series, the doll has been a major hit on the secondary market. In 1995, a second edition of a holiday doll from Hallmark is being greatly anticipated by collectors.

Of course, December 25 is but one day in the 365-day year. Mattel has developed Barbie dolls for other holiday occasions, including Valentine's Day and Easter—employing heart and egg themes, respectively—that are easily worked into new Barbie doll costumes. (Could Halloween be far-off?) Hallmark has also produced Valentine's Day Barbie dolls and Barbie doll Christmas ornaments, and it produced its first Barbie doll Easter ornament in 1995. Limited edition Barbie ornaments are available through the Hallmark Keepsake Ornament Collector's Club.

Hallmark retailed its first customized Barbie doll in 1994, and it met with great success. **Victorian Elegance Barbie** *(left) wore an elegant burgundy velvet suit trimmed in fur, with details like a fur muff and ice skates completing the ensemble.*

Hallmark's second holiday offering, **Holiday Memories,** *was packaged like the first issue Hallmark doll. Her long skirted suit is trimmed in fur.*

This third in the Hallmark Holiday Series, **Yuletide Romance,** *concluded this particular series.*

*The Winter Princess series grew with the addition of **Jewel Princess Barbie** doll.*

Bottom row, left to right: *Grocery and drugstores offer Barbie dolls throughout the year, including this **Holiday Season Barbie** available for Christmas 1996. JC Penney's **Royal Enchantment** was its 1995 customized doll offered for the holiday season. It won favor with many collectors who appreciated the gold and green gown that was priced within many collectors' budgets. Supermarkets and drugstore chains offered the **Caroling Fun** doll in 1995, following up the successful Holiday Hostess and Holiday Dreams dolls of the previous two years.*

*Hallmark's **Sentimental Valentine** added to the company's line of Victorian-inspired dolls.*

*JC Penney's **Golden Winter Barbie** was greatly favored by collectors due to its opulent costume trimmed in fur.*

*Hallmark issued this lovely Victorian doll, **Holiday Traditions,** for the 1997 holiday season.*

◆ Evening gown Barbie dolls

The roots of the Barbie doll are in the elegant gowns designers have conceived for the doll since 1959, many which were, in fact, inspired by couture designs from both U.S. and European fashion designers. Barbie doll collectors of all ages have always valued attention to evening gown details and the use of "real" fabrics like satins and silks. In the *Contemporary BARBIE* era there are scores of these dolls, favorites of both younger and adult collectors. Sometimes referred to as "glamour dolls," some collectors acquire the doll for the fantasy, others for the beautiful costumes. Regardless, these dolls comprise a large proportion of *Contemporary BARBIE*. Many of the retail store customized dolls, particularly those issued around the Christmas season, are evening-gowned dolls. Porcelain dolls that are not reproductions of vintage Barbie and family dolls can be considered evening gown dolls.

In addition to acquiring dolls wearing fabulous gowns, many collectors also highly prize evening gown fashions that are available in packages separately from the dolls, just as they were available in the 1960s. These would include the collections of fashionable outfits that are developed for both U.S. and foreign consumption such as the Private Collection, Haute Couture, Pret-a-Porter, and Beverly Hills fashion lines from the 1980s to the present day. Exciting fashion news for late 1995 was that Ann Driskill, Barbie doll and fashion designer at Mattel, had initiated the new Fashion Avenue line designed to be similar in feel to the internationally-distributed fashion lines. Based on early reviews from the Internet, they met with instant success.

Mattel is a savvy market-driven organization and has used print advertising to promote Barbie dolls throughout the Contemporary BARBIE *era. The porcelain dolls, in particular, benefited from this medium because they were targeted to adult collectors.*

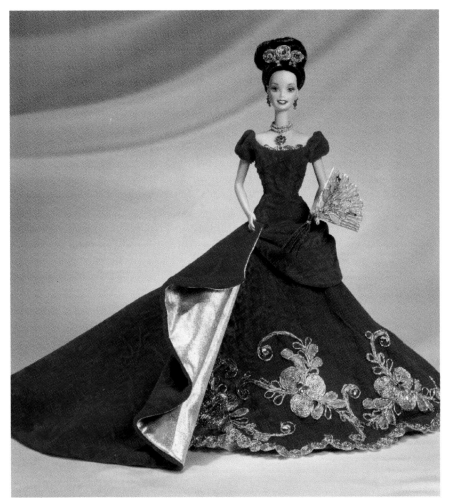

The ad for **Opening Night Barbie** promoted Janet Goldblatt, designer of the doll. Most advanced Barbie collectors are very familiar with, and highly value, Ms. Goldblatt's designs.

The Holiday Porcelain Series continued in 1997 with this exquisite **Belle of the Ball Barbie** doll (third in the series).

THE ART OF EVENING GOWN BARBIE

Barbie doll designer Janet Goldblatt has conceived some of Barbie's most glamorous and elaborate evening ensembles. Several of her personal favorites are Opening Night Barbie, Royal Splendor Barbie, Snow Princess Barbie, and the 1994 Happy Holidays Barbie. It's plain to see that Goldblatt's influences include Christian Lacroix, Valentino, Ungaro and Chanel. While harboring a passion for glamorous evening wear, Goldblatt, who has designed for Mattel for over 20 years, has also done dolls such as Bathtime Barbie, Western Fun Barbie and Animal Lovin' Barbie.

Janet Goldblatt, Barbie doll designer

The popular children's-oriented eatery, **Chuck E. Cheese,** was associated with this exclusive doll in the Barbie "food-ie" lineup.

Adding to the food-oriented Barbie dolls was **Russell Stover Barbie** doll, presented at Easter time in a basket filled with chocolates.

◆ BARBIE DOLL AS "FOODIE"

A trend in *Contemporary BARBIE* involves cross-merchandising the doll with food companies. The Barbie doll has been paired with various food producers as both special edition dolls and as premiums. Food companies that have collaborated with Barbie and family dolls since 1980 include Chuck E. Cheese, Coca-Cola, Kool-Aid, Kraft, Little Debbie, McDonald's, McGlynn's Bakery (and other regional bakeries), the Milk Marketing Board, Nabisco, Pepsi, Pizza Hut and Russell Stover. Most of these dolls tend to wear faddish fashions to appeal to younger collectors, although recently it is clear that some newer issues are targeted to the adult collector as well. This was the case with the Little Debbie Barbie, issued in 1993. Many adult collectors are interested in acquiring dolls through premiums, and many of the "foodie" Barbie dolls fall into that category.

In 1997, the line of Barbie doll Fun Fixin' sets was expanded to include the Fitness Center, Picnic Fun, Glamorous Day, Dishwasher, Stove, and Refrigerator. The latter was packaged with a plethora of items reminiscent of Barbie doll's earliest vintage kitchen accessories. The refrigerator, a licensed product manufactured by Arco Toys (#67691), was stocked with food brands including Cheerios, Del Monte ketchup, Duncan Hines frosting, Eggo waffles, Gulden's mustard, Hellman's mayonnaise, Life Saver Flavor Pops, Nabisco Chips Ahoy!, Pepperidge Farm Goldfish, Tropicana orange juice, and Wonder Bread, among others.

Mattel, Barbie and McDonald's have enjoyed a cooperative relationship for several years. Here is their 1993 offering featuring Barbie holding a party for Stacie and Todd.

◆ BARBIE THE SUN WORSHIPER

I t can be argued that the Barbie doll has been a sun lover since her inception in 1959, since the first Barbie dolls were clad in a zebra-striped swimsuit, sunglasses and stiletto slides. For collectors, the "official" sun-loving era was commemorated in 1971 with the first Sun Gold Malibu Barbie, followed by Sun Set ("Today's Together Teens"), Sun Lovin' (from 1979 to 1981—the dolls with peek-a-boo tans), Sunsational ("She's got the California look!"), and Sun Gold Malibu Barbie dolls. The Sun Gold dolls were the last to incorporate the word "Malibu" in their name. In Barbie doll's sun-loving history, after Malibu came Tropicals, Island Fun, Beach Blast and Wet 'N Wild Barbie and friend dolls.

Some collectors call this theme the "swimsuit line." They tend to be among the least expensive dolls sold each year, having been designed for mass market consumption.

Sun, beach and water fun
Contemporary BARBIE **dolls**

Sun Lovin' Malibu Barbie	1980
Sunsational Malibu Barbie	1981
Hawaiian Barbie	1982
Sun Gold Malibu Barbie	1984
Tropical Malibu Barbie	1986
Beach Blast Malibu Barbie	1988
California Dream Barbie	1988
Island Fun Barbie	1988
Wet 'N Wild Barbie	1990
Bathtime Fun Barbie	1991
Hawaiian Fun Barbie	1991
Mermaid Barbie	1991
Bath Blast Barbie	1992
Bath Magic Barbie	1992
Sun Sensation Barbie	1992
Glitter Beach Barbie	1993
Fountain Mermaid Barbie	1993
Sun Jewel Barbie	1994
Swim 'N Dive Barbie	1994
Baywatch Barbie	1995
Bubble Angel Barbie	1995
Tropical Splash Barbie	1995
Sparkle Beach	1996
Hula Hair	1997

*This **Sun Jewel Barbie** doll is typical of bathing beauty Barbie dolls that hearken back to Barbie's origins in her zebra-striped swimsuit.*

◆ BARBIE THE SHOPPER

Shopping has emerged as a prevalent theme in Barbie doll designs in the 1990s, particularly in support of department store exclusives (see the following chapter for a further discussion on the subject). What distinguishes this category from a generic fashion doll is that the doll carries a store logo shopping bag and is usually dressed in an upscale fashion. This relatively new category began in 1991 with the FAO Schwarz Madison Avenue Barbie doll, packaged with a logo FAO Schwarz shopping bag. Today, there are upwards of 13 shopping-themed Barbie dolls released in North America.

In 1993, Meijer's, a Michigan-based department store group, unveiled its exclusive Meijer's Shopping Fun doll, with a Meijer's logo bag. In 1994, Bloomingdale's unveiled its first exclusive Barbie doll—the Savvy Shopper, designed by Nicole Miller, came complete with Bloomingdale's shopping bag. Bloomingdale's followed this doll in 1995 with the hit Donna Karan Barbie doll, who, with her shopping bag, was dressed for a great day of shopping fun.

*Acclaimed designer Nicole Miller designed **City Shopper**, a red-headed beauty exclusively for Macy's.*

SHOPPING-THEME BARBIE DOLLS

SPONSOR	DOLL	YEAR
Benetton	Shopping	1991
Bloomingdale's	Donna Karan	1995
Bloomingdale's	Savvy Shopper (Nicole Miller)	1994
Bloomingdale's	Bloomie's Barbie	1996
FAO Schwarz	Barbie at FAO	1997
FAO Schwarz	Madison Avenue	1991
FAO Schwarz	Shopping Spree	1994
GAP	GAP Barbie	1996
Hudson Bay	City Style	1995
Macy's	City Shopper (Nicole Miller)	1996
Mattel	City Style ("B" logo bag)	1993
Mattel	Cool Shoppin' Barbie	1997
Meijer's	Shopping Fun	1993
Spiegel	Shopping Chic (Blonde and Black)	1995-96

She's off to the mall! Shopping Barbies complete with the appropriate shopping bags. From left: **Classique City Style Barbie**, **Benetton Shopping Barbie**, **Meijer Shopping Fun Barbie**, **FAO Schwarz Madison Avenue Barbie**.

The Grand Ole Opry was commemmorated with this special Barbie doll in 1997.

One of the most clever designs by Cecil Beaton, Barbie doll is dressed to attend Ascot from that pivotal scene in *My Fair Lady.*

Barbie as Little Bo Peep *(above) was issued in 1996, sadly still without her sheep!* **Barbie as Rapunzel** *(above left) had, appropriately, the longest hair of any doll in the Children's Collection Series. Mattel's successful line of collector dolls targeted to children continued with* **Barbie as Cinderella** *(below left) in 1997.*

Barbie hits the big time in the Big Top as FAO Schwarz continued its popular customized Barbie line with Circus Star Barbie in 1995.

Chapter 6

CUSTOM MADE

Customized product is an area of Barbie® collecting that is growing every year and greatly contributes to the sheer volume of new dolls entering the market. Beginning in the early 1960s, retail giants have been working with Mattel to create Barbie dolls consistent with their stores' image and customer base.

In the vintage Barbie doll era, Mattel had product exclusives with Montgomery Wards (the 1962 Barbie Mix 'N Match Set, #861), Spiegel (the 1962 Barbie and Ken Tennis Set, #892), Sears (the 1966 Sears Color Magic Barbie Gift Set, #1043) and JC Penney (whose 1969 catalog showed Talking Barbie, available in a Pink Premier Gift Set).

By the 1980s, customized product development was a well-entrenched tradition between Barbie dolls and retail establishments. But only the largest retailers can take full advantage of customized editions since Mattel requires a minimum run before they will produce a special item. Many customized dolls are released in the fourth quarter of the year in anticipation of the holiday gift season.

The number of department store and other consumer-branded exclusive dolls has never been greater in the doll's history, a distinctive feature of Barbie doll collecting in the 1990s. Between 1996 and 1997 alone, exclusive Barbie dolls

In 1992, Target stores offered **Wild Style Barbie,** *dressed in a Desperately Seeking Susan/Madonna-inspired combination of black "leather" jacket, print leggings, denim skirt, long gold chain and neon pink cap.*

Target's **Steppin' Out Barbie** *(left), the store's customized offering in 1995, wore a short fuchsia and black cocktail dress and was nicely accessorized. Hills offered this customized* **Blue Elegance Barbie** *doll in 1992 (right), dressed in a turquoise gown with dotted tulle and satin sleeves.*

were sponsored by Avon, Bloomingdale's, FAO Schwarz, the GAP, Hallmark, Hills, Hudson Bay (Canada), JC Penney, Macy's, Sears, Service Merchandise, Spiegel, Target, Toys 'R Us, Wal-Mart, Wessco, and Wholesale Clubs (e.g., B.J.'s Wholesale Club, Price/Costco, and Sam's Club).

FAO Schwarz
Silver Screen Barbie *from 1994.*

◆ FAO SCHWARZ

The Barbie doll went "up-market" when FAO Schwarz got into the act. The store opened its first Barbie Boutique—the 1500-square-foot "Barbie on Madison Avenue"—at its New York flagship store in late autumn 1992.

The opening of the boutique was heralded by more than 100 journalists, Kathie Lee Gifford, and, of course, an appropriate and customized Madison Avenue Barbie doll (who, with her upswept blond hairdo, dark glasses, Chanel-inspired suit and ubiquitous shopping bag, broadly resembled Ivana Trump). The entire FAO Schwarz building was wrapped in a giant pink ribbon for the event, and pink carpet stretched from Fifth Avenue to the Madison Avenue entrance. Mattel announced at a ribbon-cutting event that $50,000 from the store's initial proceeds would be donated to the Pediatric AIDS Foundation, the national organization founded by Elizabeth Glaser to help children with AIDS and fight against prenatal spread of the disease from mother to child.

FATHER OF HER COUNTRY?

FAO Schwarz, the ultimate toy store, has been offering unusual and trendsetting merchandise for 135 years. Not one to rest on their laurels, however, FAO felt it was time to offer the world something that could truly be described as revolutionary. Barbie as George Washington was the result.

George Washington, the FAO exclusive Barbie for 1997, was the second in the American Beauties Collection, and made waves by marking an unprecedented event in the 38 year history of the Barbie doll.

Barbie as George shows Barbie dressed for the first time ever as a man, in honor of the father of America. Barbie as George is resplendent in a detailed coat and vest, ruffled jabot, plumed hat, and powder white hair, and she patriotically personifies the true style and spirit of revolution. George was created for FAO Schwarz by Ann Driskill, long-time designer of exclusive dolls for FAO Schwarz. Since 1989, FAO has launched a number of exclusive, limited edition, collectible Barbie dolls which are collected avidly around the world.

This customized doll, **Shopping Spree Barbie,** from FAO Schwarz was popular with both young and older collectors. She came packaged with an FAO Schwarz shopping bag and was labeled a "souvenir" doll.

Rockette Barbie *from FAO Schwarz practices her kicks in front of her stylized box.*

Early success of the Barbie on Madison Avenue boutique resulted in eventual expansion of the facility to a two-story "townhouse." A second Barbie Boutique was created at the FAO Schwarz store in San Francisco in 1993, and today there are special Barbie Boutiques in FAO Schwarz locales across the U.S. In addition, two Barbie Boutiques run in association with the Hudson Bay Co. retail chain are located in Canada.

FAO Schwarz also joined similar efforts launched by Bloomingdale's and Meijer's stores in coming up with an appropriately-clad version of a shopping Barbie doll. In 1994, Shopping Spree Barbie (#12749) made her debut. Wearing an FAO Schwarz oversized sweatshirt and purple stirrup pants, she carried the store's universally recognizable shopping bag. (The doll's packaging bore the words "Souvenir Edition," something never before seen on a Barbie doll box).

Jewelled Splendor, issued for FAO Schwarz in 1995, was the toy store's up-market doll that year.

◆ BLOOMINGDALE'S

Hot on the heels of the FAO Schwarz up-scale shopping Barbie doll was Bloomingdale's Savvy Shopper from Nicole Miller, another customized success story involving Ann Driskill. According to Lisa McKendall of Mattel Toys, "1994 was the first year we did a special doll with Bloomingdale's: the Nicole Miller. The store could not keep them on the shelves; they sold out everything we could manufacture. Because Bloomingdale's had a long-term relationship

Another shopping doll, Bloomingdale's **"Bloomie's Barbie,"** *wore an outfit consistent with shopping mall styles.*

Bloomingdale's third exclusive doll was from Calvin Klein, wearing the designer's signature denim look with logo undergarments.

*This hard-to-find **Donna Karan Barbie** doll was a big hit with collectors. A brunette with sunglasses, and the second in Bloomingdale's customized series, she carries the famous "Big Brown Bag" from the store. . .Barbie-sized, of course!*

with Donna Karan, the store decided to follow up Miller's success with Karan." Driskill recalled: "They [Bloomingdale's] sent us actual clothes [from Karan's studio in New York]. At first they didn't know if they wanted to do an outfit from her latest line. I found a pink jacket from the current collection that really was close to 'Barbie pink,' but the style didn't scream 'Donna Karan.' We made up a prototype of this, but we knew we wouldn't go in this direction. I went to New York on vacation and visited her studio. I met with her husband [Stephen Weiss] and a bunch of other people. So they set up some actual clothes and thought we should do something from her original collection as it was going to be her tenth anniversary in her own business. The consensus was that we should not do 'the pink.' For her tenth anniversary, we thought we'd do something quintessential Karan. Everybody remembers the original turtleneck body suits with the wrap skirt and the big shawl. So we worked that up, sent it to them and they approved it. It was really fun to work on."

Bloomingdale's exclusives have proliferated collecting in the latter 1990s, with the following dolls having been issued since 1994: Savvy Shopper/Nicole Miller, Donna Karan Barbie (1995); Calvin Klein Barbie (1996); Bloomie's Barbie (1996); Ralph Lauren Barbie (1997); and, anticipated in 1998, Oscar de la Renta Barbie.

ANN DRISKILL
JUST CALL HER "MS. CUSTOMIZED PRODUCT"

I have to admit to gushing somewhat when I met Ann Driskill for the first time, but it is fair to say that the FAO Schwarz Madison Avenue Barbie is among my favorite Barbie dolls in the *Contemporary BARBIE* era. Driskill designed the doll. So how did the doll develop, anyway?

FAO Schwarz wanted a special doll to kick off the opening of the store's boutique—Barbie on Madison Avenue—in their New York flagship store. According to Driskill, "They [FAO Schwarz] wanted to see a New Yorker shopping in a realistic-type outfit. It was right up my alley because it was related to real clothes," Driskill explained. Her background was in fashion design, an area she was active in for several years prior to joining Mattel. The team at FAO Schwarz sent Driskill tear sheets of various designs from magazines. "I did lots of sketches," Driskill said, "and then we had to complete the final design in two days. It was one of the fastest development times of any doll, especially for a customized product. It was first of the series and different than anything else they had done before. . . ."

I asked Driskill about the doll's relationship to Ivana: art imitating life, or what? Driskill replied smartly, "We didn't plan it that way, but we always knew there would be an 'Ivana' connection, just as with Silver Screen Barbie, there was a 'Marilyn' connection."

SOURCE: Author's interview with Ann Driskill, August 1995.

◆ Toys 'R Us (TRU)

The leader in sheer volume for customized doll product every year is Toys 'R Us (TRU). Since the early 1980s, TRU has been associated with over 50 customized Barbie dolls.

In 1995, TRU introduced its most exclusive doll yet: Sapphire Dream Barbie (#13255), promising to be the first in a series called the Society Style Collection.

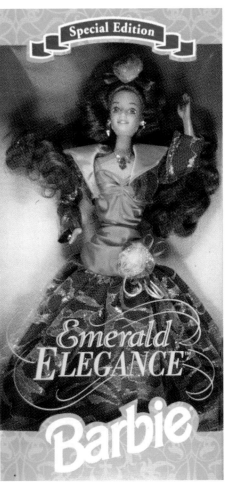

Toys 'R Us successfully appealed to adult collectors with this doll, **Emerald Elegance** (above), probably because it featured rare red hair.

Toys 'R Us offered both Caucasian and Black versions of this popular doll, **Radiant in Red** (left), in 1992.

Dressed in a rich blue velvet gown cinched at the waist with a gold and crystal brooch, her ensemble is topped with a sheer gold-painted wrap.

TRU has about 450 stores in the U.S. and, like Mattel, is optimistic about growth overseas. TRU currently operates in Canada, the United Kingdom, Germany, Singapore, Hong Kong, France and Japan, among other countries. It is likely that TRU's growing involvement as a major retail entity overseas will play a significant role in Barbie's presence in the global market.

See the Appendix for a complete list of customized TRU dolls, all identified with the prefix "TRU."

In 1994 Mattel celebrated fifteen years of Hispanic Barbie-and-family dolls with the **Quinceañera Teresa** *doll. She features the Teresa face mold, a favorite among adult collectors.*

Barbie received her letter in fashion excellence in this **Back to School** *doll (top), offered through supermarket and drugstore chains in 1993. Toys 'R Us offered collectors the* **Purple Passion** *glamour doll (bottom) in 1995.*

Toys 'R Us went up-scale with its first in a series called the High Society Collection in 1995. **Sapphire Dream's**
gown of royal blue velvet was warmly greeted by many adult collectors.

◆ SEARS

Sears was arguably the first department store to sponsor customized Barbie dolls in the contemporary era. The company marked its 100th anniversary with the Celebration Barbie doll (#2998) in 1986. According to that year's Sears Wish Book (the firm's holiday catalog), Barbie was dressed "in her most glamorous gown ever." The ensemble consisted of a long pink-and-silver skirt worn over a silver lamé jumpsuit. But this doll also wore something that hadn't been seen for a decade: a wrist tag. It read: "Celebration™ Barbie® doll Sears 100th Anniversary."

Sears offered an exclusive Black Barbie doll in 1990—Lavender Surprise Barbie (#5588). The company did not sponsor another Black exclusive doll until 1992, when Shani doll was offered in a gift set (#5882).

Sears' exclusive dolls

Year	Doll	Stock No.
1986	Celebration Barbie	2998
1987	Star Dream	4550
1988	Lilac & Lovely	7669
1989	Evening Enchantment	3596
1990	Lavender Surprise (Caucasian)	9049
1990	Lavender Surprise (Black)	5588
1991	Southern Belle	2586
1992	Dream Princess	2306
1992	Blossom Beautiful	3817
1993	Enchanted Princess	10292
1994	Silver Sweetheart	12410
1995	Ribbons & Roses	13911
1996	Evening Flame	15533
1997	Blue Starlight	17125

◆

*To celebrate the company's centennial in 1986, Sears commissioned this **Celebration Barbie** doll. This custom would be repeated in future years by Wal-Mart, FAO Schwarz, and even Mattel itself in 1995.*

◆ OTHER STORES

For the complete list of custom dolls by store, please refer to the Appendix: Comprehensive List of *Contemporary BARBIE* Dolls.

Barbie dolls have been sponsored by these retailers and other organizations

Ames	Meijer's
Applause	Mervyn's
Avon	Nabisco/Oreo
Bloomingdale's	Osco
Child World/Children's Palace	Planet Hollywood
Chuck E. Cheese	Sears
Disney	Service Merchandise
FAO Schwarz	Shop-Ko
Fred Meyer's	Singapore Airlines
GAP	Spiegel
Hallmark	Supermarkets nationwide
Harley-Davidson	Target
Hills	Toys 'R Us
Home Shopping Club	Venture
JC Penney	Wal-Mart
Kmart	Wessco
KB Toys	Wholesale clubs (Sam's Club, Costco, BJ's Wholesale Club, Price Club)
Kraft Foods	
Little Debbie/McKee Foods	Winn-Dixie
Macy's	Woolworth
McGlynn's Bakery	

*Wal-Mart's 1994 **Country Western Star** (above) was done in Caucasian, Black and Hispanic (Teresa) variations. Service Merchandise store and catalog stocks of the 1995 customized **Ruby Romance** (right) were quickly depleted.*

*In 1994, Service Merchandise scored a major hit with collectors with this **City Sophisticate** doll, featuring a gold and black ensemble with velvet beret.*

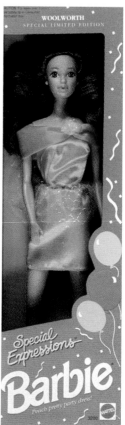

GAP Barbie (above) debuted in 1996 richly packaged with a full complement of GAP-style clothing and accessories. A so-called supermarket special in 1991, **Trailblazin' Barbie** (above right) came dressed in a red bandana-print trimmed outfit and capitalized on the western fashion trend used throughout the Contemporary BARBIE era. This first Hispanic doll for Woolworth's in 1992 (below right) was from the store's customized **Special Expressions** series.

*Wessco sponsored the customized **International Travel Barbie** doll (left), exclusively available through duty free airport terminals and through TWA. Wessco's second **International Traveler Barbie** doll (above) was smartly dressed for globe-trotting.*

JC Penney's **Arizona Jeans Barbie** doll (above left) was among several denim-clad Barbie dolls issued in 1996. She was followed by a second version in 1997. JC Penney dazzled collectors with **Night Dazzle Barbie** in 1994 (above right). Her costume was a variation based on a ready-to-wear outfit for the European market.

Hills **Polly Pocket** (left) was a surprise hit among collectors in 1994, incorporating the tiny Barbie-pocket-size dolls popular with young girls.
This 1993 example of a shopping Barbie doll, **Shopping Fun** (far right), was customized for Meijer's, a Midwestern retail chain, and came complete with shopping bag. Later versions of similar shopping dolls, from Bloomingdale's to Spiegel, came with similar carry bags.

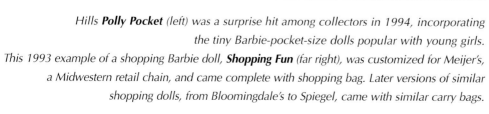

Clockwise from top left: **Fifties Fun Barbie** *was a Warehouse Club exclusive in 1996. Its poodle skirt is reminiscent of the iconic 1960s outfit, Saturday Night Date. JC Penney's added* **Winter Renaissance Barbie** *doll to its long line of exclusives in 1996. Warehouse Clubs continued their popular offerings with this desirable* **Silver Royale Barbie** *doll in 1995. Avon nurtured its relationship with Barbie doll collectors with the* **Spring Blossom Barbie** *doll, available only through Avon representatives.*

The first **Disney Fun Barbie** *doll from 1990 (left) was packaged with a mouse balloon and wore an outfit made with mouse-printed fabric. In 1993, Disney and Mattel paired up for a second* **Disney Fun Barbie** *doll (right). This one came complete with Mickey Mouse ears (á la the Mouseketeers) and fabric printed with Mickey Mouse silhouettes.*

◆ PREMIUMS

Cross-merchandising the Barbie doll with other brands, primarily in the form of premiums, is not a story or technique exclusive to the contemporary era. The Barbie doll has worked with a range of consumer products and brands since the 1960s. Barbie's first premium, offered in 1962, was a free *Barbie* magazine earned with box tops from Kellogg's Corn Flakes. Another early Barbie doll premium was a tie-in with Carnation food products in 1963. The most famous premium campaign for Barbie in the vintage era was arguably the Twist 'N Turn Trade-In Barbie doll offered by Mattel in 1967. Regardless of source or type, contemporary era Barbie doll collectors have savored the opportunity to take advantage of a variety of premiums since 1980.

The majority of premium programs occurred between 1989 and 1992 via the "Pink Stamp" program. Regular Barbie merchandise and special items were available through the redemption of pink stamps found in select Barbie costume packages. The final version of the program offered five items for joining the program, a number of products in exchange for stamps alone, or a "speed plan" which was a combination of stamps and cash.

In 1989, Ralston-Purina, Inc. began a "Breakfast with Barbie" promotion. Each Breakfast with Barbie cereal box showed a 1989 Barbie doll next to a bowl of cere-

McGlynn's Bakery Barbie doll was a much sought-after doll in very limited distribution.

BARBIE AIDS THE CHILDREN'S MIRACLE NETWORK

The Barbie doll teamed up with the world's largest retailer. For the first time, a "CMN Barbie" was offered exclusively at Wal-Mart stores, with $1 from each sale designated to support hospitals affiliated with the Children's Miracle Network (CMN).

"Sales of these dolls will raise a half-million dollars to help children who are fighting life-threatening diseases and injuries," said Nikki Goode, CMN coordinator for Wal-Mart. The CMN Barbie had long hair in blonde or brunette, and wore a lavender evening outfit. Mattel manufactured a onetime supply of only 500,000 of these dolls.

As it does annually, the Children's Miracle Network broadcast was held nationwide May 31 and June 1, and was aired on various local television affiliates. The CMN Barbie is the second toy that has helped Wal-Mart stores raise money for charitable causes in local communities. By conducting auctions and fundraisers of the Tickle Me Elmo doll (manufactured under license by Tyco, a company acquired by Mattel in 1997), Wal-Mart stores raised more than $200,000 for local charities in December, 1996.

According to Mattel's 1996 Annual Report, Wal-Mart is among the top three retailers of Barbie dolls. On average, one Barbie doll is sold in a Wal-Mart store every seven seconds.

SOURCE: *PR Newswire*, 28 May 1997

al. Featured dolls included SuperStar Barbie, Cool Times Barbie, Dance Club Barbie, Beach Blast Barbie, and the 1989 Happy Holidays Barbie doll.

Regional bakeries in 1991 offered a "Specialty Deco-Pak Barbie Doll," which was a ballerina Barbie that could sit (perhaps pirouette?) on top of a decorated cake (#1511 for the Caucasian doll, #1534 for the Black doll). They resemble 1991's My First Barbie doll, but differ in hairstyle, face paint and costume. In 1995, McGlynn Bakery also offered the doll as a premium.

Kraft General Foods, Inc., has offered Barbie doll premiums through its Kool-Aid Wacky Warehouse division. Kool-Aid's first special edition Barbie doll offering in 1993 was the so-called Collector's Edition Barbie Doll (#10309). A year later, Kool-Aid celebrated Barbie's 35th anniversary with a Kool-Aid Wacky Warehouse Barbie premium (#11763). The offer expired December 31, 1994, and required a completed form, 300 Kool-Aid points and $1.50 for postage and handling. (For readers who are not Kool-Aid fans, the "deal" equated to 200 quarts of Kool-Aid consumption, calculated at three points per two quart sugar-sweetened package). Seen another way, and based an average retail price of 50¢ for a one-quart packet of drink mix in 1993, the doll's cost would translate to $100 per doll. While this sounds unattainable, in fact the premiums were very successful.

Kraft Foods, Kool-Aid's parent company, offered a special edition Barbie doll (#11546) through the company's Kraft Treasures premium facility. This doll required 220 points, amounting to about 74 boxes of Kraft macaroni and cheese dinner, or an equivalent cost of about $50 per doll.

McKee Foods Corporation holds the trademark on Little Debbie®—the snack line introduced in 1960, one year after Barbie doll entered the market. By 1993, both were mega-brands in their respective categories. When the two came together for a 1993 premium—Little Debbie Barbie (#10123)—the doll effectively captured the quintessential Little Debbie personality. She wore a blue and white checked dress and a sparkling-white apron customized with an iron-on Little Debbie label.

*Barbie doll was paired with a favorite American snack food in this **Little Debbie Barbie.** She was dressed in the costume of this longtime American icon. A second version is due out in 1996.*

◆ POETIC LICENSE

In 1991, Mattel launched Barbie For Girls, an "umbrella concept" designed to expand the licensing potential of Barbie. Barbie Boutiques were set up with major retailers across the United States, providing a vehicle to promote and sell such licensed items as the World POG Federation's POG™ milk caps, Western Publishing's coloring books, Colorforms' stick-on books, Enesco's collectible figurines, and Wundies' sleepwear.

The licensing program has met with great success. The categories suitable for licensing arrangements with the Barbie doll brand are exploding, from publishing and fashion accessories to entertainment. The latter area even included the Barbie doll moving into a Nintendo game, not to mention a physical fitness exercise video.

To enforce licensee consistency in using the Barbie doll brand, Mattel publishes detailed annual style guides that assist licensees in packaging and promoting their products. Once a company has secured a license associated with the Barbie doll brand, they must follow through in a consistent way from the image of the product, the colors used, and the packaging that will contain the product. "Barbie pink" packages, for example, utilize very specific colors—combining a specified background color with accent colors in very precise proportions.

Companies that have licensed the Barbie brand

APPAREL/ACCESSORIES

A Wish Come True	Dress up apparel and accessories
The Haddad Apparel Group, Ltd.	Outerwear, jackets, snowsuits
H.H. Cutler Company	Coordinates, separates, sets
Hope Industries	LCD watches, toy jewelry
i care International	Sunglasses
IMT Accessories	Hair accessories
JJ's Mae/Rainbeau	Bodywear
Kahn Lucas Lancaster, Inc.	Coordinates, dresses
KidNATION, Inc.	Childrens footwear
Knitwaves, Inc.	Knit coordinates, separates
Mamiye Brothers, Inc.	Swimsuits, coordinating cover-ups
Meltzer Industries Corp.	Blanket sleepers
Messer Import Corporation	Accessory footwear, slippers
Pyramid Handbags	Fashion bags, rainwear
Relic Watches (Fossil, Inc.)	Metal analog watches
Riviera Trading, Inc.	Hair accessories, fashion jewelry, sunglasses
Sara Lee Hosiery - L'eggs	Tights
Sara Lee Knit Products - Hanes	Panties, fashion daywear
Wundies, Inc.	Sleepwear, robes, cotton short/long under wear, daywear

CONSUMER ELECTRONICS

Kalimar, Inc.	Cameras
KIDdesigns, Inc.	Childrens electronics

FOOD

Russell Stover Candies, Inc.	Everyday and seasonal chocolates
Wilton Industries, Inc.	Baking and confectionery supplies

HEALTH/BEAUTY AIDS

Colgate-Palmolive Company	Toothbrushes
Tsumura International	Bath and beauty products

GIFTS/DECORATIVE ACCESSORIES

Anagram International, Inc.	Mylar balloons
Basic Fun, Inc.	Sculpted 3-D keychains
Hallmark Cards, Inc.	Stockings, stocking hangers
Matrix Industries, Ltd.	Frames, jewelry boxes, ornaments

HOME FURNISHING/HOUSEWARES

The Bibb Company	Bedding
Borden Decorative Products, Inc.	Wall borders
ERO Industries, Inc.	Slumber bags, play tents, flotations, swim items
Franco Manufacturing Company	Beach, bath towels
The Thermos Company	Lunch kits
Zak Designs, Inc.	Melamine dinnerware

PUBLISHING/STATIONERY

Colorbök Paper Products	Activity kits, stationery products
Colorforms	Colorforms
Craft House Corporation	Arts and crafts products
Disney Book Publishing, Inc.	Interactive storybooks
Golden Books	Storybooks, color and activity books
Grolier Enterprises, Inc.	Direct mail book club
Hallmark Cards, Inc.	Greeting cards, stationery, giftwrap
Impact, Inc.	Back-to-school stationery
Tara Toy Corporation	Rubber stamps
The Miner Group, Inc./Mello Smello	Stickers

SPORTING GOODS

Brookfield Athletic Company	Rollerskates, ice skates, accessories
PTI	Bicycle helmet, accessories
Rand International	Bicycles, accessories

TOYS/GAMES

Rubie's Costume Co., Inc.	Halloween costumes
Spectra Star	Kites
Strombecker Corporation	Miniature china tea sets
Tara Toy Corporation	Doll and accessory carrying cases

SOURCE: Mattel, Inc. Marketing

BARBIE PICKS HER ACCESSORIES

Mattel has added a new twist by joining forces with Benetton and Reebok, marking the first time the toy maker has linked up with national apparel makers. The denim-clad All-American Barbie comes with two pair of Reebok high-top sports shoes, and there is also a Benetton Barbie, whose outfits can be found (life-size) in Benetton clothing stores. One industry analyst describes the links with Benetton and Reebok as "nice wholesome tie-ins" for Mattel. Although the lines are not expected to generate dramatic profits for any of the companies, they will increase market exposure for all concerned. And exposure is cru-cial for survival in the competitive world of toys, where companies are fighting over static sales of about $13 billion. Increased licensing is another relatively painless way to improve consumer exposure. This year Mattel is expanding its licensed products to include Barbie dresses, trousers, shorts, bedding, T-shirts, and a range of birthday party goodies. Larry Carlat, editor of *Toy & Hobby World* magazine, agrees that licensing the Barbie name could be extremely lucrative. I can see little girls saying, "I want to go to the Barbie store" someday.

SOURCE: *Financial Times*, 21 February 1991

The Hills department store offered this exclusive in 1996, a combined treat for teddy bear and Barbie doll collectors.

The series of holiday-timed Avon dolls expanded in 1996 with the release of the **Winter Velvet Barbie** doll.

*Bob Mackie's 1995 offering,
Goddess of the Sun, had the
golden sequins of the first Gold
Mackie and the surreal "flames"
reflected in Neptune Barbie's
earlier mermaid costume.*

Chapter 7

PURE COUTURE

Not everyone can afford to buy full size original Bob Mackie, Christian Dior, or Nicole Miller ensembles, but buying these famous designs for the Barbie® doll is in the realm of financial possibility for many collectors. As Anne Parducci, marketing director of collectible Barbie dolls at Mattel, noted, "Barbie allows people to dream. We don't want to forget that she is about fashion, beauty and glamour. She allows a woman to dream about being in that gown. . . ."

Avid Barbie collectors highly prize the couture-designed evening gown dolls of the *Contemporary BARBIE* era. This segment of Barbie doll collecting generally represents the ultimate in terms of sophistication, attention to detail and, more often than not, price.

◆ BOB MACKIE

To many collectors, Bob Mackie represents the créme de la créme in Barbie dolls. As of autumn, 1995, these high-end dolls were selling on the secondary market for as much as $1,000 for Mackie's first Gold Barbie doll, and over $1,000 for the Empress Bride Barbie doll. Mackie designs Barbie dolls and costumes consistent with his designs for Hollywood, Broadway, and the Follies Bergere.

As *People* magazine described in 1994, "Bob Mackie [has] worked with more stars than Carl Sagan." In fact, Mackie's exposure early in life to Hollywood movies and glamorous stars such as Betty Grable and Rita Hayworth are evident in his designs for the Barbie doll. After he attended Chouinard Art Institute in Los Angeles (which ironically was the alma mater of Charlotte Johnson, the first designer of Barbie doll outfits), Mackie was discovered by legendary costumer Edith Head in 1961 while working as a novice designer at Paramount Studios. He soon found himself designing for Marlene Dietrich, Mitzi Gaynor and Ann-Margret, and later for Cher,

*Bob Mackie's **Queen of Hearts**.*

Diana Ross, Bernadette Peters and Carol Burnett. Mackie has won six Emmy Awards, plus Oscar nominations for *Funny Girl, Lady Sings the Blues* and *Pennies from Heaven.*

In 1997, Mackie starred in his first infomercial for the Barbie doll to promote the Jewel Essence Collection, a five-doll series. The dolls were available exclusively via the infomercial, direct from Mattel's Barbie Collectibles division. The dolls included Diamond Dazzle, Emerald Embers, and Ruby Radiance, sold as a set of three. In addition, Sapphire Splendor and Amethyst Aura were available to complete the set of five.

In a recent interview, Mackie talked about his showy fashion aesthetic. He said, "I'd rather be recognized for glitz than for khaki-colored canvas." Looking at his Barbie doll designs, Mackie should be a happy man. He is well-loved by legions of Barbie collectors.

*A sketch by Bob Mackie of his 1996 Barbie doll, **Goddess of the Moon**. Bob Mackie's ninth design for Barbie featured the doll, for the first time, with a "prop"—a silvery moon.*

*The tenth Barbie doll by Bob Mackie was **Madame du Barbie** issued in 1997.*

*Every Bob Mackie Barbie doll comes packaged with a copy of Mr. Mackie's sketch of the doll. Mackie's **Empress Bride Barbie** sketch is shown here.*

Bob Mackie's Barbie doll designs to date

Issued	Doll	Stock No.
1990	Gold	5405
1991	Starlight Splendor	2703
1991	Platinum	2704
1992	Empress Bride	4247
1992	Neptune Fantasy	4248
1993	Masquerade Ball	10803
1994	Queen of Hearts	12046
1995	Goddess of the Sun	14056

Issued	Doll	Stock No.
1996	Goddess of the Moon	14105
1997	Madame Du Barbie	17934
1997	The Jewel Essence Collection	
	Amethyst	15522
	Diamond	15519
	Emerald	15521
	Ruby	15520
	Sapphire	15523

Savvy Shopper, Bloomingdale's first customized Barbie doll, designed by Nicole Miller, was an instant hit. The doll wears a silk coat, in typical Nicole Miller style, over a little black dress. Of course, she carries her Bloomingdale's shopping bag.

◆ NICOLE MILLER

Barbie, the Savvy Shopper, was Nicole Miller's first Barbie doll design, created expressly for Bloomingdale's in 1994. Retail priced at $65, this doll has been a secondary market treasure, fetching between $90 and $120 in 1995. She is dressed in a proto-typical Nicole Miller silk print coat (similar in lines to the navy taffeta coat from the highly prized 1960 ensemble, Easter Parade) and the proverbial "little black dress" in black velvet, complemented by matching velvet bag and fuchsia spike heels. Of course, she carries her Bloomie's shopping bag wherever she goes!

While her design for Bloomingdale's first Barbie doll exclusive was superb, Miller generally designs wonderful clothes and accessories for people substantially larger than 11½ inches. Her silk-based goods inspired by the Barbie doll include pajamas, vests, totebags and wallets, which Miller designed in both 1994 and 1995. The 1994 design commemorated the 35th anniversary and can sometimes be found on dealers' lists.

Miller is considered to be one of the most witty fashion designers practicing today. Her clients include Demi Moore, Meryl Streep and Linda Evans. She attended the prestigious Rhode Island School of Design before moving to New York City.

Thanks to Nicole Miller's Barbie doll, designer Barbie dolls have become big business at Bloomingdale's. The chain sold $1 million worth of the doll in 1994, excluding catalog sales. According to Bud Konheim, president of Nicole Miller, the company did about $3 million in full size ready-to-wear sales at Bloomingdale's chain-wide in 1994.

Nicole Miller has more Barbie projects in the works. Mattel created a redheaded designer Barbie doll based on Miller, which debuted in 1996 as a Macy's exclusive called City Shopper.

◆ BILLYBOY*

"Le Nouveau Theatre de la Mode" was BillyBoy*'s special exhibit of international high fashion designers who each contributed a design for Barbie in 1985. BillyBoy* was one of the first Barbie observers to recognize and document the haute couture aspects of Barbie, as recorded in his book: *Barbie, Her Life and Times.* His two dolls created for Mattel include Le Nouveau Theatre de la Mode and the Feelin' Groovy (aka Glamour-a-Go-Go) Barbie. These are highly prized and valued on the secondary market. BillyBoy* subsequently left the Barbie doll behind to create an entire spinoff line of fashion dolls called "Mdvanii and Friends."

BillyBoy* began collecting Barbie dolls when he was 13. Ever joking, in an interview with *People* (December 2, 1985), BillyBoy* claimed

BillyBoy*'s **Le Nouveau Theatre de la Mode Barbie** *poses on a Patron Original Christian Dior Paris design.*

BILLYBOY* AND LE NOUVEAU THEATRE DE LA MODE

Le Nouveau Theatre de la Mode Barbie doll was designed for a major Barbie fashion show held in two railroad cars that toured France in 1985. The collection featured 600 Barbie dolls, many dressed in custom outfits from 70 top designers, including: Pierre Cardin, Hermes, Jacqueline de Ribes, Jean-Paul Gaultier, Yves Saint Laurent, Thierry Mugler, Frederic Castet, and Sonia Rykiel. Yves St. Laurent had his atelier craft a tiny version of the famous St. Laurent pea coat for BillyBoy*'s Barbie, as well as a replica of the safari outfit the model Verushka wore on a cover of *Paris Vogue* in 1968. The great Alexandre de Paris—Jacqueline Onassis' Paris hairdresser of choice—did Barbie's hair. Marc Bohan, of Christian Dior, created a lovely green and black strapless sheath for Barbie, an exact miniature of one he made for Princess Caroline of Monaco. Ungaro added four ensembles, Hanae Mori offered three, and Kenzo created a Japanese-style jacket with straight, wide pants and multi-colored straw hat. Andrée Putnam, interior designer, created a room exclusively for Barbie and Ken. The 400-piece Barbie exhibition was sponsored by Mattel, S.A., the French affiliate of Mattel Toys.

The exhibition also made a nine-city tour which started in New York in February 1985 and stopped in Chicago, Dallas and Philadelphia, among other cities. At a party in New York to celebrate the occasion, Andy Warhol unveiled his painting of Barbie, and 1,300 guests danced until dawn to Barbie and the Rockers. Warhol was rumored to have given BillyBoy* the ubiquitous 1985 portrait of Barbie.

to be "a product of the Flintstones and the Jetsons." In an interview with the Franklin Mint *Almanac* in 1987, BillyBoy* referred to Barbie as, "Nice and responsible and sweet and kind and loving...cool to the max, neat-o, snazzy, grooved out, hyper, ultra super stuff."

BillyBoy* is reputed to own 11,000 Barbie dolls and some 10,000 other dolls, along with a huge collection of couture garments from Elsa Schiaparelli, Dior, Chanel, Balenciaga, Patou, Lanvin, and other designers.

This ad for BillyBoy*'s **Feelin' Groovy Barbie** *doll was based on bright, energetic colors and a dynamic layout to reflect the attitude of both designer and doll. It sharply contrasted with other ads in the 1986 doll magazine in which it was placed.*

◆ CHRISTIAN DIOR / GIANFRANCO FERRÉ

*Released in 1995, the **Dior Barbie** created by Gianfranco Ferré was based on an early couture design.*

When Mattel announced at Toy Fair 1995 that a new Barbie doll would be on the market from Dior, many collectors immediately contacted their dealers. Within several months of the announcement, rumors spread that the doll was pre-sold out.

The Christian Dior Barbie doll was designed by Gianfranco Ferré, a favorite designer among many of Hollywood's fashion elite since the early 1980s.

Gianfranco Ferré became the new designer at the House of Christian Dior in 1989, and all of Paris was struck by the irony that an Italian would be dictating French fashion. In protest, Princess Caroline of Monaco took her business elsewhere. So Ferré wears two hats, designing his own line of couture as well as providing expert direction for the House of Dior.

Ferré first burst into the Milan fashion scene in 1978. His trademark is using luxurious fabrics, such as silk organza and cashmere finished off with rich details and embroideries. Ferré's work for Dior tends to be cut in the elegant Dior mold, identified by big shoulders and cinched waists, but with a splash of wit.

Ferré's academic background wasn't in fashion, but architecture. He moved on to design jewelry and accessories for a friend and was "discovered" by the then-influential editor of Italian *Vogue,* Anna Piaggi. She liked his work, and asked him to make some baubles for a Vogue photo shoot. You've come a long way, Gianfranco!

In 1997, a second Christian Dior Barbie was issued, based on the designer's "New Look" style of cinched waistline. "So new! So upbeat!" were the words that greeted Christian Dior's celebrated New Look, launched over 50 years ago. During the course of his decade-long reign over French couture—and by extension, global fashion—Christian Dior, inventor of the New Look and of the fashion show as theater, revealed how he had cast a spell over 25,000 women a year, from Caracas to Buckingham Palace.

Having considered a career as an architect, a diplomat, a museum curator, and a composer, Dior eventually opened an art gallery in 1928. The collapse of the world economy closed the gallery within three years. It is unclear exactly when or how he did it, but he subsequently started selling fashion sketches. Eventually, the major couture designers began to notice and to buy his dress designs. Dior introduced the New Look in Paris to an exclusive audience of couture clients and fashion magazine editors in February 1947. The first rustle of voluminous skirts were mixed. The yards of rich material that blossomed out from cinched waists, sexy lifted busts, and rounded shoulders, rudely brushed aside the residual misery of the war's clunky cork shoes, short slit skirts (for cycling), squarecut jackets, and stocking lines drawn on the back of the leg.

Dior also launched a perfume with his first collection, realizing the profit potential of licensing. He opened branches in major cities. He kept his name in the headlines by raising and lowering hemlines. Until his early death in 1957, Christian Dior was fashion's emperor.

Barbie strolls near the Eiffel Tower wearing Christian Dior's New Look, the second Dior-inspired Barbie doll.

*Bloomingdale's second customized doll, the **Donna Karan Barbie,** inspired by Karan's earliest designs, was snapped-up by collectors directly via the store's toll-free telephone number. The brunette version is difficult to find.*

(For more information on the evolution of this doll, see Chapter 6, Custom Made).

◆ DONNA KARAN

Christian Dior and Gianfranco Ferré were not the only big-names in the world of fashion to design a Barbie doll in 1995. After the success of Nicole Miller's Barbie doll in 1994, Bloomingdale's did not have to think twice about commissioning a second exclusive. The retail giant chose a quintessential American fashion designer for Barbie number two: Donna Karan.

Based on the excellent sales results of the Miller Barbie doll the year before, Bloomingdale's bought two-and-a-half times as many of the Donna Karan dolls. Most of the dolls were already pre-sold prior to release in the fourth quarter of 1995.

Like the Nicole Miller costume, Karan's clothing is somewhat of a departure for Barbie. The outfit is more reminiscent of a tailored European Pret-a-Porter or Haute Couture Moderne fashion than a typical sequined or glittered outfit. Karan's Barbie is dressed in pieces from the first Donna Karan New York collection, introduced 10 years ago: a turtleneck bodysuit, black sarong skirt, red "cashmere" oblong scarf, gold jewelry, black beret and black faux crocodile belt and bag. The doll retailed for $65. She was available as both blonde and brunette; the brunettes were rumored to be more scarce.

One Bloomingdale executive was quoted as saying that, "Barbie is part of the Bloomingdale's theater. The Bloomingdale's customer is not interested in stores that, decor-wise, are glitzy, with tons of mirror and tons of chrome. She wants the excitement of theater. Theater is Donna Karan dolls."

Karan, a junior designer at Anne Klein early in her career, launched her own ready-to-wear line in 1985. She won an instant following by appealing to America's modern business-woman—the exec with lots of cash, but little or no time to spare for shopping. Her clothes looked nothing like Brooks Brothers-for-women or John Molloy's model of dressing for success. She produced seven easy pieces that managed to be both professional and feminine. Her second line of comfortable sportswear—DKNY—included the kind of things every woman wants, but can rarely find: a faded pair of khakis, the perfect white T-shirt, and a boxy blazer. The idea for the clothes evolved, Karan says, because she was sick of wearing her husband's jeans.

In an interview in *Newsweek* magazine's issue of January 3, 1994, Donna Karan said, "The future of fashion will focus on technology—in fabric and personal electronics." So into the body skimmer, ladies, and strap on the info-wrist that contains an electronic Filofax and mobile telephone!

◆ ERTÉ

W hile Erté's Stardust doll is not based on the Barbie persona, *per se*, she
is nevertheless highly prized among many Barbie enthusiasts. Erté
created magazine covers for *Harpers Bazaar* innovating the Art Deco
style. Long famous for his fashion as featured in the Ziegfeld Follies, Erté's creations were also featured in the 1994 production of *Stardust* on Broadway. The
dress worn by the doll was worn in the show. The doll stands about 13½ inches
tall; has outstretched arms characteristic of Erté's mannequins; and features a fully
hand-beaded dress with a headpiece in a star design. Each doll was numbered and
retailed originally for $650.00. In 1997, Mattel released the second porcelain
Stardust Erté doll.

*Erté's **Stardust** doll was the
breathtaking physical incarnation
of a two-dimensional Erté design
originally created for a theatrical
production. Below, typical Erté
Art Deco fashion designs.*

CHARLOTTE JOHNSON 1915-1997

With great sadness, Mattel announced the death of one of the original members of the Barbie doll family. Charlotte Johnson, the first fashion designer for Barbie doll, died January 22, 1997, following a long illness.

Originally a dress designer and teacher at a Los Angeles art school, Ms. Johnson was "discovered" while Mattel was searching for someone to help start a new doll project in 1956. Three years later, the Barbie doll was introduced. Ms. Johnson was an integral member of the Barbie team during the early years, and created memorable wardrobes for the dolls until 1980. Perhaps her most valuable asset to the company,

and one that would help place Barbie at the pinnacle of the doll industry, was her ability to anticipate trends so that Barbie doll fashions would be current upon their release. She accomplished this by frequenting Paris fashion shows and getting an early peek at upcoming styles. This trend has continued to this day and keeps Barbie on the cutting edge of fashion design.

Ms. Johnson's innovation and creativity helped make Barbie doll an international phenomenon. She will be missed by the many fans that she touched through her artistry.

SOURCE: Mattel, Inc., Press Release

The **Escada Barbie's** dramatic pink and black gown was based on a couture design by the Spanish design house.

◆ ESCADA

Escada is rumored to be one of Jill Barad's favorite designers. Thus, it was a natural for Escada Barbie to surface in 1996, wearing a reproduction couture gown. Escada has been a Munich, Germany-based fashion house with a broad range of branded apparel, accessories and fragrances since the early 1970s. Its brands of Escada and Laurel are among the toniest European women's favorites. In the U.S., the Escada brand often ranks among the top three best-sellers in designer-level fashion in stores like Neiman-Marcus and Saks Fifth Avenue. One of the reasons for the company's success in the U.S. is the influence of fashion consultant Todd Oldham, who is also known as one of the clothing stylists of Fran Drescher of "The Nanny" fame. Oldham, the baby face of MTV's "House of Style," has been part of Escada's inside design team.

◆ CALVIN KLEIN

Bloomingdale's, one of the Barbie doll's best department store friends, issued the Calvin Klein (aka CK) Barbie in 1996. The doll was clothed in Calvin Klein denim apparel, including a CK logo T-shirt, windbreaker, denim jacket, miniskirt, shirt, backpack, and CK underwear worn á la Marky Mark (e.g., designer name showing on the panties' waistline). The doll was available from

Bloomingdale's via mail order catalog, toll-free telephone number, and through the company's web site at http://www.bloomingdales.com/barbie. While issued as an exclusive to Bloomingdale's, the doll later appeared in direct-to-consumer advertisements by Mattel itself.

Calvin Klein is often called fashion's Frank Lloyd Wright. In the more than 50 collections he has produced since 1968, Calvin Klein has remained a devout modernist. "I've always believed in simplicity," Klein has said. "I've never been one to see women in ruffles and all kinds of fanciful apparel. To me it's just silly."

Richard Martin, curator of the Costume Institute at the Metropolitan Museum of Art, has called Klein, "The true American Puritan. Even as his style has evolved over time, it's always about eliminating anything that is not necessary, and always thinking of the garment as being pure as possible."

Some fashion observers believe that Klein has provided the basic aesthetic adopted by the GAP, J. Crew and Banana Republic—all retailers of a type of American uniform. Klein has been successful at tapping the *hautest* levels of couture while also tapping the youth market. Nearly ten years after the launch of his famous underwear, the youth market took notice. When hip-hop musicians decreed that underpants must be seen, the small print specified that they must be Calvin's, thus firing-up the brand for the youth market all over again.

Beyond Marky Mark, Klein made icons out of Brooke Shields ("Nothing comes between me and my Calvins") and fresh-faced Kate Moss, who, with Klein's exposure, defined a new generation of supermodel. Today, the CK aesthetic pervades a broad range of consumer goods, from fashion to fragrance and home furnishings.

Calvin Klein Barbie.

◆ ANNE KLEIN

Anne Klein was the mother of contemporary American style. The woman behind the label was, during and after her lifetime, one of the most important figures in American fashion. Donna Karan, who joined Anne Klein & Co. as a design assistant in 1968, said that Anne Klein constantly told her, "Fashion is not just about making a blouse or a skirt, but about a lifestyle. And to use my eyes. Anne Klein must have said it a million times, and now I hear myself saying it all the time: 'God gave you two eyes. Look at everything.'"

Most of the American public is perhaps not even aware that the original designer and founder of the company, Anne Klein, passed away in 1974, and that she is not Calvin's sister or even his mom. Since Klein's death, several designers have led the fashion house's design team. Louis Dell'Olio joined the company in the year in which Klein died, and worked closely with Donna Karan. Later, Richard Tyler assumed the mantle of head designer.

Dell'Olio has said that "Anne Klein has not been given nearly enough credit. She broke all the rules and developed a whole new vocabulary which all of us—Calvin, Ralph, Donna, everybody—followed."

Anne Klein, who had trained originally as an illustrator, instinctively understood the need for a coherent wardrobe for the active woman. To her mind, all women worked, whether they stayed home or went to an office.

BARBIE ON RODEO

Escada Barbie wore a strapless black-and-gold lace gown, and a signature evening bag. Versace Barbie chose a sparkling gown of leopard print chiffon.

Decked out by exclusive designers, 20 unique Barbie dolls went up for sale and dozens of vintage dolls on display stared out from glass cases. The charitable Barbie auction drew about 25,000 onlookers and raised more than $80,000 for children's charities.

"Barbie is the most fashionable girl in the world," declared Ron Michaels, president of the Rodeo Drive Committee, which sponsored the event along with Mattel, the toy company that makes the Barbie doll.

The starting bid on most of the designer-dressed dolls was $1,000. The most expensive item on the auction block was a Barbie carrying case designed by Louis Vuitton, which sold for $16,500.

A Barbie in a black dress set with real diamonds, and accessorized with emeralds and rubies, went for $4,000. Another doll costumed as Dorothy from *The Wizard of Oz*, wearing 18-karat gold shoes studded with real rubies, brought $3,500.

SOURCE: Associated Press, 9 December 1996

◆ BILL BLASS

Bill Blass's first design for the Barbie doll was typical Blass: feminine, with gusto. The doll features a Blass trademark: the cowl dress. Born in 1924, the always-a-gentleman Blass has Midwestern roots. He has claimed that the good manners that marked his wonder years in his native Indiana are missing in the fashion industry today. Blass has also said "I refuse to be characterized as 'the grand old man' of the industry—even though I am!"

Blass's mentor was the late Norman Norell, a fellow Hoosier. "Norell was really the last designer in our country to have a totally American viewpoint," Blass has said of Norell. He asserts that Norell taught him that great American fashion is based on cleanness and simplicity.

Janet Goldblatt designed 1997's **Bill Blass Barbie** *doll based on a designer gown.*

◆ RALPH LAUREN

It's hard to believe that Ralph Lauren was born Ralph Lifschitz in the Bronx, New York. His designs for *The Great Gatsby* back in 1974 make you think he grew up in Block Island High Society. But that goes to show what a design genius the man is.

He studied business science at the City College of New York in the late 1950s and worked in fashion retail and sales for several years. His career in design began with a stint as a designer for the Polo Neckwear Division of Beau Brummel in New York in 1967, which he then fashioned into the company Polo Fashions. Ralph Lauren Womenswear was founded in 1982, the beginning of what is now one of the most significant global fashion houses. He's received seven Coty Fashion Critic Awards, and the Council of Fashion Designers of America Lifetime Achievement Award in 1992, among many other commendations.

After he recieved world acclaim for his designs in *The Great Gatsby* (who could forget Robert Redford in that tailored pinstripe suit), Lauren created clothes for the active women of the 1970s. His look has changed little since then: it's classic, tailored sensibility epitomizing quality and style.

*In 1997, Bloomingdale's offered the exclusive **Ralph Lauren Barbie** doll, shown in this advertisement.*

There's a first time for everything. Here are the "first" ethnic contemporary Barbie dolls for the mass American market. From left: Tropical Miko, Hispanic, Native American, Black and Hawaiian.

Chapter 8

COLOR ME BARBIE®

A close-up of the 1997 Classique Romantic Interlude (African-American version).

The *Contemporary BARBIE* doll continually evolves to reflect the times in which she is created. And, the times in the U.S. 'are a changin' insofar as American demographics are concerned. According to the U.S. Bureau of the Census, Hispanics will eclipse African-Americans as the nation's largest minority group in 2010. By 2050, the U.S. population will be just about evenly divided between its various minority groups on the one hand and non-Hispanic whites on the other. Beyond 2050, there may never again be a majority ethnic group in the United States.

Another way of looking at these numbers is that while the overall U.S. population is projected to grow by 15 percent by the year 2010, growth rates are projected to be much higher among minorities—22 percent for African-Americans, 56 percent for Hispanics, and 86 percent for Asians and Pacific Islanders.

Key features forecasted for U.S. ethnic diversity include:

◆ Hispanics, who represent 9 percent of the U.S. population today, will comprise 14 percent in 2010, and 23 percent in 2050.

◆ African-Americans, who represent 12 percent today, will represent 13 percent in 2010, and 16 percent in 2050.

◆ Asian-Americans will remain the fastest-growing minority group—increasing from 3 percent of today's population to 10 percent in 2010.

◆ The number of Native American Indians will double from 2.1 million today to 4.3 million in 2050, but their share of the total population will continue to hover at around 1 percent.

◆ As for non-Hispanic whites, their share of the population will drop from 76 percent today to 53 percent in 2050. Their actual numbers will grow from 188.6 million to 205.8 million in the period.

◆ Nearly one in eleven U.S. residents—about 9% of the American population—was foreign-born in 1994, the highest percentage of foreign-born since World War II, and nearly double the 1970 level of 5%, according to the Census Bureau. Of the 23 million foreign-born people living in the U.S. as of March 1994, one in five arrived here between 1989 and 1994. More than one-fourth of the immigrants between 1990 and 1994 came from Mexico and Russia. This growing foreign-born population is profoundly reshaping American society and, thus, American consumer demands.

Growing ethnic diversity in the U.S. has played a role in the design of Barbie dolls since the mid-1960s. In 1967, "Colored Francie" (#1100) was presented as the first Black doll in the Barbie product line. Francie was the first so-called "colored" friend of Barbie (which is the way her ethnicity is treated on the doll's packaging).

In 1968, Mattel introduced two additional Black dolls to Barbie's world: Talking Julia (#1128) and Talking Christie (#1126). Talking Julia was based on a hit television series and was, according to the promotional booklet, endowed with "Diahann Carroll's lovely voice and starry-eyed looks!" Talking Christie was

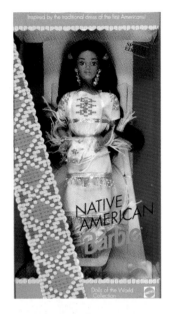

*Mattel finally recognized the contributions of Native American women by issuing the **Native American Barbie** dolls in 1993 (top), 1994 (above) and 1995 (right).*

described as a "sweet talker [who] says many charming phrases." In 1977, Mattel presented Hawaiian Barbie (#7470), a new ethnic variation, complete with ukelele and windsurfer. The doll used the Steffie head mold.

Not until 1980 were Black and Hispanic dolls named "Barbie" introduced. Mattel implemented an advertising campaign for Black Barbie in targeted media, and this resulted in tremendous sales. This convinced Mattel of the market viability for the concept of Black fashion dolls. Black and Hispanic Barbie dolls were not made with the regular Barbie doll face mold; instead, they were constructed with the Steffie doll mold (as was the previously-noted Hawaiian Barbie). Steffie—one of Barbie's friends—was sold only from 1972 to 1973, but since then her head mold has often been used in Mattel's production of ethnic dolls.

Following the introduction of Black Barbie in 1980, Mattel continued to conduct focus groups with Black mothers and daughters and found that they felt "very underrepresented" and wanted more authentic African-American dolls. In 1991, Mattel introduced a new line of African-American fashion dolls led by Shani (the Swahili word for "marvelous"). Shani had two best friends: Asha and Nichelle. Each had a different skin tone, intended to reflect differences among African-American people. To promote Shani, Mattel tied into *Ebony* magazine's Fashion Fair, where three Black models wore replicas of Shani's outfits. Ads for the doll featured the headline: "Now here's a doll that can make a real difference in her life." Accessories included kente cloth outfits and other ethnic fashions. In place of Barbie's own signature fashion color—pink—the dolls featured a warmer gold. Based on Mattel's belief (supported by market research) that all little girls, regardless of race, love playing with hair, the dolls had long flowing hair.

The first Hispanic Barbie doll, issued in 1980, was dressed in what can be best described as a Mexican-style holiday outfit: white off-the-shoulder blouse, red skirt and black mantilla. Giving Mattel designers the benefit of the doubt, suffice it to say that she was dressed more as an International Barbie doll or Doll of the World than a Barbie doll that reflected the lifestyle of an American-Hispanic teenager. More mainstream Hispanic versions of the Barbie doll were welcomed by con-

sumers later in the 1980s, with Sun Gold Malibu in 1984, Day-to-Night Barbie in 1985, and Dream Glow Barbie in 1986. By the mid-1990s, collectors grew to value the Hispanic doll, Teresa, as one of the most attractive friends in Barbie's world.

In 1993, Mattel issued the first Native American Barbie doll, followed by second, third and fourth editions each year thereafter. Furthermore, the Native American doll, complete with papoose, was issued as a member of the American Stories collection in 1996. This doll was followed with the American Stories American Indian in 1997, the last in the series.

Ethnic dolls (including Asian, Black and Hispanic) named "Barbie" proliferated through the latter 1980s in the *Contemporary BARBIE* era. Given the reshaping of American demography, they will remain an evolving, integral component of Barbie's world.

Ethnic dolls in the *Contemporary BARBIE* era

Year	Doll	Stock No.
1980	*Black Barbie*	1293
1980	*Hispanic Barbie*	1292
1981	*Sunsational Malibu*	4970
1982	*Magic Curl Barbie* - Black	3989
1983	*Twirly Curls* - Black	5723
1983	*Twirly Curls* - Hispanic ("Ricitos")	5724
1983	*Spanish Barbie*	4031
1984	*Sun Gold Malibu*	4970
1984	*Crystal Barbie* - Black	4859
1984	*Great Shapes* - Black	7834
1984	*My First Black Barbie*	9858
1985	*Astronaut Barbie* - Black	1207
1985	*Day-to-Night* - Black	7945
1985	*Day-to-Night* - Hispanic	7944
1985	*Dream Glow Barbie* - Black	2422
1985	*Dream Glow* - Hispanic	1647
1985	*Peaches 'n Cream*	9516
1986	*Magic Moves Barbie* - Black	2127
1986	*Tropical Barbie* - Black	1022
1986	*Hispanic Tropical*	1649
1986	*Mi Primera Barbie*	5979
1987	*Jewel Secrets Barbie* - Black	1862
1987	*Super Hair Barbie* - Black	3206
1988	*Fun to Dress Barbie* - Black	1373 and 7668
1988	*My First Barbie* - Black	1281
1988	*My First Barbie* - Hispanic	1282
1988	*Perfume Pretty Barbie* - Black	4552
1988	*Animal Lovin' Barbie* - Black	4824
1989	*Feelin' Fun Barbie* - Black	4809
1989	*Feelin' Fun Barbie* - Hispanic	7373
1989	*SuperStar Movie Star* - Black	1605
1989	*Mexican Barbie*	1917
1989	*UNICEF* - Black	4770
1989	*UNICEF* - Hispanic	4782
1989	*UNICEF* - Asian	4774
1989	*Wedding Fantasy Barbie* - Black	7011
1989	*Woolworth Special Expressions* - Black	7326
1990	*Dance Magic Barbie* - Black	7080
1990	*Disney Barbie #1*	9835
1990	*Fashion Play Barbie* - Black	5953
1990	*Fashion Play Barbie* - Hispanic	5954
1990	*Flight Time Barbie* - Black	9916
1990	*Flight Time Barbie* - Hispanic	2066
1990	*Happy Birthday Barbie* - Black	9561
1990	*Happy Holidays Barbie* - Black	4543
1990	*Ice Capades Barbie* - Black	7348

*The first **Hispanic Barbie** doll was available in 1980, along with the first Black Barbie doll.*

Factoid

Woolworth's 1992 Special Expressions Hispanic Barbie (#3200) was the first Hispanic customized Barbie doll.

Wholesale clubs offered the **Fantastica** doll in 1992, using the Teresa face mold.

This special effect doll, **Locket Surprise**, came in both Black and Caucasian versions in 1993.

Year	Doll	Stock No.
1990	*Fun to Dress Hispanic Barbie*	7373
1990	*Sears - Lavender Surprise* - Black	5588
1990	*Summit Barbie* - Black	7028
1990	*Summit Barbie* - Hispanic	7030
1990	*Summit Barbie* - Asian	7029
1990	*Woolworth Special Expressions* - Black	5505
1991	*American Beauty Queen* - Black	3245
1991	*Bathtime Fun Barbie* - Black	9603
1991	*Bob Mackie Starlight Splendor*	2704
1991	*Costume Ball Barbie* - Black	7134
1991	*My First Barbie* - Black	9944
1991	*My First Barbie* - Hispanic	9943
1991	*Marine Corps Barbie* - Black	7594
1991	*Navy Barbie* - Black	9694
1992	*TRU - Barbie for President* - Black	3940
1992	*Bath Blast Barbie* - Black	3830
1992	*Spanish Barbie*	4963
1992	*Bath Magic Barbie* - Black	7951
1992	*Fashion Play Hispanic*	3860
1992	*Birthday Party Barbie* - Black	7948
1992	*Birthday Surprise Barbie* - Black	4051
1992	*Kmart Pretty in Purple Barbie* - Black	3121
1992	*My First Barbie* - Black	3861
1992	*My First Barbie* - Hispanic	3864
1992	*Snap 'n Play Barbie* - Black	3556
1992	*Sparkle Eyes Barbie* - Black	5950
1992	*Army (Desert Storm)* - Black	5618
1992	*Army (Desert Storm) Gift Set* - Black	5627
1992	*Teen Talk Barbie* - Black	1612
1992	*Totally Hair Barbie* - Black	5948
1992	*Woolworth Special Expressions* - Hispanic	3200
1992	*TRU - School Fun Barbie* - Black	4111
1992	*TRU - Fashion Brights Barbie* - Black	4112
1992	*TRU - Cool 'N Sassy Barbie* - Black	4110
1992	*TRU - Radiant in Red Barbie* - Hispanic	4113
1992	*TRU - Spring Parade Barbie* - Black	2257
1992	*Woolworth Sweet Lavender Barbie* - Black	2523
1992	*Woolworth Special Expressions Barbie* - Black	3198
1993	*Bedtime Barbie* - Black	11184
1993	*Classique - Evening Extravaganza* - Black	11638
1993	*Earring Magic Barbie* - Black	2374
1993	*Wholesale Clubs Festiva Barbie* - Hispanic	10339
1993	*Fountain Mermaid Barbie* - Black	10522
1993	*Happy Holidays Barbie* - Black	10911
1993	*Locket Surprise Barbie* - Black	11224
1993	*My First Barbie* - Black	2767
1993	*My First Barbie* - Hispanic	2770
1993	*Paint 'N Dazzle Barbie* - Black	10058

Year	Doll	Stock No.
1993	*Romantic Bride Barbie* - Black	11054
1993	*Ruffle Fun Barbie* - Hispanic	12435
1993	*Secret Hearts Barbie* - Black	3836
1993	*Fun to Dress* - Hispanic	2763
1993	*TRU - Dream Wedding Set* - Black	10713
1993	*TRU - Moonlight Magic Barbie* - Black	10609
1993	*TRU - Police Officer Barbie* - Black	10689
1993	*TRU - School Spirit Barbie* - Black	10683
1993	*Wal-Mart - Superstar* - Hispanic	10711
1993	*Twinkle Lights Barbie* - Black	10521
1993	*Western Stampin' Barbie* - Black	10539
1993	*Woolworth Special Expressions* - Black	10049
1993	*Woolworth Special Expressions* - Hispanic	10050
1994	*TRU - Astronaut Barbie* - Black	12150
1994	*Bicycling Barbie* - Black	11817
1994	*Birthday Barbie* - Black	11334
1994	*Camp Barbie* - Black	11831
1994	*Dance 'n Twirl Barbie* - Black	12143
1994	*Dr. Barbie* - Black	11814
1994	*Dress 'N Fun Barbie* - Black	11103
1994	*Dress 'N Fun Barbie* - Hispanic	11102
1994	*Glitter Hair Barbie* - Black	11332
1994	*Gymnast Barbie* - Black	12153
1994	*Happy Holidays Barbie* - Black	12156
1994	*My First Barbie Ballerina* - Black	11340
1994	*My First Barbie Ballerina* - Black	13065
1994	*My First Barbie Ballerina* - Hispanic	11341
1994	*My First Barbie Ballerina* - Asian	13064
1994	*My Size Bride Barbie* - Black	12053
1994	*Airforce Thunderbird Barbie* - Black	11553
1994	*Airforce Thunderbird Set* - Black	11582
1994	*Swim 'N Dive Barbie* - Black	11734
1994	*TRU - Emerald Elegance Barbie* - Hispanic	12353
1994	*Wal-Mart - Country Western Star* - Black	12096
1994	*Wal-Mart - Country Western Star* - Hispanic	12097
1995	*Baywatch Barbie* - Black	13258
1995	*Birthday Barbie* - Black	12955
1995	*Birthday Barbie* - Hispanic	13253
1995	*Bubble Angel Barbie* - Black	12444
1995	*Butterfly Princess Barbie* - Black	13052
1995	*TRU - Fire Fighter Barbie* - Black	13472
1995	*TRU - Teacher Barbie* - Black	13915
1995	*Cut 'n Style Barbie* - Black	12642
1995	*Dance Moves Barbie* - Black	13086
1995	*Happy Holidays* - Black	14124
1995	*Hot Skatin' Barbie* - Black	13512
1995	*My First Barbie Princess* - Black	13065
1995	*My First Barbie Princess* - Hispanic	13066

Wholesale clubs offered the **Festiva** *doll in 1993, following the success of the Fantastica in 1992. Here are two variations of the doll: one with a scarf-as-mantilla (above), and the other with the scarf tied under Barbie's chin (bottom).*

This 1994 **My First Black Barbie** *doll was designed for a young girl's entry into the world of Barbie dolls.*

Year	Doll	Stock No.
1995	*My Size Princess Barbie* - Black	13768
1995	*Ruffle Fun Barbie* - Black	12434
1995	*Slumber Party Barbie* - Black	12697
1995	*Wholesale Clubs Fantastica Barbie*	3196
1995	*Strollin' Fun Barbie & Kelly* - Black	13743
1995	*Supertalk Barbie* - Black	12379
1995	*Sweet Dreams Barbie* - Black	13630
1995	*Wal-Mart Country Bride Barbie* - Black	13615
1995	*Wal-Mart Country Bride Barbie* - Hispanic	13616
1996	*American Stories Native American* - Native American	14715
1996	*Avon Winter Velvet* - Black	15571
1996	*Avon Spring Blossom* - Black	15202
1996	*Career Collection - Pet Doctor* - Black	15302
1996	*Career Collection - Teacher* - Hispanic	16210
1996	*Classique - Starlight Dance* - Black	15819
1996	*DOTW - Ghanaian* - Black	15303
1996	*DOTW - Native American IV* - Native American	15304
1996	*GAP Barbie* - Black	16450
1996	*Happy Birthday* - Black	14662
1996	*Happy Birthday* - Hispanic	14663
1996	*Happy Holiday* - Black	15647
1996	*Jewel Hair Mermaid* - Black	14587
1996	*My First Tea Party* - Black	14593
1996	*My First Tea Party* - Hispanic	14875
1996	*My First Tea Party* - Asian	14876
1996	*My Size Barbie* - Black	15910
1996	*Ocean Friends* - Black	15429
1996	*Olympic Gymnast* - Black	15124
1996	*Oshogatsu #1* - Asian	14024
1996	*Pretty Hearts Barbie* - Black	14474
1996	*Pretty Hearts Barbie* - Hispanic	14475
1996	*Shopping Fun* - Black	15801
1996	*TRU - Crystal Splendor* - Black	15137
1996	*TRU - Dr. Barbie* - Black	15804
1996	*TRU - Got Milk? Barbie* - Black	15122
1996	*TRU - Got Milk? Barbie* - Hispanic	15123
1996	*Wal-Mart - Skating Star* - Black	16691
1996	*Wal-Mart - Skating Star* - Hispanic	15511
1996	*Twirling Ballerina* - Black	15087
1996	*Wal-Mart Sweet Magnolia* - Black	15653
1996	*Wal-Mart Sweet Magnolia* - Hispanic	15654
1997	*101 Dalmations Barbie* - Black	17601
1997	*American Stories - American Indian* - Native American	17313
1997	*Angel Princess* - Black	15912
1997	*Avon - Spring Petals* - Black	18657
1997	*Avon - Winter Rhapsody* - Black	16354
1997	*Barbie and Ginger* - Black	17369
1997	*Birthday Barbie* - Black	15999

Year	Doll	Stock No.
1997	*Birthday Barbie* - Hispanic	.16000
1997	*Blossom Beauty* - Black	.17033
1997	*Bubbling Mermaid* - Black	.16132
1997	*Career Collection - Dentist Barbie* - Black	.17478
1997	*Classique - Romantic Interlude* - Black	.17137
1997	*DOTW - Puerto Rican* - Hispanic	.16754
1997	*Flower Fun* - Black	.16064
1997	*GAP Barbie* - Black	.18548
1997	*Happy Holidays Barbie* - Black	.17833
1997	*Hula Hair Barbie* - Black	.17048
1997	*Jewelry Fun My First Barbie* - Black	.16006
1997	*Jewelry Fun My First Barbie* - Hispanic	.16007
1997	*Jewelry Fun My First Barbie* - Asian	.16008
1997	*Kay-Bee Glamour Barbie* - Black	.18595
1997	*Military - Ponytails Barbie* - Black	.18142
1997	*Oshogatsu #2* - Asian	.16093
1997	*Runway Collection - In the Limelight* - Black	.17031
1997	*Shoppin' Fun Barbie and Kelly* - Black	.15757
1997	*Splash 'n Color* - Black	.16174
1997	*Splash 'n Color* - Hispanic	.16172
1997	*Target - 35th Anniversary* - Black	.17608
1997	*TRU - Crystal Splendor* - Black	.15137
1997	*TRU - Career - Paleontologist* - Black	.17241
1997	*TRU - Sapphire Sophisticate* - Black	.16692
1997	*Wal-Mart - 35th Anniversary* - Black	.17616

KITTY BLACK-PERKINS ON THE FIRST BLACK BARBIE DOLL

"The first Black Barbie that we did had short hair. She had on a red bodysuit with gold trim, and a long red wrap skirt. At that time one of my idols was Diana Ross. I really loved the way she dressed. When I designed the fashion for that doll, I thought 'this is the way to go,' the way that I would visualize Diana Ross if she were a Barbie doll.

"There was a lot of controversy about the color of the dress [red] and about the length of the hair [short], as well. I wanted to do something different than what we had done with Barbie's long hair before. I thought the short haircut was adorable. What I didn't know at the time, because at that time we didn't rely on a lot of market research, was that half of the play with the doll was [and still is] in the hair. What we know now through our market research is that it doesn't matter what color the child is, they like that long hair! That's one reason why a lot of Black kids will buy Barbie—for the length of the hair.

"A lot of the Black kids own white Barbies and a lot of white kids own Black Barbies. Color doesn't matter to a child.

"When we did Shani in 1991, we capitalized on some of the information from the research that we found when we did the first Black Barbie doll. That was the reason we opted to go with long hair instead of short hair. Another selling feature with Shani was that we did three different skin tones with her. We wanted the child to make a purchase that was most 'like me.' So, of course, Black people come in all different shades and colors. This was how we wanted our line to be reflected.

"Now Shani really is a part of Barbie's world. . .we have made her a part of the whole fashion doll world. Kids will mix Shani together with Barbie dolls. . .and that is one of the really neat things about watching them play. They don't have any problem with putting a ballerina Barbie with a Shani doll to go shopping or whatever. . . . It doesn't matter to them."

SOURCE: Author's interview with Kitty Black-Perkins, August 1995

BYRON'S BARBIE DOLLS

Byron Lars signed with Mattel to produce a line of collectible African-American Barbie dolls. There have already been Black Barbie dolls, but this was be the first sold through direct marketing rather than in toy stores. The first doll was available in April 1997. Lars introduced the doll, "In the Limelight," at New York's Fashion Cafe April 29. The doll wore a satin opera cape over a chocolate brown sheath with faux fur collar and cuffs and rhinestone brooch.

"I'm really thrilled about it," said Lars. "It's funny. I never thought of doing one before, but when I got that call, you would have thought the President of the U.S. called and asked me to make him a tuxedo."

Lars said he couldn't disclose what fashions Barbie will wear, but said, "It's even more upscale than my collection." But designing for a doll wasn't all fun and games; Lars said he learned a few things about proportion.

"It's hard to make things translate as readable and wearable," he said. "Something that would look awesome on a model didn't work on the doll, like matchy looks."

SOURCE: *Women's Wear Daily*, 25 March 1996, p13; *Women's Wear Daily*, 7 May 1997, p9

*Byron Lars wowed collectors with his first African-American glamour doll, **In The Limelight**, first in the Runway series.*

Toys 'R Us packaged a special **Fashion Brights Barbie** doll with a weekend of outfits in 1992.

The last in the Great Eras series, the **Chinese Empress Barbie** (above left) wore in a richly detailed, authentic period costume. Note the long sleeves covering the dolls hands.

Oshogatsu Barbie (far left) was issued in late 1995 to celebrate the Japanese New Year. She had a lush costume and gorgeous face mold. The second doll (left) commemmorating the Japanese New Year was **Oshogatsu Barbie II.**

Ken's been playing a Prince ever since he first donned the costume in 1964 (#772). Here he is as Rapunzel's Prince.

Chapter 9

CONTEMPORARY KEN®

He's been called Good Looking Ken, Super Dance Ken, Party Time Ken, Beach Fun Ken, Dream Date Ken, Dream Glow Ken, Perfume Party Ken, Rappin' Rockin' Ken, Dance Magic Ken (who's dressed in a Saturday Night Fever-inspired tuxedo with silvery lamé lapels), and even Baywatch Ken. But until recently, he's been, arguably, just one of the Barbie doll's many accessories. In 1996, Ken turned 35. While Mattel threw the Barbie doll a Barbie Festival in Orlando, Florida, for her birthday, little fuss was made over the Ken doll's 35th birthday.

Ken might be considered the Barbie doll's first accessory. He was first introduced in 1961 as part of her wedding collection. Since then, Ken has been the most patient boyfriend anyone could ever want. Someone has written that Ken has expressed his love for Barbie through the clothes that he has worn—always coordinating with Barbie. It is true that Barbie doll's and Ken doll's ensembles were named for recreational activities and for the outfits themselves: sock-hops, drive-ins, cook-outs, and the sort of activities that typically engaged such mass media icons as Troy Donahue and Sandra Dee in their movies of the late 1950s and early 1960s.

Up until that point, male dolls had not succeeded well in toy markets, but requests for a boyfriend for Barbie were endless. Against Mattel's wishes, but motivated by popular consumer demand, the company introduced the Barbie doll's steady Ken in 1961. As Barbie was named after the Handlers' daughter, Barbara, so Ken was named after their son, Ken Handler.

Unlike G.I. Joe, Ken was not intended as a doll for boys to actively play with. Ken was more the psycho-social adjunct to a little girl fantasizing about the Barbie doll's life. Beauregard Houston-Montgomery has written this about Ken: "Despite

Totally Hair Ken *wore a Pucci-inspired print shirt and was packaged with Dep™ to ensure the perfect hairstyle.*

35 YEARS OF THE KEN DOLL'S HAIR

1961-63	Flocked hair Ken
1963-67	Ken gets a butch haircut, painted on
1968	Ken disappears for a year
1969-72	Painted-hair Ken returns
1973	Mod Hair Ken introduced with rooted hair, á la the Beatles.
1974-76	Return to painted hair Ken
1977	The Now Look Ken debuts with rooted hair
1978-91	Back to the painted helmet-hair look
1992	Totally Hair Ken, rooted in a 1990s way
1993-94	Return to plastic hair, but hipper style
1995	Shavin' Fun Ken, with rooted hair and some facial growth
1996	Cool Shavin' Ken with rooted hair and a razor
1997	Big Brother Ken with Little Brother Tommy

SOURCE: *Orange County Register*, 15 April 1996, pE01

image fluctuations that cast him as macho ("All Star Ken"), flashy ("Rocker Ken"), and sensitive ("Animal Loving Ken"), to this day Ken remains Barbie's constant complement in her pursuit of pinktinted consumerism."

The initial promotions for Ken promised: "And now. . . presenting Ken. He's a Doll! Ken is the ideal boyfriend for Barbie, the Teen-Age Fashion Model. A complete wardrobe of exclusively-tailored men's clothes is available for Ken. . . plus the 'right' accessories in the latest men's style. . . sports, business, semi-formal, and formal wear."

Ken had coordinating outfits for fraternity parties, lawn picnics, drive-ins, and beach blanket bingo parties. From cummerbund to keys, pennants to Panama hat, Ken was as accessorized as Barbie was. Collateral products were developed to support the Ken concept: magazines ran comic book-type stories about Barbie and Ken; a series of books was published by Random House; and Barbie and Ken sang on a record released in 1961—"Barbie Sings!" (songs included "Barbie," "My First Date," "The Busy Buzz," "Instant Love," "Nobody Taught Me," and, "Ken."

GIRLS, PARENTS NOT ONLY ONES BUYING "EARRING MAGIC KEN" DOLL

After years of playing second fiddle to Barbie, Ken is coming into his own as a doll that makes dollars for Mattel, Inc. But not any old Ken. It's Earring Magic Ken—a new model that sports an earring, faux-leather vest, lavender mesh shirt with rolled-up sleeves, black pants, and two-tone hairdo. And it is not only girls and their parents who are buying. It's also gay men.

The Wall Street Journal reported that interest in the doll first spread in February, after the *Gay Advocate* ran a blurb on the Ken doll's wardrobe. Since then, buying the doll has become an opportunity for some gay men to tweak the sensibilities of those with more conventional views of gender and toys.

"How much more middle America can you get than Barbie?" asks Randy Snyder, a member of Gays and Lesbians Against Discrimination. It's like "a pariah setting foot in one of America's sanctuaries," adds Dennis McNult, a San Francisco-area resident.

"A couple of years ago there was Desert Storm Ken in khaki fatigues, and as soon as he heard President Clinton was going to lift the ban on gays in the military he comes out as Earring Magic," jokes Rick Garcia, a gay lobbyist in Chicago. He says that the doll's outfit—right down to the two-tone hair—evokes the hot gay fashion style of the late 1970s and early 1980s.

Stores around the country report thinning stocks of the doll. And at FAO Schwarz in Chicago, there's a waiting list. Because of the demand, some retailers in San Francisco are marking up Earring Magic Ken to $17-24 apiece. Earring Magic Barbie usually sells for $11.

SOURCE: *The Wall Street Journal*, 30 August 1994

Some highlights of the Ken doll's life include:

◆ The Ken doll's reappearance in 1969 with a whole new look, face, and body. Some have called this transformation: "From Geek to Sleek."

◆ In 1982, a Black Ken was introduced following the introduction of the first Black Barbie doll in 1980. Hispanic Ken followed shortly thereafter.

◆ In 1991, Mattel honored the 30th anniversary of Ken with the creation of a porcelain Ken doll to accompany a porcelain Barbie doll issued the same year. The porcelain Ken was a reproduction of the first doll, with brunette hair "flocking" (a felt-like substance that served as Ken's "hair" in the earliest issues of the Ken doll circa 1961). The doll wore Tuxedo Set (#787), and included a pair of boxer shorts and sock garters.

◆ As Earring Magic Ken, he was immediately dubbed "Gay Ken" by New York *Newsday*, and "Fey Ken" by *Genre*, a publication purportedly documenting the gay lifestyle (see sidebar). The doll was unique in several respects, including his first ear piercing and two-toned hair. According to Dan Savage in the *NUCITY* 'zine, "On closer inspection, the Ken doll's entire outfit looks like three-year-old rave wear. A Gaultier purple faux-leather vest, a purple mesh shirt, black jeans and shoes." (*NUCITY*, 18 June-1 July 1993)

◆ In 1992, Ken was reinvented. Ironically, this was accomplished by giving him a face mold originally designed for Allan, the Midge doll's boyfriend.

In some ways, Ken is the Rodney Dangerfield of Barbie doll's world—he just can't seem to get much respect. That is, at least among adult collectors. At auction, a number-one Barbie doll mint in its original box can sell for as much as $10,000. Ken, in a similar condition, might fetch $300.

But the Ken doll's Dangerfield status might be changing. Until 1995, Ken was always a part of the Barbie line, advertised literally as an accessory to the Barbie doll and her friends. He was an enthusiastic partner for volleyball at the beach, for going bicycling, or as a dependable last-minute date to the dance. But in 1995, Ken finally got his own television commercial—as Shavin' Fun Ken—after 34 years in media limbo. Cool Shavin' Ken (#15469), introduced in late 1996, was also singularly promoted; he was coupled with Old Spice After Shave. For more formal occasions, Great Date Ken (#14837) was released.

Mattel based the Ken doll's redesign on a survey of the little girls who play with Barbie and family dolls. "We asked girls if Barbie should get a new boyfriend or stick with Ken," said Lisa McKendall of Mattel. "They wanted her to stay with Ken, but wanted Ken to look a little cooler. Ken and Barbie both reflect mainstream society; reflect what little girls see in their world. What they see their dads,

*In 1961, Ken wore this outfit, **Dreamboat** (#785), on dates with Barbie.*

brothers, and uncles wearing, they want Ken to wear." Today, McKendall says that contemporary Ken dolls' hairstyles have "kind of a Melrose Place style to them."

The number of contemporary Ken dolls is growing each year, owing in part to the success of the Hollywood Legends Collection. Ken has played leading men to the Barbie doll's starring roles in cinema classics since the beginning of the series in 1994. He first starred as Rhett Butler in *Gone with the Wind*; followed that success as Henry Higgins in *My Fair Lady*; and rounded out his screen adventures with the pivotal *Wizard of Oz* roles—The Scarecrow and the Cowardly Lion (looking truly like Bert Lahr).

The Ken doll's latest role is as Big Brother to little brother, Tommy. This is the first time that Ken has been packaged with a sibling (Barbie has been an older sister since Skipper's emergence in 1964). Perhaps this is the ultimate contemporary Ken, demonstrating his nurturing, caring side to an eager public. Now, *that's* something worthy of our respect!

Now Look Ken, *issued in 1972, wore the men's fashion of the time: a white leisure suit and bandana.*

Shavin' Fun Ken, *with rooted hair, could magically "shave."*

A doll custom-made for Doll Forum participants on Compuserve—known as Compuserve Barbie, poses on a CPU.

Chapter 10

CYBERSPEAKING
ABOUT BARBIE®

S
ome sixteen years have elapsed since IBM introduced its first personal computer. Since then, computers have become a ubiquitous feature of our daily lives at work, home, and school. Today, more than one in three Americans age three and above have used a computer. Largely because they are more concentrated in occupations where computer use is high (in technical, sales and administrative support jobs, for example), women use a computer at work more than men.

And, by mid-1997, millions of Americans, both male and female, are surfing the Internet. By July 1996, 35 million U.S. residents age 16 and over had accessed the Internet or online services in the previous three months. Furthermore, 75 percent of Web users sent or received messages in March 1996 (Source: IntelliQuest phone survey, April/May 1996). The median Internet-user's age has been estimated at between 30 and 34 years (Source: SRI and Nielsen). Internet users are generally upscale: 25 percent have an annual household income of $80,000-plus, while 50 percent hold professional/managerial jobs (Source: Nielsen).

Computer technology—indeed, technology in general—has impacted the Barbie doll since she first "spoke" in 1968 (thanks to a miniature tape player). While Talking Barbie (who spoke in both English and Spanish), Talking Christie, Talking Julia (the 1960s television series starring Diahann Carroll as a nurse), and Talking Stacey (who spoke with a British accent) can still be found in dealers' lists to this day, most of the time these dolls are listed as being "mute." The first Talking Barbie uttered six different phrases, had bendable legs, and had "real" eyelashes.

Throughout the years, Mattel's product developers have created a variety of talking Barbie and family dolls; however, not until the 1990s was the "talking" done by a computer chip. In fact, by the 1990s, the Barbie doll entered the cyberworld in several key ways:

◆ Computer chips were implanted into dolls such as Teen Talk Barbie, who uttered the controversial phrase, "Math class is tough!" and "Let's go shopping!" and Supertalk Barbie, introduced at Christmas 1994, whose chip allowed Barbie to say at least 100,000 different phrases.

◆ In 1991, Radio Shack packaged an Earring Magic Barbie with software for becoming a "Barbie Fashion Designer."

◆ Computer chips were also implanted in Barbie allowing her to move in fairly random ways, such as the Dance Magic Barbie doll.

The hiring of Doug Glen, first recruited to head up Mattel Media in 1995, was very strategic indeed: Glen was familiar with the marriage of Hollywood effects companies and videogames. He came from Lucasfilm Games before going to Sega, where he launched Sega's multimedia videogame product line.

According to an article in the Feburary 9, 1996, issue of *The Wall Street Journal*, Mattel spent about $4 million in the initial 18 months developing its interactive division, in the hopes that Barbie would lure girls to the computer. Rather than

*Radio Shack packaged the **Earring Magic Barbie** doll with Barbie Design Studio software, marking the first time a Barbie doll ever came packaged with software for the personal computer.*

Talk with me Barbie *astounded visitors to Mattel's 1997 Toy Fair exhibit.*

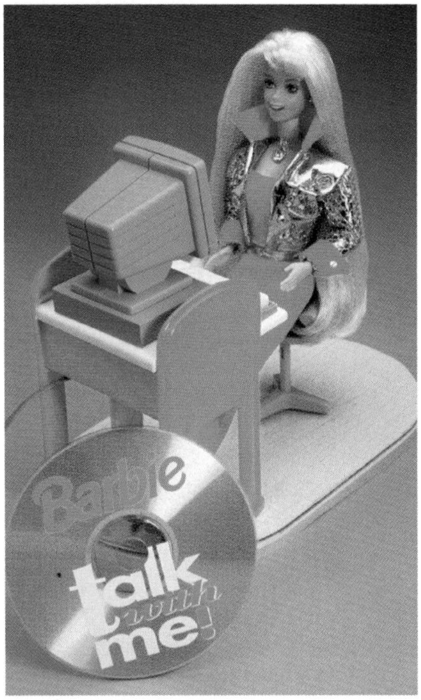

targeting computer owners, Mattel targeted Barbie owners who would pick up the package and say, "Oh yeah, we have a computer I could play this on."

When Glen was appointed Chief Strategy Officer by Mattel in 1997—a new position—this was a signal to the marketplace that technology *per se* would be integral to the future of the toy industry.

It was appropriate that Toy Fair 1997 occurred about the same time of that announcement. This is because at Toy Fair, there was indeed one significantly large step for technology made by the Barbie doll. It was the unveiling of Talk with Me Barbie, the first programmable talking Barbie doll. Here was a doll whose lips really moved when she talks (with the touch of a button on her back). Data is transmitted to an infrared receiver stored in the doll's necklace.

How is this incredible feat accomplished? The doll came with her own Barbie doll-sized personal computer that linked to a PC. The CD-ROM software allows personalization, including name, birthday, and favorite colors, and allows the participant to choose what Barbie doll talks about in categories such as makeup, shopping, parties, career, vacation and pets. For a suggested retail price of around $90, this was anticipated as a big seller for Christmas 1997.

Talk with Me Barbie, however, is just the tip of the technology iceberg in the world of the Barbie doll. A broad range of all things cyber that impact the Barbie doll will be played out in the following ways:

VIA MATTEL'S OFFICIAL WEBSITE ON THE INTERNET—1997 ushered in the era of Mattel's first official Barbie doll website (URL address: http://www.barbie.com). Because by its nature the Internet is actually a global network of networks, Barbie Collectibles On-Line is rumored to have thousands of "hits" (i.e., online inquiries) every week. Mattel uses

BARBIE BOOTS UP

Barbie, who has become the best-selling girls' brand ever, is poised to strut into, and perhaps change forever, the male-dominated world of multimedia software and video games. . . . After almost a year of buildup, Mattel is rolling out a line of seven interactive products led by three Barbie programs. Unlike such shoot-'em-up, beat-'em-up boy toys as Doom and Mortal Kombat, the Barbie titles are notably pacific and based on creative play. "The demand will be many times higher than Mattel thinks it will be," predicts Gary Jacobson, a senior vice president at the brokerage Jefferies & Co., who has followed Mattel for a decade. "The orders (from retailers) are large."

There are few sure things in the $36 billion global toy business; indeed, previous interactive games aimed at girls have been largely a flop. Although the mission is child's play, creating a toy or game that sells is not: the process generally takes a couple of years and requires big up-front costs. Toy manufacturers pray for a product's sales to double after the launch of TV ads and for demand to exceed supply temporarily.

The most hotly awaited Barbie title is Fashion Designer (suggested retail price: $39.99), produced by the Hollywood special-effects studio Digital Domain (*Interview with the Vampire*, *Apollo 13*). The product lets users create as many as 15,000 different outfits that Barbie models in a 3-D walk down a runway. . . .

For the Barbie doll's corporate mom, Mattel President and C.E.O. Jill Barad, the line represents the first test of her stewardship of the company. She envisions launching Barbie into cyberspace and inspiring legions of girls to follow her there, as one of the keys to Mattel's growth.

SOURCE: *Time*, 11 November 1996, pp48-50.

the site to inform collectors about new issues of dolls, to provide a
baseline of information about Barbie doll collecting, and overall, to
promote the collectability of the doll. The site is graphic-intense, featuring colorful images of the newest Barbie dolls available on the market. Browsers can also learn more about Barbie doll history on the site.
Finally, Mattel's website has offered dolls exclusive to visitors of the
site, such as the Midnight Waltz in a brunette version.

VIA THE INTERNET AND COMMERCIAL ONLINE SERVICES—Beyond Mattel's
official website, there has been a proliferation of unofficial sites prof-
fered by individual collectors, publishers, and dealers on the Internet.
These can be located by using the various Internet search engines (e.g.,
Alta Vista, Deja News, HotBot, Infoseek, and Yahoo) and typing in
the words, "Barbie doll." Trying to assemble a complete roster of
Barbie-doll-related sites on the Internet is a futile pursuit; new sites are
added to the Web every week, and oftentimes old sites are withdrawn.

In addition to browsing websites to learn about Barbie dolls, collectors use the Internet, and specifically commercial online services and
electronic mail, to communicate about the hobby. The Internet links
collectors globally, allowing cyber-savvy collectors to enact cross-border
trades (for example, I have traded dolls unique to the American market

BARBIE FETCHES A QUEEN'S RANSOM ON EBAY'S AUCTIONWEB

Doll lovers and other collectible fans may want to check out that toy box in the attic.

eBay Inc. announced that its online auction service, AuctionWeb, was the site for an auction which brought $7,999 for the seller of a mint condition, 1959 "Suburban Shopper" Barbie doll. The doll, which still belonged to the original owner, was a rare display model which came with its original outfit and pink dis-play box. Some experts have speculated that less than 5,000 display Barbie dolls were distributed.

According to the seller, the doll was originally pur-chased at a small San Diego "five and dime" store in the summer of 1959. One of only a handful of Barbie dolls available at the store, this doll appealed to the lit-tle brown-haired girl because it was the only brunette. Apparently the store owner only stocked a few dolls at the time because she was unsure whether or not the dolls would sell.

"This may well be the highest value collectible Barbie transaction completed over the Internet," says eBay Inc. President Jeffrey Skoll. "It surely is a testa-ment to the power and potential reach of Internet com-merce. While most of the items offered on our online auction service sell for considerably less, this is an excellent example of how AuctionWeb brings together a more widespread audience of buyers and sellers with common interests than was conceivable before online access became so readily available. We expect to see more of these types of transactions as the Internet becomes a standard household commodity."

AuctionWeb is designed to allow consumers to easi-ly buy and sell a range of goods. Anyone may browse the site, and a simple registration process allows visitors to bid on or offer an item for sale in any of 60 cate-gories. One of the largest online auction services, AuctionWeb hosts an average of 20,000 simultaneous auctions daily, with more than 2,000 new auctions each day. The site receives more than 6 million hits per week.

AuctionWeb may be accessed at: www.ebay.com

SOURCE: *Business Wire*, 13 February 13 1997

with a Barbie doll "E-Pal" in France). This mode of communication and commerce will grow as more Barbie doll collectors become comfortable with navigating the Net.

There are active Barbie doll collecting bulletin boards on the largest commercial online services including America Online, CompuServe, the Microsoft Network and Prodigy. Other more generic antiques and collectibles sites, such as *Antique Trader's* Collectors Super Mall home page, CSM OnLine (http://www.csmonline.com), have begun to emerge on the World Wide Web and are anticipated to continue to burgeon over the next several years. Electronic auction houses, such as eBay, are a new source for secondary market dolls, as well.

These various aspects of the Internet are being closely scrutinized by Mattel, Inc. In 1995, an online Web magazine featured two Barbie dolls in a somewhat compromising position. Mattel issued a cease-and-desist order posthaste. The company will continue to monitor any potential violations of the brand image and name to preserve its valuable intellectual property.

IN THE EMERGENCE OF ELECTRONIC COMMERCE—The Internet supports the world of electronic commerce. Electronic commerce is conducting or enabling the exchange of goods and services via electronic networks among trading partners. In the context of Barbie doll collecting, electronic commerce is exchanging dolls and Barbie-doll-related collectibles via computers, the Internet and online services.

There are many sources for buying Barbie dolls online, most notably Mattel itself (through its direct-to-consumer division Barbie Collectibles); doll dealers; and retail channels such as FAO Schwarz, JC Penney, Spiegel, the Bay (premier Canadian retailer) and electronic retailer QVC (via its online iQVC site). With the advent of secure

GENDER BLENDER, AN INTERVIEW WITH DOUGLAS GLEN, THEN CEO OF MATTEL MEDIA.

Wired: What is the basic difference between software games that are designed for boys and those created for girls?

Glen: Play patterns. Playtime allows boys and girls to construct a fantasized version of what their life will be like when they get older. For boys, those fantasies lean toward the primordial, the male as defender of the tribe. . . . For girls, occupying the role of observable adult women is more attractive. That's why we have Teacher Barbie, Astronaut Barbie, and Doctor Barbie. Girls also play more cooperatively. A group of girls will often agree on a joint goal and work toward it. . . .

Wired: What can media-savvy kids teach adults about navigating this (information) overload?

Glen: Rather than shift in design, we'll see a shift in the audience. The multimedia revolution has been confined to a small part of the global population. There are only a few million people who have been loyal consumers of PC multimedia entertainment. But now, around one-third to one-half of American kids grow up with multimedia, taking it for granted as one of the ways we play and take in new information. This is the generation that will set expectations for the masses.

SOURCE: *Wired,* November 1996, p190.

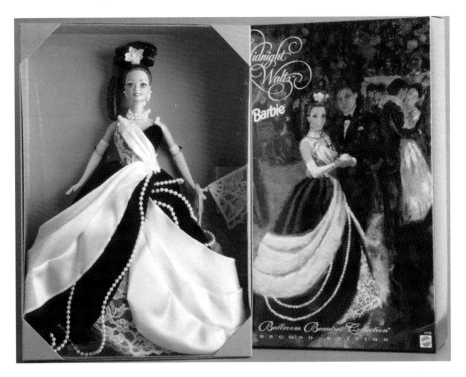

This brunette **Midnight Waltz Barbie** doll was available solely from Mattel's Barbie
Collectibles site on the World Wide Web.

    online financial transactions, electronic commerce will become a grow-
ing mode for purchasing Barbie dolls, particularly for those collectors
who tend to spend a lot of time Internet surfing, and who wish to stay
out of shopping malls and save hassle and travel time.

IN THE DEVELOPMENT OF "CONVERGED" PRODUCTS—Talk with Me Barbie is
just the latest in an evolving lineup of Barbie dolls that began with the
first talking Barbie doll in the '60s. As we approach the millenium and
beyond, new computer technologies will provide the basis for new
applications beyond "just talking." Emerging technologies such as arti-
ficial intelligence, lasers, and sensors will support dolls that can "do
what I do," which is the goal of Mattel vis-a-vis their target audience
of young girls into the next century.

ON CD-ROM—Various computer games have been licensed and targeted to
the younger Barbie doll consumer. One of the first was the "Barbie and
Her Magical House" CD-ROM, available in 1994. In this game, participants helped Barbie decorate, cook, and move the Ken doll's picture
around the room. Also available that year, Nintendo's Game Boy
Barbie Game Girl had her steer through a mall to meet Ken for a date,
and search for fashion treasures for a fantasy ball. In a series of
videogames available from Hi Tech Entertainment in 1995, Barbie
mountain bikes, shops, and performs other tasks. Mattel licensed these
and other vendors to create new computer games using the Barbie persona.

For "Barbie Makeover Magic," Mattel Media teamed with Academy Award-winning special effects house R/GA Digital Studios. The Mattel media team worked with director James Cameron's company, Digital Domain, to develop the smash hit, "Barbie Fashion Designer"—a successful 1996 Christmas gift for young girls.

The history-making success of the Barbie Fashion Designer CD-ROM will be an important landmark in Mattel corporate history. Not only was this product one of the hottest Barbie-doll-related products of the Christmas 1996 season, but the software was, in fact, the brainchild of a child-brain: that of E.J. Rifkin. It was E.J.

(Elizabeth Joy) Rifkin, an eight-year-old, who was the real genius behind the product. Her father, Andy, was a toy and game inventor who, after working with E.J. on the project, landed a job at Mattel Media. His precocious daughter wanted to run fabric through the computer printer, and the seed for the product was sown.

E.J., along with the NASA scientists who found life on Mars, was subsequently honored by *Popular Science* magazine for her personal contribution to computing. E.J. said, "Before all of this (notoriety), I thought I wanted to be a movie star, but instead, I'm an inventor. I'm even more proud of that." (Source: *The Dallas Morning News*, 25 November 1996, p1C)

"And I thought math class was tough!" complaints **Teen Talk Barbie** *as she learns how to surf the Net. She is pictured with her 1994 Home Office.*

BARBIE AT THE CYBERCAFÉ

On November 10, 1994, at The Kitchen on West 19th Street in the Chelsea section of New York City, Barbie cyberhistory was made. The Kitchen joined cybersalons in far-ranging sites that included Santa Monica, Paris, Jerusalem, Tokyo, Berlin, Managua and Maui. This electronic café event, later called "Café Barbie—An Inter-Continental Salon," commemorated the 35th anniversary of the Barbie doll. Using state-of-the-art hardware largely donated by manufacturers and audio-visual communications lines installed by NYNEX, The Kitchen's performance space was fitted out as a balance of traditional café amenities such as espresso and biscotti completed by a computerized video installation. Speakers included a star-studded panel with personalities such as Betty Friedan, Lauren Hutton, Raquel Welch and Camille Paglia. Also on hand for the event was the Barbie Liberation Organization, the group notorious for entering toy stores and switching Barbie doll voice boxes with those of G.I. Joe.

*The **Barbie Hairstyler CD-ROM** expanded Mattel's line of edu-tainment software.*

There's a lot to be proud of. Barbie Fashion Designer has sold more than one million units worldwide as of August, 1997, encouraging Mattel Media to expand its Barbie interactive franchise.

In 1997, Mattel introduced Barbie Magic Hairstyler, Barbie Ocean Discovery, and Barbie Print & Play—a productivity tool to design and print invitations, post-cards and other items.

Another planned CD-ROM title, Barbie Magic Fairy Tales, is a fantasy story starring Barbie as Rapunzel. It adds the modern twist of allowing Barbie to rescue the prince (her faithful pal Ken) from the wicked spell of the evil witch. The strategy was another effort to appeal to girls' desire to identify with the heroine, and at the same time help them master challenges.

Barbie Print 'N Play is a CD-ROM used for making stationery, invitations, coloring book pages, cards, and other ephemera using templates and clip-art images of Barbie and her world. The program comes with pink stationery, notecards, postcards and stickers that are inkjet and laser-printer compatible.

There is more to follow. As personal computers, online network subscribers, Internet surfers, and specialty collecting networks proliferate the world over, the Barbie doll, too, will be taking her place on the cyber-stage. Mattel has strategic alliances with several technology companies to create innovative new approaches for Barbie-related games, both for pure fun and for education (in media circles, known as edu-tainment).

Plans to develop Barbie doll adventures via virtual reality technologies are already under discussion. "The idea," Mattel's Jill Barad said in an interview with *Investor's Business Daily* in April, 1995, "is to bring value to where children will be spending their time and having her [Barbie doll] add value to their time. Those children online or on the Internet will be able to interact with Barbie in very special ways." Such "special ways" could include Barbie taking little girls on a journey, and explaining new opportunities open to them as they travel in her world.

Abbe Littleton's Midnight Gala, *the sixth Classique doll in the series, was issued in 1995.*

Abbe Littleton
1995

Chapter 11

"Mommy, Where Do Barbie® Dolls Come From?"

It is no small miracle that a Barbie doll ultimately finds its way to a toy store shelf. If you think the process begins and ends with the talented Barbie doll designers, you're mistaken. For each doll conceived by a designer, there is an extensive and dedicated team deployed that performs multiple functions and roles. The team works together to bring a beautiful, safe doll to the market.

According to Barbie doll designer Cynthia Young, a multidisciplinary team is involved with the designer from the initial concept. The team is "a wonderful blend of experts doing what they know best." Designers present ideas to the team and the group votes on which ones will work "best." Young described the complex, interactive brainstorming process: "The designer makes a Barbie sketch, drawing a picture like the Butterfly Princess dress, showing the butterflies and what the doll does. The group agrees that this is a good idea and recommends that a 3-D model be made up. The designer brings the model to the group's next meeting. The group critiques the model: 'Take off some butterflies, change the colors.' Designers and others at the team meeting have ideas about face paint, whether the doll's mouth should be open or closed. They will say things like, 'Don't use a closed mouth, the doll looks too serious. We want her to look younger.' Everyone adds all of their critiques, additions and edits. Then it goes back to the designer and she has to design it the way the group wants it. That's when she'll bring it back, when they say, hopefully, 'That's good. . .let's go for it'!"

The many individuals, sections and departments that have roles in the doll's development as it moves from concept through production include:

◆ *Manufacturing,* to determine the viability of producing the doll on time.

◆ *Costing,* to determine how the company will financially fare on the doll.

◆ *Time management and scheduling,* to calculate when the doll is needed for the market.

◆ *Chemical and Safety Laboratories,* to identify potential quality and health issues with the planned doll.

◆ *The Hair Department,* to work closely with the designer in creating an appropriate hair style for the doll, to be consistent with both the designer's vision and the various constraints set by costing, scheduling, and safety.

◆ *Face painting,* again to work closely with the designer to realize makeup that is consistent and complementary to the design.

- *Face sculpting,* to create a new head mold, or to select an existing head mold.
- *Engineers,* to provide input on technical aspects of the doll, such as computer chips for speaking, pliability for bending the dolls, etc.
- *Textiles,* for designing and then sourcing the fabrics for the dolls.
- *Production pattern making,* to design the pattern for the costume.

Once the designer has conceptualized the [final] doll, she drapes, pins and sews fabric to it. Kim Burkhardt and her colleagues in the soft goods and fabrics area then have to actually produce the pattern for the gown. This is no easy task. Burkhardt, with a B.A. in Textile Science, has to carry through the designer's vision for the doll's costume, whether it's based on a fabric that wholesales for $80 per yard or is to be hand-painted. "We do whatever it takes to create the vision. Our job is to think about how to create the costume within a budget."

An example: For Barbie doll designer Abbe Littleton's popular 1995 Classique, Midnight Gala, Littleton had originally used gold metallic lace over the black velvet gown. However, the actual layout made the costume impossible to reproduce. As an alternative fabric, the textile engineer on the project, Wendy Wilson, worked out an engineered glitter print. After careful consultation with the designer, production, marketing and accounting team members, this was the resulting fabric for Littleton's doll. "We do our best to maintain the designer's vision, but a big part of our job is meeting marketing's product margin," Burkhardt explains.

"From the very start, we're working with another person on every single Barbie doll design. A production designer is looking at how we're putting the doll and costume together for production, and she is also responsible for putting together the patterns. Once we receive a doll design, we know fairly quickly how we're going to approach the product. We do a lot of 'translating' of fabric. The designer will layer up several fabrics, but we have to figure out how to make it into one layer of fabric," Burkhardt described.

The Hollywood Legends doll—Barbie as Maria in *The Sound of Music*—provides an example of this process. The designer, Janet Goldblatt, originally had envisioned glitter on the skirt of the dress. On the bodice, Goldblatt used a novelty raw silk with a metallic yarn woven into it, "far more expensive than anything we could have chosen to use," Burkhardt said. "On the skirt, Goldblatt had used a very large human-sized tapestry pattern," Burkhardt continued. "The designer cut a segment out of the fabric that she thought looked best for the skirt. Our dilemma is that we can't get the feeling we wanted through repeating the pattern. The designer initially resisted the change, but they know there are certain elements that don't work. We have a group here that designs our textile art that designed the floral motif for Maria's dress. As we sent the fabric out to the vendor, our vendors in the Orient started working on it, and through some color adjustment and throwing glitter on the product, it worked. They hit the bodice with a golden metallic foil without using glitter, and this very effectively translated the designer's original feeling."

The textile designers are sensitive to Barbie doll collectors' wants. They understand that collectors want to see quality fabrics on the dolls. Burkhhardt said: "Collectors would enjoy seeing 'real' designer fabrics being used, not just our standard Barbie fabrics." Burkhardt believes that the upcoming 1996 porcelain

How Abbe Littleton was Meant to Work at Mattel, Inc.

Abbe Littleton

"When I joined Mattel, it was like it was meant to be. I always loved to draw, and I loved fashion. Even as a kindergartner, I was attuned to what everybody wore. After completing design school, I did design in downtown L.A. in the garment industry. I worked there for five years. I saw an article about Carol Spencer in a magazine and thought, 'What a dream job!'

"I always loved dolls. My mother and I have always been into miniatures. I played with my Barbie dolls even when I was 19 years old. My girlfriends would make fun of me until I opened the case on the floor and then they would get into it, too.

"My very first job out of college was at the factory at Mattel. My mother worked at the factory when I was a little girl. I had a lot of Mattel inside of me! I knew who Ruth and Elliot Handler were as a kid. So I had a lot of exposure to the product and knew where she was made since I was a young girl.

"When I was working in the garment industry, I saw an ad in *Apparel News* for a job with Mattel. I went for a first interview at Mattel, and they gave me a naked doll and said, 'Bring the doll back dressed.' So I had designed my wedding dress, and I decided to do the same design in red. I used a Valentine theme and made a box of chocolate out of erasers that I painted red. I took a feather boa and cut out little tiny red hearts out of sequins.

"This doll got me the job! I later found out that Mattel was coming out with a Valentine themed doll, Lovin' You Barbie. I couldn't believe I got the job. It was so ironic, because when I was in Girl Scouts, the first badge I got was Toymaker for making a doll."

SOURCE: Author's interview with Abbe Littleton, November 1995

Rose Bride doll will satisfy collectors' desires for beautiful "adult" fabrics on the Barbie doll. This doll was designed by Demaris Vidal, who happened to be a wedding gown designer prior to joining Mattel. "The original design for the doll was absolutely fabulous, but when we got done costing the doll, we couldn't make it as originally conceived," said Burkhardt. The original design used embroidered net covered in iridescent sequins with seed pearls. "There was no way it was going to happen with the budget that we had," Burkhardt added. "The production designer and I sat down and really looked at the doll. We glitter-flocked a net in an engineered pattern and created a very shimmery, very delicate fabric on the net so that it could take a scalloped edge. By doing this, we didn't have to put any sequins on it, as the fabric was shimmering on its own. We did all of the appliques this way, allowing us to add back in a lot of rosettes, keep the faux pearls on the doll, use really nice jewelry. It was the first time we've ever approached doing an engineered print." The labor in this is enormous; Burkhardt noted. "In the case of these dolls, instead of laying-up 30 at a time, we have to lay them up one at a time."

When the group finally agrees on a design, it is transferred onto a Computer Design, Inc., CAD system. Once designed, the patterns are transferred to the product development department and from there to manufacturing support where Mattel makes certain that designs are ready to go to the overseas plants in Indonesia, Malaysia and the People's Republic of China.

The plants utilize high technology manufacturing equipment. A complicated dress design, such as the jewel-laden Christian Dior, relies on special machine attachments for creating intricate designs. The plant has a special attachment that combines the hemming of the doll's skirt with the joining of sequins at the very edge of the skirt. Then, production workers hand-sew small accents on clothing such as bead buttons. It is not surprising that turnaround time for doll clothing, from concept to store shelf, can take up to 24 months.

Paulette Bazerman of Mattel Toys, Hong Kong, oversees much of this process. "I am Barbie's stepmother," Bazerman proudly asserts. "The designer trusts me to be their eyes. I have to make sure that Barbie is well taken care of. Once Barbie leaves home, I am watching her through boarding school. Boarding school is when Barbie doll leaves California and lands in the Hong Kong office, our Asian headquarters. Our office supervises the manufacture of Barbie dolls which is done in two factories in China, one in Malaysia and one in Indonesia. There are also fabric soft goods that get utilized in Italy and Mexico. Barbie doll's cars and vans, accessories, horses, and beds are all made in Italy and Mexico. These accessories need soft goods, such as the horse's blanket, pillows for the bed. . .these get made in China and are shipped. We just completed the My Size Barbie, which is made

Mattel's Barbie production plant in the Republic of China.

Barbie doll assembly line floor within the plant in the Republic of China.

in Mexico with clothes made in China. The final assembly is done in either Mexico or Italy."

Bazerman is well prepared for this choreographed logistical dance. "My background is in the garment industry in New York City and Los Angeles, so I went from women's clothing to Barbie clothing. Now I watch over collector and customized Barbie dolls, as well as ensembles such as the Fashion Avenue line."

Bazerman's team consists of textile engineers and final pattern-makers that provide the sewing standards to the plants throughout Asia. "When the dolls arrive here in concept form from California, their ensembles have glued and pinned fabrics which might have come from somebody's sweater," she said. "These are not in a manufacturable form, either for the fabric or the pattern. So it's still in concept form when we receive them. I have a group of 14 sample makers and a manager who make the prototypes that we're doing. The sample makers hand-decorate [e.g, hand-glitter] and make the prototypes for packages, toy shows, catalogs and television commercials. Of the 320 different Barbie items, I get about half of them. I have a colleague that has the same responsibilities covering the other half of the items."

Through each step, Bazerman is there to manage the many "moments of truth" in the manufacturing process. More complex dolls, generally beloved by collectors, often require modifications along the way. Sometimes there have to be compromises. Bazerman has to make a "call" on budgets and timing, ensuring the high level of quality that the designer intended. "I always want to make it gorgeous," she noted. "It's easy when you have a lot of money. . .even on beaded costumes, you'd think that was easy, but it's not. . .every single one is hand done. . .that's difficult to control. It's fairly straightforward for 100 of them, but think about 50,000 units of a doll. No other garment manufacture makes as much clothing as we do."

Echoing Cynthia Young's description of the multi-disciplined group, Bazerman described the team as follows: "Everybody is a specialist. Think of the design cen-

There are many small steps in the completion of a Barbie doll. The rooting of the Barbie head, shown at right, is one of the most time consuming and important.

ter as doctors; the specialists are dermatologists who paint the dolls' faces. Then we transfer them out to sub-specialists. Hong Kong is the fabric costume specialist. Next door are the people who know how to find the vendors who make the fabrics. This is difficult, since 99% of these vendors make fabric for the garment (i.e., human-sized) industry. And we invent fabrics all the time. They figure out how to find the fabric in a back-and-forth dance with the vendors. This process alone can take four weeks or as long as a year."

Dolls that must be turned around quickly are particularly challenging. One of the quickest turnaround-time Barbie dolls was the Target Baseball Barbie. The designers in California wanted to capitalize on the baseball frenzy at the time (think *Field of Dreams,* and you get the idea). "We try not to put new fabrics [i.e., fabric requiring design "from scratch"] on a doll like this," Bazerman said. "We had to go into the open market and find some stripes to give it top priority and capitalize on the baseball trend. Now we're working on Olympic Barbie the same way. Baywatch Barbie also had a quick turnaround. In these situations, the whole team has to work fast, design fast."

All this activity would be fathomable for a few dolls at a time. However, Bazerman admitted: "We have 50 projects on our plate at any one time." How are all these balls juggled at once? "Everything is managed on a computer," she said. "My secretary prints out flow charts every Monday and we manage the various projects in real time. My bottom line is to get it done!"

Another way of fast-tracking dolls is by working very closely with the team. Bazerman said, "Ann Driskill is coming to Hong Kong in November with the team, including managers of marketing, costing and planning. We will lock ourselves in a room for two weeks and go from concept to approval in the office in real time. This is how to get things done!"

"We've come a long way since 1985 when there were only two textile people and three pattern people. Today we have 50 such professionals," Bazerman said from her sophisticated high-rise office on Canton Road in Kowloon, chock full of glitter. . . .

Now, fast-forward from the glitter in Hong Kong to the glitter back at Mattel's corporate offices in El Segundo, California. Once the dolls are manufactured in Asia in a first run-through, along comes Judy Schizas from the Corporate Product Integrity group (CPI). To prevent potential pitfalls along the way, CPI is involved throughout the process. This function fills the crucial safety and quality assurance (QA) roles. Each doll is tested for its age-grading and has to meet every requirement for that group. CPI's laboratory conducts all kinds of testing. The CPI engineers write specifications, instructing the manufacturing plants how to test the toys. Manufacturing plants located outside of the United States must meet all requirements established by Mattel's CPI group in El Segundo, CA. Once CPI receives the manufactured doll, they perform audits in the CPI lab.

It seems that there are more types of testing than there were variations of Teen Talk Barbie dolls. Tests include:

◆ *Transit tests,* where CPI puts doll packages on "shake machines" to simulate the workout that the boxes will get when packed and shipped.

◆ *Drop tests,* a series of different drops to see if earrings fall off, if hair covers the doll's face, if the doll breaks even though it is hooked down. Schizas described: "We drop the doll from different attitudes. . .on her head, her arms, her bottom!"

◆ *Aging tests,* where CPI puts the doll in an oven to determine shelf life.

◆ *Humidity tests,* where the doll is placed in an environmental chamber. One scenario in a humidity test is a Barbie wearing black trousers: if the doll gets damp, do her legs get stained black? "We try to figure this out before it happens by doing these little tests," Schizas said.

◆ *Function tests,* where every doll's legs, head and arms have to move.

◆ *Abuse tests,* where both reliability and safety abuse are tested. Schizas emphasized: "When we say abuse, we mean *very* abusive abuse. We pull arms and legs off, to determine how secure they are. We do bite and hair-pull tests. We conduct abrasion tests to see if the paint comes off of the doll's face."

◆ *Heavy elements test,* where the face paints and other chemicals are checked for lead and other elements.

◆ *Flammability tests,* "from the doll figure itself to her underpants," said Schizas. Every piece of material has to burn at a slow rate.

◆ *Life tests,* where the doll's arms are rotated a certain amount of times, knees are bent a number of cycles, and heads are turned a prescribed number of cycles.

DESIGNING THE STAR TREK GIFTSET

Robert Best recalled: "I remember one of my assignments for a collectible Barbie doll was the Star Trek giftset. This was appropriate, since I was born in Florida while my father was working at Cape Kennedy. Initially, the project was difficult for two reasons. First, being relatively new to the Barbie doll design team, I was getting familiar with a different craft. Coming from working with the designer Isaac Mizrahi in New York and with Louis Dell'Olio at Anne Klein to working in 'Barbie-size' was a huge leap. There are very specific things that you can only learn by working on the doll. When you start working on that scale, the limitations become clear. It was a whole introduction about being attuned to very small details.

"Second, I wasn't a 'Trekkie,' so I had to become familiar with the designs. I started by asking Paramount Studios (the producer of the Star Trek properties) what the costumes were made out of. Paramount sent me swatches and later sent me photographs and images. I rented all of the Star Trek movies and immersed myself into the project."

Robert Best then succeeded in going where no other Barbie doll designer had gone before. . . .

SOURCE: Author's interview with Robert Best, August 1997

◆ *Chemical and biological testing,* where if a doll is designed to go into the water, it must meet chemical and biological testing. This test focuses on mold inhibitors.

◆ *Other safety and health issues:* Even feathers for Bob Mackie dolls are sent out to labs to be tested, to make certain that they contain no bacteria.

After all of that abuse, it is interesting to note that only about four percent of dolls go back to the drawing board for retooling. Not until every test is completed does the doll move ahead to the manufacturing line to be prepared for production. From there, everything is sent to Asia for mass production.

Barbie dolls have never been manufactured in the U.S. Since 1959, the dolls have been made overseas. Manufacturing has occurred in Japan, Singapore, Malaysia, Indonesia, Mexico and the People's Republic of China (PRC). Currently, Mattel operates two plants in Malaysia, two plants in the PRC, and one plant in Indonesia. Barbie dolls are also being made in a new world-class manufacturing facility in Jakarta, Indonesia. Managing the mix of dolls coming off the line is a challenge; just ponder for a moment the many distinctions—some obvious and others more subtle—between a porcelain evening gowned doll, a Mackie vinyl Barbie doll, and a main line hair play doll, and you begin to appreciate the logistical challenge.

Larry Morgan of Mattel International is responsible for overseeing Asian manufacturing operations. "A funny thing happened on the way to Indonesia," he told me. To establish the manufacturing plant in Indonesia, Mattel had to obtain approval from the country's investment approval board BKPM, which advises President Suharto. The Mattel team presented their business case to a huge group of people to review. "They didn't know who we were when we walked into the meeting," Morgan recalled. "As part of our presentation, we brought our toy catalogs, which we opened to illustrate our business. As soon as we opened to the first page, their eyes lit up. They said, 'Barbie! Barbie!' They knew who *she* was, even though they didn't know Mattel!"

Just a few Barbie heads waiting for assembly.

*Robert Best created this sketch of his masterful **Portrait in Taffeta Barbie** doll.*

THE BARBIE DOLL MEETS THE COURIER

The Couture Collection was unveiled in 1996, bringing many new collectors into the Barbie doll collecting fold. The first two dolls have been designed by Robert Best. I asked him about the origins of this charming collection:

"The Couture Collection was really the result of brainstorming between design and marketing. We wanted to do a line that was different in a number of ways. It embodies adult sophistication. It is different because it is as meticulous about real details and finishes as possible. We wanted it to be 'the best of the best.'

"The Couture Collection is a line that is very close to me because it's about my vision. I was told, 'Design something glamorous.' Given those parameters, the sky was the limit!

"For Portrait in Taffeta (the brown gown) I thought, 'What's the color that I haven't seen on a Barbie doll?' And brown was so popular at the time as 'the new black.' I thought that I would love to do a brown gown. Using that color as a springboard, I went looking for fabrics in velvet and taffeta. I used a rich combination of the two. Playing with the fabric, I came up with the doll's total design. I wanted something that was grand, elegant, awe-inspiring."

As with any couturier, Robert Best depends on a team to develop and realize his designs. "I must give homage to the entire team involved in this process. In particular, Nini Lwin, my sample maker, has done every prototype for all of the dolls I've designed at Mattel. She has been instrumental in making everything as beautiful as it is. Her hands make it all come together. She sews these tiny seams, she lines things, things I never thought possible on this scale. I ask, 'Can we pad this?' or 'Let's put this without a dart.' When I challenge her with something, she always delivers.

"I never know if people are going to love or hate these things. I do something that I like and I hope others will. It's all about enjoying my craft and loving the art of creating something."

Mr. Best, I have good news for you: The Couture Collection is loved by legions of collectors!

SOURCE: Author's interview with Robert Best, August 1997

Happy Holidays

Special Edition

1995 Happy Holidays Barbie *sold out so quickly that Mattel issued vouchers for additional dolls to be made available Spring 1996.*

BARBIE® ECONOMICS

The Barbie doll is big business. In 1992, *Financial World* magazine calculated a market value for Mattel, Inc., of $2.3 billion. But the bean counters found that when the value of the Barbie doll brand name was factored in, the company's market value increased to $4.5 billion.

That kind of brand equity only happens through diligence, sound strategic planning and no small amount of luck. This chapter focuses on the business side of Barbie doll, including advertising and the globalization and management of the brand.

actoid

Between 1990 and 1996, sales of Barbie dolls more than doubled, reaching nearly $1.8 billion in 1996.

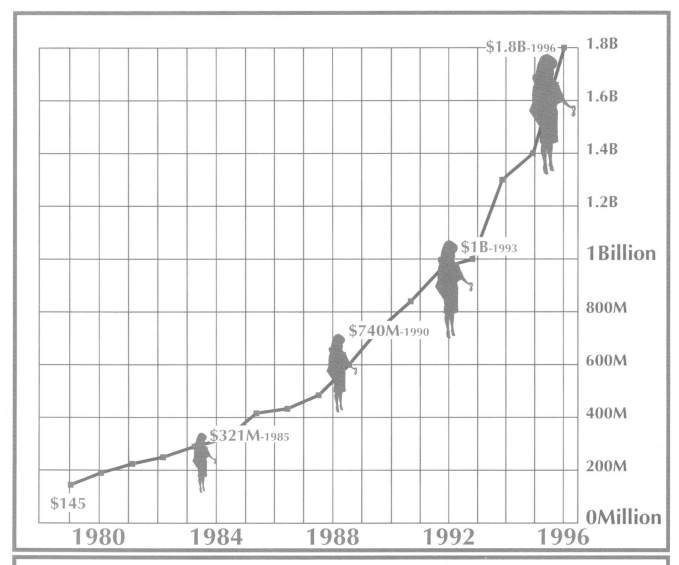

$1.8B-1996 1.8B
1.6B
1.4B
1.2B
$1B-1993 1Billion
800M
$740M-1990
600M
400M
$321M-1985
200M
$145
0Million

1980   1984   1988   1992   1996

BARBIE WORLDWIDE SALES
1980—1996

◆ ADVERTISING

One contemporary art medium is particularly relevant in a discussion about *Contemporary BARBIE*: the applied art of Madison Avenue known as advertising. Since the Barbie doll's introduction in 1959, advertising has played a key role in promotion of the doll. When the doll was first unveiled at New York Toy Fair in 1959, television advertising time was purchased during programs such as "The Mickey Mouse Club." In addition to TV ads, Barbie ads have been placed in print media—particularly magazines. Today, ads for the Barbie doll go well beyond traditional television and magazine promotions, and have evolved into thirty-minute infomercials and offers through electronic catalogs over on-line computer services, along with the proliferation of print catalogs.

It is informative to review Mattel's advertising for the Barbie doll since her inception. The changing ad campaigns reveal much about the language and social mores prevalent at any given time. In the course of compiling material for this book, I had the opportunity to review and analyze some sixty minutes of Barbie doll television commercials.

FASHION DOLL WARS BREAK OUT IN EUROPE

The fashion doll sector represents four percent of toy sales in Europe, but is dominated by one perennial brand. Every other toy segment is populated by several, if not dozens, of hotly competing brands. The situation in Europe is different from the U.S., inasmuch as until recently every major country had at least one distinctly national 11½-inch fashion doll competing against the distinctively Californian girl, Barbie. Germany had Petra, the U.K. had Sindy, and France had Perle. Going back to the early 1980s, some of these brands dominated the sector. Each was developed in one country for sale just in that country, so the name, packaging, clothing, accessories and advertising all reflected one national culture. As Barbie grew in strength in Europe during the 1980s, it displaced these national dolls from sector leadership. Then Hasbro acquired Sindy in the U.K. and embarked on a strategy of marketing fashion dolls across Europe, acquiring Perle in France and Petra in Germany, both of which have subsequently disappeared. But Sindy replaced them. Hasbro management is committed to the long-term success of Sindy in Europe. While Sindy has been nibbling at Barbie's share in several European countries, in the U.K. Barbie hit back hard last year. . . . In fact, Barbie in Europe is beginning to benefit from the warm, nostalgic memories of women who are the first generation of young mothers who themselves as children played with Barbie, and who are predisposed to buy Barbie for their daughters. Except in the U.K., Sindy does not have this advantage.

SOURCE: *The Toy Book*, July 1996, pp14-15

The Barbie doll was first advertised on television in 1960, back in the, "You Can Tell It's Mattel. . .It's Swell" era. The first commercial jingle was sung to the strains of an orchestra:

> Barbie you're beautiful
> You make me feel
> My Barbie doll is really real
>
> Barbie's small and so petite
> Her clothes and figure look so neat
> Her dancin' outfit rings a bell
> At parties she will cast a spell
> Purses, hats and gloves galore
> And all the gadgets gals adore
>
> Male voiceover: "Barbie dressed for swim and fun is only $3. Her lovely fashions range from $1 to $5. Look for Barbie wherever dolls are sold."
>
> Some day I'm gonna be
> Exactly like you
> 'Til then I know just what I'll do
> Barbie
> Beautiful Barbie
> I'll make believe that I am you
>
> Male voiceover: "You can tell it's Mattel, it's swell!"

Goddess of the Sun™ Barbie
She wears a shimmering Bob Mackie gown with over 11,000 hand-sewn sequins and beads.

Enchanted Evening® Barbie
A reproduction of one of Barbie doll's most popular vintage fashions from 1960.

Poodle Parade™ Barbie
A charming reproduction of a 1965 Barbie doll and nostalgic fashion.

Summer Sophisticate™ Barbie
This Spiegel exclusive has her own unique and sophisticated retro look.
#15591 $59.99

Victorian Lady™ Barbie
She takes a step back in time, wearing an authentic Victorian gown with elegant bustle and marabou headpiece.
#14900 $59.99

*This brochure illustrated the **Spiegel Summer Sophisticate Barbie** doll, as well as promoting other dolls.*

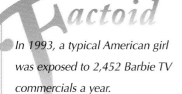

Now fast-forward through years of Beach Boys/Jan & Dean-style surfing music, and Maureen McCormick (later famous as Marsha from the "Brady Bunch") promoting the New Living Barbie.

In 1972, the "Surprising Barbie" era of ads began. . .

Hey! How can you make your Barbie's arms and legs move like that? Hey! You're making her walk!

Meet new Walk Lively Barbie.
She comes with her own walk and turn stand.
Just put her in and push her along.
Look, she even turns around.

There's a Walk Lively Ken and Steffie, too.
Now we can pretend she's going for a walk in the park with Ken.
You can also make her walk off the stand.
See how her head turns?

[Song]
With surprising Barbie there's always something new
Lots of fun and surprising things to do
Surprising Barbie. . . Barbie. . .Barbie. . .

AVON + MATTEL = MEGA-CO-BRANDING

Meet the newest Avon lady: Barbie. Avon Products Inc. has teamed up with Mattel Inc. to launch a line of Barbie cosmetics and toiletries for children. The line will include lip balms, perfumes, shampoos, conditioners, bubble bath and hand creams, aimed at girls aged six to twelve.

They will range in price from $1 to $7.50 and will be available beginning in the last three months of 1997 in the United States, Canada, and certain Latin American markets, with markets in Europe and Asia under consideration.

Avon, the direct seller of beauty products and related products, also said it will again market Barbie dolls designed for Avon by Mattel. Last year, Avon sales representatives marketed the dolls. They were Avon's best-selling gift product ever, generating $40 million in sales, the company said. Avon said the alliance with Mattel is expected to boost Avon's net sales by $100 million annually.

The products will be promoted heavily through Avon's 440,000 U.S. sales representatives as well as in the Avon U.S. sales brochure during two, two-week sales campaigns during the important holiday gift-buying season. The brochures will feature a Mattel product on the cover and dedicate the first ten pages of each brochure to Mattel brands and licensed properties. Avon's U.S. brochure reaches an estimated 15 million women during each two-week sales campaign. The two companies also said that they will launch a global line of licensed Barbie cosmetics, fragrance and toiletry products for children. The line will include perfumes, shampoos, conditioners, bubble bath and hand creams. The line is expected to launch in the fourth quarter 1997 in the U.S., Canada and certain markets in Latin America. Additional markets in Europe and Asia are also under active consideration.

SOURCE: *Reuters*, 1 May 1997

Then in a few years, Barbie promoted the "We Girls Can Do Anything" campaign. . .

> Here's Day-to-Night Barbie
> [Song]
> We girls make working lots of fun
> Right, Barbie?
> Day-to-Night Barbie
> We can work from nine to five
> And then change in a sec' for an evening with Ken
> Secret turnaround skirt, fabulous hair
> We girls can do anything
> Right, Barbie?
> Day-to-Night Barbie has a change-around outfit
>
> Ken doll sold separately.

BARBIE DOLL: JAPAN'S NEW LOOK

Young women all over Japan will be dressing like Barbie starting fall 1997, if all goes as Mattel Inc. plans. The toy maker will soon introduce a Japanese line of clothes, shoes, underwear, pajamas, hats, gloves, and other accessories for young adults, all fashioned after the world's most beloved piece of hourglass-shaped plastic.

Go ahead, laugh! Then listen to Sayaka Hata, 20, as she scoops ice cream cones at the corner Häagen-Dazs shop: "I love Barbie so much. I want to be Barbie. I know this is going to be the biggest hit ever. People are going to buy it for sure." Hata and her friends actually went shopping last summer to find clothes like Barbie doll's, without much success. Now she's thrilled that she'll be able to dress like a doll she considers a role model: "She's cute, pretty, perfect—pretty much everything I want to be."

Mattel is now investing in Japan's love of Barbie, its passion for brand names, and the explosive and lucrative nature of fads and fashion trends here. Japan is the only country where Mattel will sell Barbie clothes for young women aged 15 to 25, and published reports say the company is counting on annual sales reaching $90 million a year.

"Many young women want to look like Barbie," said Kaoru Kondo, who runs the bustling Barbie section at Kiddy Land on Tokyo's fashionable Omotesando Boulevard. "Barbie has a perfect body and really cool-looking outfits," she said. "Right now, the whole fashion trend is really into 1960s and '70s items—just like the ones the original Barbie used to wear."

Kiddy Land spokesman Kenichiro Fujii said women from their twenties to their forties (and a handful of men) are buying Barbie dolls that cost up to $100, as well as Barbie picture frames, watches, books and notebooks that run up to nearly $250.

"We are not only thinking about selling clothes, we want to sell the concept of Lady Barbie," said a spokesman for Itochu Fashion System Co., which will produce the clothes under a license from Mattel. "She is the symbol of an independent, self-confident, new type of woman."

Adrienne Fontanella, a Mattel vice president, said market research in Japan showed strong interest among Japanese young adult women in the Barbie doll's lifestyle. "We're really into marketing her persona: her energy, her spirit, her lifestyle," Fontanella said. "She has this great energy. She's always on the go. She can be anything she wants to be."

Which isn't necessarily true of many Japanese women. In this male-dominated society, women still face discrimination in almost every other facet of their lives. "That's exactly why it works here," Fontanella said. "They can dream and aspire to be anything they want to be through her. It's her attitude that gives them confidence."

SOURCE: *The Washington Post*, 16 December 1996, pA20

From "We Girls Can Do Anything," the ad campaigns shifted to, "We're into Barbie. . . ." This campaign was successfully and intensively used for California Dream Barbie, Island Fun Barbie, Perfume Pretty Barbie, Cool Times Barbie, Animal Lovin' Barbie, Doctor Barbie, Style Magic Barbie, Dance Club Barbie, Western Fun Barbie, Wet 'n Wild Barbie, Lights and Lace Barbie, Hawaiian Fun Barbie, and Costume Ball Barbie.

Then, rap music began to be used in some ads. . . .

> *[3 young girls rapping]*
> There's a brand new Barbie
> In a brand new mood
> She's a teenage Barbie
> With a cool attitude
> Feelin' fun is her name
> Havin' fun is her game
> Ooh, those clothes
> Ooh, that hair
> She's got friends everywhere
> She's where it's happening
>
> You put it together
>
> Feelin' Fun
> Feelin' Fun Barbie.

The "You've Got Something Special Era," which began around 1991, has been the basis for ads for Totally Hair Barbie, Sun Sensation Barbie, Rollerblade Barbie and Sparkle Eyes Barbie.

THE ORIGINS OF "WE GIRLS CAN DO ANYTHING"

Upon joining Mattel, one of Jill Barad's first tasks was to update the image of Barbie, which was introduced two decades earlier. By 1985, more than a few mothers who had grown up playing with the doll viewed her as a flighty and inappropriate role model for their daughters. Sales of Barbie were flattening out at around $320 million annually, well behind the then-popular Cabbage Patch Kids, and even top managers at Mattel thought the Barbie doll's growth might have been permanently stunted.

"I thought Barbie was wonderful," Ms. Barad says. "But that's not what people I'd run into would say. My sister said, 'All this stuff about power and leadership is only for boys. What's there for girls? What's Barbie doll's job?'"

After posing the problem to the company's ad agency, Ogilvy & Mather, Ms. Barad's marketing team settled on a slick campaign titled "We Girls Can Do Anything." The plan was to transform Barbie into an ambitious career girl capable of moving up the corporate ladder just as fast as her boyfriend Ken. Thus, Ms. Barad's team introduced Day-to-Night Barbie, who could work in her pink business suit and then hit the discos in a pink gown. Aspirational themes continue today.

The "We Girls Can Do Anything" campaign was a hit, and sales bounced up to $415 million in 1986.

SOURCE: *The Wall Street Journal*, 5 March 1997, pA1

The tone of child-directed ads radically shifted in 1994 to target adult consumers. Mattel's first Barbie doll infomercial was produced to promote the Classique line. The infomercial was hosted by Pam Dawber (of "Mork and Mindy" fame) who interviewed several Barbie collectors in the typical infomercial living room set-up. During the course of the infomercial, viewers were introduced to Janet Goldblatt, Carol Spencer and Kitty Black-Perkins. The purchase offer included three Classique dolls with a bonus special gift—a Barbie collector's video filmed in part at the 1993 Barbie convention held in Baltimore, Maryland.

The second Barbie doll infomercial, which started airing in 1994, was the Scarlett Infomercial hosted by Leeza Gibbons, ex-"Entertainment Tonight" and current talk show host. Infomercials promoting Barbie as Eliza Doolittle in *My Fair Lady* and the Bob Mackie Jewel Essence Collection were aired in 1996 and 1997 respectively. Mattel credits these infomercials with very effectively attracting and communicating to new collectors. Count on seeing more of them in the future!

◆ GLOBAL BARBIE

Mattel is more than a toy company: It's a global marketing company. It is clear that the company's major growth area looking to the year 2000 is outside of the United States. That's because there are twice as many children in Europe three times as many in South America and fifteen times as many in Asia as there are in the United States. In Europe, by the year 2000, more than 20 percent of the 40 million children in the European Community under the age of 10 will be living in the United Kingdom. And, Barbie already has a good start in Europe. Due to aggressive marketing efforts in the early 1990s, the typical girl in Italy had almost as many Barbie dolls (seven) as her American counterpart. In France and Germany, the average girl had five Barbie dolls.

Mattel maintains 34 marketing offices overseas. Further facilitating international expansion is the surging growth of Toys 'R Us into foreign markets. The huge toy chain has 234 stores from Germany to Malaysia, and plans to open at least 50 new stores overseas every year for the foreseeable future.

UNICEF Barbie dolls, like those shown here, helped to expand Barbie's global presence.

BARBIE GOES GLOBAL

To grow market share overseas, Mattel is also working closely with other consumer-driven companies such as Avon. Using Avon's network in other markets where awareness of Barbie exists but retail distribution is limited, Mattel plans to use the network in China, Indonesia, Russia and Brazil. Although the doll is already manufactured in China, it has never been widely available to Chinese consumers.

Mattel is planning to develop a new international Barbie for the Chinese market, but the company has no immediate plans to introduce career Barbie dolls such as the Dr. Barbie, Dentist Barbie, or Teacher Barbie popular in the U.S. and Europe. Instead, the doll will be a traditional Barbie doll who plays with pets and goes to school. "In Japan we found that little girls were encouraged to stay little girls," Jill Barad has said, adding that Mattel will eventually conduct test marketing in China. Mattel also doesn't plan to make the new doll look Asian. Several years ago, it launched a Barbie in Japan with Asian eyes and a less-prominent bustline, but the doll flopped. Little girls around the world prefer the well-known American doll rather than a local version.

HONG KONG HANDOVER BARBIE

DATELINE: 30 May 1997—"Handover Barbie" will step out today, in Hong Kong's swanky Peninsula Hotel. Bidding will start at HK$50,000 ($6,457) for the limited edition of seven diamond-studded dolls decked in Ch'ing dynasty imperial robes.

The auction is the latest symptom of souvenir fever heating up ahead of Hong Kong's transfer of sovereignty to China. The occasion has spurred a new industry of memorabilia, from badges and T-shirts to the exclusive limited editions of jewelry and ornaments beloved by Hong Kong's highrollers.

"Hong Kongers can smell money," says Mr. Ronnie Chan, chairman of Hang Lung Development, one of the territory's big developers. And while diplomats and democrats fret about postcolonial politics, the July 1997 handover is giving off a powerful aroma.

Ms. Yvonne Ngau, marketing manager at Mattel East Asia, said a limited edition Barbie doll—without diamonds—had already sold out in spite of its HK$539.90 price ($70.00).

SOURCE: *Financial Times*, 30 May 1997

CHADOR-CLAD DOLL IS IRAN'S ANSWER TO BARBIE

Barbie is getting competition. But Iran's new "Sara" doll isn't the type to show off her figure in a swimsuit.

"Sara" wears long, flowing clothes and wraps, or similarly modest Iranian national costumes. She is Iran's latest attempt to resist what authorities consider cultural corruption from the West.

And in contrast to Ken, that guy always hanging around Barbie, Sara's companion doll—Dara—is safely her brother. He wears the long coat and turban of an Islamic cleric.

"Barbie is an American woman who never wants to get pregnant and have babies. She never wants to look old and this contradicts our culture," said Majid Ghaderi, who designed the new dolls. "Barbie is like a Trojan Horse," Ghaderi added. "Inside it, it carries its Western cultural influences, such as makeup and indecent clothes. Once it enters our society, it dumps these influences on our children." Ghaderi is director of the amusement department at the government-sponsored Institute for the Intellectual Development of Children and Young Adults.

The project to design Sara and Dara dolls began two years ago, and they are expected to hit the market next summer (1997). They long have been used as educational characters in elementary schools; their names are simple in Farsi script.

"We are also planning to introduce them in theaters, cartoons, puppet shows and computer games," Ghaderi said. In the computer game, Sara will travel to different parts of Iran and wear each region's local costumes.

Barbie dolls are considered anti-Islamic and importing them is prohibited. However, dozens of shops in Tehran display original all-American Barbie dolls, some wearing only a swimsuit.

Shopkeepers said they do not expect the Iranian dolls to compete with Barbie, but said they would display them. A genuine "Barbie-at-the-prom" sells for $40, while a three-foot-tall bride model goes for as much as $700 in a country where the average monthly salary is $100. Iranian imitations run about one-fifth of the price.

SOURCES: Associated Press, 24 October 1996; *Chicago Tribune*, 25 October 1996, p4; *The Allentown Morning Call*, 25 October 1996.

Mattel has implemented an aggressive direct mail campaign to sell Barbie dolls to collectors since 1996. A direct mail brochure from Barbie Collectibles (left) features **Holiday Caroler Barbie**.

One small step for Barbiekind....1994 and
1986 Barbie dolls on the moon....

Chapter 13

READING THE PINK TEA LEAVES

Where do you want to see Barbie® in the year 2001? Given that the designers work on a two-year lead time, I didn't think the question would be too difficult for Barbie doll designers to forecast.

I asked everyone with whom I met at Mattel about the future of the Barbie doll. While Mattel designers cannot share specific plans, it is interesting to note the company-line response, which goes something like this: "Barbie will go places she's never gone before. . .places that haven't even been imagined yet." She could be in a movie, have her own theme park, and star in a Broadway musical. To those readers who may be cynical about such a possibility, ponder this: Who just a few years ago would have thought that Disney would ever consider refurbishing Times Square in New York to create a Disney neighborhood of attractions?

One intriguing possibility is that the Barbie character will be in a feature film. According to Mattel, they have been approached more than once to do a big-screen movie deal. But even with major studio interest over the years in the Barbie doll, Mattel has not yet received a satisfactory script. Even avid Barbie doll collector Demi Moore's production company, Moving Pictures!, has shown interest in a Barbie film project.

One certainty is that collectors will have a broad range of Barbie dolls from which to choose. . .and careful choosing is required. A glance at the *Contemporary BARBIE* doll list in the Appendix quickly reveals that the number of dolls named Barbie brought to market has grown each year—over 100 in 1997 alone. Given the cost of living indices for shelter, food and clothing, very few collectors can afford to buy, display or store every doll that comes on the market; nor is every doll available to every collector—limited editions being a case in point.

Mattel marketing management realizes that the collector market segment, particularly new collectors, is its fastest growing segment (domestically speaking). The Mattel team of designers, market management, engineers, production staff and accountants are working hard to attract new collectors, and to convert them to dedicated collectors. Their strategies are working; Mattel estimated that as of August 1995, there were well over 100,000 avid collectors with the following demographic characteristics:

- ◆ 90% of avid collectors are women (yes, Virginia, 10% are men).
- ◆ The median age of avid collectors is 40 years.
- ◆ Avid collectors buy more than 20 Barbie dolls each year.
- ◆ 45% of avid collectors spend upwards of $1,000 a year.

*The past meets the future: Nostalgic reproduction **Poodle Parade Barbie** doll wore a very desirable, rare outfit.*

Mattel is working hard to attract new collectors to Barbie's world. Market research shows that there are some 28 million women between the ages of 25 and 45 who grew up playing with Barbie. This age group certainly represents many who are already avid collectors. The 35th anniversary, the success of the 1994 and 1995 releases of Nostalgic Barbie dolls, and the success of the Hollywood Legends Barbie as Scarlett series have demonstrated a fertile and as yet relatively-untapped market of baby boomers.

There are several ways that this phantom group might be enticed into the world of Barbie doll collecting. Here, for example, are just a few of the things we might expect:

◆ Barbie dolls will be "cross-germinated" with themes attractive to baby boomers, such as those with complementary collections (e.g., Star Trek, movie characters, and the like) or childhood memories and "tastes," via food tie-ins. Barbie dolls tie in well with adult brands such as Avon, Coca-Cola, Russell Stover and the like.

◆ Fashion fantasies and character dolls will be increasingly important in the future.

◆ Ethnic variations will continue to grow in importance given the changing demographics of the U.S. as well as the phenomenon of immigration on a global basis.

As we approach the year 2000, it is incredible to believe that the Barbie doll as a force in American popular culture will be over 40 years old. . . like many of her avid collectors. As this most successful of fashion dolls approaches the millenium, there are signposts to expect along the way. . . .

COLLECTIONS GO GLOBAL. American collectors are acquiring dolls from overseas as never before—particularly on the retail market. Access to these dolls is enhanced by the Internet and commercial online services. As soon as a new collector doll is announced in an overseas market, American collectors can jump on the Web via e-mail, or make a long distance call, to order a doll almost as soon as it is released. In 1996, this could be done for some very limited dolls such as the

Hamley toy store's first exclusive shopping doll; the Easy Chic doll, in a very limited edition of 250, sold at the United Kingdom's most exclusive retailers such as Hamley's, Selfridge's and Harrod's; and the International Happy Holidays Barbie doll. If dolls tailored to overseas markets grow, Americans will have a whole new cache of dolls from which to choose; however, Mattel may choose to focus on developing a global product which appeals to a broader range of collectors throughout the world. The first signs of this are the multilingual packages that are often found in toy stores that sell main line/mass market dolls.

THE INTERNET BECOMES A HOT RETAIL AND PROMOTIONAL CHANNEL. Hundreds of thousands of Barbie doll collectors are already surfing the Net. The number of online collectors will exponentially grow as personal computers continue to penetrate households, and as the cost of going online continues to drop. Furthermore, electronic commerce on the Internet—that is, actually doing business online—is becoming more accessible to consumers through the use of encryption to protect credit card numbers and identities, as well as a growing number of banks that are implementing procedures to facilitate online transactions for consumer markets. New dolls will be sold on the Internet, from initial selection through to final payment. There will also be many more online auctions, both static lists and virtual online, real-time auctions, for vintage Barbie dolls and merchandise. Finally, infomercials, initially a cable television-based promotional medium, will plug into the Internet.

WHAT WILL THIS MEAN TO THE TRADITIONAL RETAILERS OF BARBIE DOLLS? The way we shop for *everything*—from groceries to cars to clothing—is changing. The structure of retail has shifted under our feet, as mom-and-pop stores on Main Street have given way to big box retailers in the suburbs and exurbs. . . and beyond. This is also happening to retail channels for the Barbie doll. A growing legion of specialty doll dealers is going the way of the corner grocer, hardware store, and butcher. We have already seen the influence of the mega-retailers such as Target, Toys 'R Us, and Wal-Mart on the distribution of Barbie dolls to the retail market. But even these large sources will be cannibalized by the next generation of the distribution channel. . . .

MATTEL AS ONE-STOP-SHOP. Mattel's site on the World Wide Web—www.barbie.com—is just a hint of what's to come. The site is, for the moment, strictly an educational (read: promotional) vehicle for the Barbie doll. If the company chooses, it can grow its direct distribution of dolls to collectors through the use of print catalogues, toll-free telephone numbers, and computer-based order forms. . . and increase its profit margins at the same time. What rational business planner wouldn't advocate that approach? Collectors might be able to acquire more Barbie dolls directly from Mattel a few years from now. Will they like it? If the price point is right, the service level is high, and the doll arrives at the doorstep intact, box and all—then collectors would cotton to the new distribution channel. In addition, if the company offers exclusive, unique dolls only available through their direct channel, collectors will acquire desirable dolls.

WHO ELSE WINS? The U.S. Postal Service, UPS, Federal Express, and DHL—these are other winners in the move toward direct-to-consumer sales. According to Unity Marketing, direct mail is perhaps the most effective way to reach new doll collectors. Unity's 1995 survey, "The Market for Collectible Dolls," found that 43 percent of collectors started collecting dolls in earnest because they had saved some from their childhood. But another 42 percent report beginning their hobby by ordering dolls through the mail. And the major home shopping networks—QVC and the Home Shopping Network—will continue to benefit from doll sales as part of their product line. Live television shopping is a perfect forum for featuring dolls; collectible doll sales by television shopping channels increased 33 percent between 1994 and 1995 (Source: Unity Marketing report, "The Market for Collectible Dolls").

TECHNO-DRIVEN TOYS BECOME THE NORM. In 1996, the Barbie Fashion Designer CD-ROM was among the hottest selling electronic toys of the season. Then, 1997 brought Talk with Me Barbie, the first personalized "talking" Barbie doll. The toys-to-computer trend will be a major transforming force on Barbie dolls and related products. These will go way beyond CD-ROMs as we know them today, and will reach beyond young girls. Instead, computer technologies will shape the actual dolls and features. Sensors and innovations in plastics will be integrated with the most popular fashion doll of all time. No doubt that the doll will be positioned to be the most popular techno-doll of all time, too.

So, what's left for Barbie, the doll who seems to have been "everywhere" and done "everything?" The pink tea leaves reveal that Barbie will be more global, work at new careers, model fabulous new fashions, demonstrate even more interesting special effects, further exploit computer technology, and have the potential to eat into every collector's retirement funds if they don't strategically plan their Barbie doll collections.

As Kitty Black-Perkins told me, "Barbie in the year 2000 is not too far away. We're thinking about a lot of opportunities where she could go. . .but they take her to another level, to a broader range of people who love her. Now that we've had a generation of people who have played with her and love her, there are so many different ways to enjoy Barbie. It can be as a child, or it can be as an adult. There's a lot of room for loving her. . . ."

Porcelain Silken Flame Barbie

Goddess of the Moon, *Bob Mackie's ninth design for Barbie featured the doll, for the first time, with a "prop"—a silvery moon.*

Chapter 14

VALUING *CONTEMPORARY* BARBIE® DOLLS

The first edition of *Contemporary Barbie* offered a comprehensive list of dolls and values at a single point in time. Since publication of that book in the spring of 1996, the secondary market for contemporary (post-1980) dolls has undergone a transformation that could be considered, in Wall Street-speak, a technical correction. Some collectors characterize the fall in the secondary market price of some dolls as a mild decline that will be short-lived; others who perceive the world in terms of half-empty glasses consider the current state of the secondary market as a Pink Depression that could be protracted.

Still, the secondary markets for certain dolls and series remain strong. At auctions, on vintage doll dealers' lists and via the Internet, the strongest contemporary Barbie dolls are early issue Bob Mackie's, the earliest issue FAO Schwarz exclusive dolls, and certain other store exclusives.

The fact is that values are constantly changing based on a complex web of economic and emotional factors. Barbie doll values on the secondary market move in ways well beyond a traditional supply and demand analysis. Since mid-1996, several factors have worked against a strong secondary market for contemporary Barbie dolls. These include the following collector concerns and perceptions:

WHAT'S AN "EXCLUSIVE"? Some store exclusives showed up in Mattel direct mail catalogs several months after issue, and at deeply-discounted prices. For example, the Barbie Collectibles direct mail catalog sent to collectors in the spring of 1997 had a back cover featuring the Calvin Klein Barbie doll at a price of $33. There was no mention of Bloomingdale's, the store that originally sold the doll, and no mention of the original $70 price. Collectors who received the catalog and had previously purchased the doll at full-retail price expressed extreme chagrin at the time.

WHAT'S "LIMITED"? Many collectors purchase dolls on the retail market that are termed as limited editions because they believe that the production runs on these dolls will enhance their "collectibility," i.e., value on the secondary market at some later date. As a policy, Mattel does not disclose production numbers on dolls on a regular basis; however, in the case of certain dolls, this magic number became a key issue for collectors who use limited editions as a parameter for buying new dolls. An example of a limited edition doll that wasn't as limited as originally promoted was the Mattel 50th anniversary Barbie doll issued in 1995. This doll has not held its original retail value even two years after issue.

QUALITY AS JOB #1. Dolls, when released, often look quite different from prototypes. Collectors pre-order dolls based on Toy Fair photos and reviews. This is one of the major issues that continues to provoke many collectors. A recent example: Many collectors were displeased with the 1996 Poodle Parade doll due to her head and hairstyle. In a positive response, Mattel subsequently manufactured replacement heads for this doll and made them freely available to any collector who contacted the company. Collectors take quality, attention to detail, and variations from prototypes very seriously.

HOARDING HURTS. Every holiday shopping season brings with it a news story on Big Box retailers whose customers are raiding the first shipments of Happy Holidays Barbie dolls to hoard for future financial appreciation. This strategy simply doesn't work in the world of Barbie doll collecting. Hoarding en masse began in the early 1990s, and the strategy quickly failed to reap large rewards. Instead, hoarders found themselves stuck with caseloads of dolls in pink boxes—some in very large boxes indeed—creating household storage problems. On a smaller scale, a practice of buying two or more dolls—"playing" with one out of the box, and keeping one or more never to remove it from the box—also came into vogue for some collectors. These storage-hungry collectors are also more the poorer, at least in the short run. It remains to be seen what will happen five, ten or even twenty years from now when these dolls are dumped on a mass basis to the secondary market.

Having said this, remember the key factors that have typically enhanced the values of contemporary Barbie dolls:

◆ The first doll in an excellent series has tended to become a strong collectible.

◆ Quality is key: in the original doll, its packaging, and keeping it that way.

◆ Limited editions that are truly limited (under 100,000 in number) would tend to hold their value more than mass quantity (e.g., Happy Holidays Barbie) dolls, which can be issued in numbers greater than one million.

◆ Wild cards—unforeseen events—can eventually impact the value of a Barbie doll. A doll can become controversial based on a story in the press; a fad could develop that wasn't anticipated, such as the emergence of Mel Odom's Gene (Ashton-Drake Galleries) as a competitor for the Barbie doll; or, a designer could really take off, making their doll(s) more valuable at some future time.

Barbie as Scarlett, *part of the Hollywood Legends Series, was creatively packaged in a gold foil box with a star cutout.*

The best way to feel confident about current secondary market Barbie doll values is to invest a great deal of time getting smart: reviewing vintage doll dealers' lists, doll collecting magazines, and auctioneers' prices realized lists; and, staying in touch with online contacts via the World Wide Web, electronic doll collecting lists or with virtual collecting friends on commercial online services. While the 'Net is full of misinformation and disinformation, it is also populated with knowledgeable collectors and has the advantage of being "immediate." Often we have seen trends being recognized by collectors communicating over the Internet months before they are written about in print publications; however, if you are more comfortable with a printed source for value information, consider *Miller's Price Guide*, or the *Barbie Bazaar Price Guide*.

The moral of the Barbie doll valuation story is this: Don't buy massive quantities of any doll with the objective of cashing in some time down the road. Trite as it sounds, stick to the new-old Barbie doll collecting cliche: Buy a doll that you like or love. You may have to live with it for a very long time!

CONTEMPORARY BARBIE
1980-1997

DOLL	MATTEL NO.	YEAR	VARIATION/COMMENT
◆1980			
Beauty Secrets Barbie	1290	1980	Blonde
Beauty Secrets Pretty Reflections Giftset	1702	1980	Blonde
Black Barbie	1293	1980	First African-American Barbie
Golden Dream Barbie	1874	1980	Blonde "big" hair
Golden Dream-Glamorous Nights Set	3533	1980	w/fur coat
Hispanic Barbie	1292	1980	First Hispanic Barbie
International-Italian	1601	1980	
International-Parisian	1600	1980	
International-Royal	1602	1980	
Kissing Barbie	2597	1980	
Pretty Changes Barbie	2598	1980	
Rollerskating Barbie	1880	1980	
Sun Lovin' Malibu Barbie	1067	1980	
◆1981			
Happy Birthday Barbie	1922	1981	
International-Oriental	3262	1981	
International-Scottish	3263	1981	
Magic Curl Barbie	3856	1981	Blonde
Magic Curl Barbie	3989	1981	African-American
My First Barbie	1875	1981	
Sunsational Malibu Barbie	1067	1981	Blonde
Sunsational Malibu Barbie	4970	1981	Hispanic
◆1982			
Angel Face Barbie	5640	1982	
Fashion Jeans Barbie	5313	1982	African-American
Fashion Jeans Barbie	5315	1982	Blonde
International-Eskimo	3898	1982	
International-India	3897	1982	
Pink & Pretty Barbie	3554	1982	
Pink & Pretty Modeling Set	5239	1982	
Twirley Curls Barbie	5579	1982	Blonde
Twirley Curls Barbie	5723	1982	African-American
◆1983			
Twirley Curls Barbie ("Ricitos")	5724	1983	Hispanic
Twirley Curls Giftset	4097	1983	Blonde
Ballerina Superstar Barbie (Mervyns)	4983	1983	Blonde
Ballerina Superstar Barbie (Mervyns)	4984	1983	African-American
Barbie & Friends Giftset	4431	1983	Blonde
Barbie & Ken Camping Out Giftset	4984	1983	Blonde
Dream Date Barbie	1982	1983	

DOLL	MATTEL NO.	YEAR	VARIATION/COMMENT
Fashion Play Barbie	7193	1983	Four outfit variations
Great Shapes Barbie	7025	1983	Blonde
Great Shapes Barbie	7834	1983	African-American
Happy Birthday Barbie	1922	1983	
Happy Birthday Giftset	9519	1983	
Hawaiian Barbie	7470	1983	
International-Spanish	4031	1983	
International-Swedish	4032	1983	
Loving You Barbie	7583	1983	
My First Barbie	1875	1983	
Party Time Barbie	4798	1983	
Playtime Barbie	5336	1983	

◆1984

DOLL	MATTEL NO.	YEAR	VARIATION/COMMENT
Crystal Barbie	4598	1984	Blonde-25th anniversary
Crystal Barbie	4859	1984	African-American-25th anniversary
Day to Night Barbie	7929	1984	Blonde
Day to Night Barbie	7944	1984	Hispanic
Day to Night Barbie	7945	1984	African-American
Dreamtime Barbie	9180	1984	Pink and Blue versions
International-Irish	7517	1984	
International-Swiss	7541	1984	
Loving You Barbie	7072	1984	
My First Barbie	1875	1984	White
My First Barbie	9858	1984	African-American
Sun Gold Malibu Barbie	1067	1984	Blonde
Sun Gold Malibu Barbie	4970	1984	Hispanic
TRU-Dance Sensation Giftset	9058	1984	Blonde

◆1985

DOLL	MATTEL NO.	YEAR	VARIATION/COMMENT
Astronaut Barbie	1207	1985	African-American
Astronaut Barbie	2449	1985	Blonde
Billy Boy Le Nouveau Theatre du Mode	6279	1985	
Dream Glow Barbie	1647	1985	Hispanic
Dream Glow Barbie	2248	1985	Blonde
Dream Glow Barbie	2422	1985	African-American
Happy Birthday Barbie	1922	1985	
International-Japanese	9481	1985	
Music Lovin' Barbie	9988	1985	
Peaches 'n Cream Barbie	7926	1985	Blonde
Peaches 'n Cream Barbie	9516	1985	African-American
Tropical Malibu Deluxe Giftset	2996	1985	Blonde

◆1986

DOLL	MATTEL NO.	YEAR	VARIATION/COMMENT
Tropical Malibu Barbie	1017	1986	Blonde
Tropical Malibu Barbie	1022	1986	African-American
Tropical Malibu Barbie	1646	1986	Hispanic
Dancin' Action Rocker Barbie	3055	1986	
Fabulous Fur (Mervyns)	N/A	1986	
Fun Time Barbie	1738	1986	Blonde in blue w/watch

DOLL	MATTEL NO.	YEAR	VARIATION/COMMENT
Fun Time Barbie	1739	1986	African-American in pink w/watch
Fun Time Barbie (w/watch)	3718	1986	Blonde in pink w/watch
Fun Time Barbie (w/watch)	3717	1986	Blonde in lavender w/watch
Gift Giving Barbie	1922	1986	
International-Greek	2997	1986	
International-Peruvian	2995	1986	
Jewel Secrets Barbie	1737	1986	Blonde
Jewel Secrets Barbie	1756	1986	African-American
Magic Moves Barbie	2126	1986	Blonde
Magic Moves Barbie	2127	1986	African-American
My First Barbie	1788	1986	Blonde-Pink Tutu
My First Barbie	1801	1986	African-American-Pink Tutu
My First Barbie	5979	1986	Hispanic-Pink Tutu
My First Barbie Giftset	1879	1986	Pink Tutu
Porcelain-Blue Rhapsody	1708	1986	
Rocker Barbie	1140	1986	
Rocker Barbie	3055	1986	2nd issue
Sears-100th Anniversary Celebration	2998	1986	Blonde
Super Hair Barbie	3101	1986	Blonde
Super Hair Barbie	3206	1986	African-American
Tennis Star Barbie	1760	1986	
Vacation Sensation Barbie	1675	1986	Pink Set

◆ 1987

DOLL	MATTEL NO.	YEAR	VARIATION/COMMENT
American Beauties Mardi Gras Barbie	4930	1987	
Beach Blast Malibu Barbie	3237	1987	Blonde
Billy Boy Feelin' Groovy	3421	1987	aka Glamour-a-Go-Go
California Dream Barbie	4439	1987	
Cool Times Barbie	3022	1987	
Doctor Barbie	3850	1987	
Fashion Play Barbie	9429	1987	
Fun to Dress Barbie	1372	1987	Blonde
Fun to Dress Barbie	1373	1987	African-American
Fun to Dress Barbie	4558	1987	Blonde
Fun to Dress Barbie	7668	1987	African-American
Gift Giving Barbie	1205	1987	
International-German	3188	1987	
International-Icelandic	3189	1987	
Island Fun Barbie	4061	1987	
Olympic Skating (Calgary)	4549	1987	
Perfume Pretty Barbie	4551	1987	Blonde
Perfume Pretty Barbie	4552	1987	African-American
Porcelain-Enchanted Evening	3415	1987	1960 Barbie doll reproduction
Sears-Star Dream Barbie	4550	1987	
Wal-Mart-Pink Jubilee	4589	1987	

◆ 1988

DOLL	MATTEL NO.	YEAR	VARIATION/COMMENT
Animal Lovin' Barbie	1350	1988	Blonde
Animal Lovin' Barbie	4824	1988	African-American
Feelin' Fun Barbie	1189	1988	Blonde

DOLL	MATTEL NO.	YEAR	VARIATION/COMMENT
Feelin' Fun Barbie	4808	1988	Blonde-second issue
Feelin' Fun Barbie	4809	1988	African-American
Feelin' Fun Barbie	7373	1988	Hispanic
Happy Holidays Barbie	1703	1988	
International-Canadian	4928	1988	
International-Korean	4929	1988	
My First Barbie	1280	1988	Blonde White Tutu
My First Barbie	1281	1988	African-American-White Tutu
My First Barbie	1282	1988	Hispanic-White Tutu
Porcelain-Benefit Performance	5475	1988	1967 Barbie doll reproduction
Sears-Lilac & Lovely Barbie	7669	1988	
Sensations Barbie	4931	1988	
Style Magic Barbie	1283	1988	
Superstar/Movie Star Barbie	1604	1988	Blonde
Superstar/Movie Star Barbie	1605	1988	African-American
TRU-Show N Ride Giftset	7799	1988	
TRU-Tennis Star Giftset	7801	1988	Barbie & Ken
Vacation Sensation Giftset	1675	1988	
Wal-Mart-Frills & Fantasy	1374	1988	

◆1989

DOLL	MATTEL NO.	YEAR	VARIATION/COMMENT
American Beauties Army	3966	1989	
Dance Club Barbie	3509	1989	
Dance Club Hot Dancin' Giftset	4917	1989	w/cassette player
Dance Magic Barbie	4836	1989	Blonde
Dance Magic Barbie	7080	1989	African-American
Dance Magic Giftset	5409	1989	
FAO Schwarz-Golden Greetings	7734	1989	
Flight Time Barbie	2066	1989	Hispanic
Flight Time Barbie	9584	1989	Blonde
Flight Time Barbie	9916	1989	African-American
Fun-to-Dress Barbie	4808	1989	Blonde
Fun-to-Dress Barbie	4939	1989	African-American
Fun-to-Dress Barbie	7373	1989	Hispanic
Garden Party Barbie	1953	1989	
Happy Holidays Barbie	3253	1989	
Hills-Party Lace Barbie	4843	1989	
Ice Capades Barbie	7348	1989	African-American
Ice Capades Barbie	7365	1989	Blonde
International-Mexican	1917	1989	
International-Russian	1916	1989	
Kmart-Peach Pretty Barbie	4870	1989	
Porcelain-Wedding Party Barbie	2641	1989	1959 Barbie doll reproduction
Sears-Evening Enchantment	3596	1989	
Target-Gold N Lace Barbie	7476	1989	
TRU-Denim Fun/Cool City Blues Giftset	4893	1989	
TRU-Party Treats Barbie	4885	1989	
TRU-Pepsi Spirit Barbie	4869	1989	
TRU-Sweet Roses Barbie	7635	1989	
UNICEF Barbie	1920	1989	Blonde

DOLL	MATTEL NO.	YEAR	VARIATION/COMMENT
UNICEF Barbie	4770	1989	African-American
UNICEF Barbie	4774	1989	Asian
UNICEF Barbie	4782	1989	Hispanic
Wal-Mart-Lavender Looks Barbie	3963	1989	
Wedding Fantasy Barbie	2125	1989	Blonde
Wedding Fantasy Barbie	7011	1989	African-American
Wedding Fantasy Giftset	9852	1989	w/6 dolls
Winn Dixie-Party Pink Barbie	7637	1989	
Woolworth-Special Expressions	4842	1989	Blonde
Woolworth-Special Expressions	7326	1989	African-American

◆1990

DOLL	MATTEL NO.	YEAR	VARIATION/COMMENT
All Stars Barbie-Aerobics	9099	1990	
Applause-Style Barbie	5313	1990	
Barbie & the Beat Barbie	2751	1990	Blonde
Bathtime Fun Barbie	9601	1990	Blonde
Bathtime Fun Barbie	9603	1990	African-American
Bob Mackie Gold Barbie	5405	1990	
Cool Looks Barbie	5947	1990	
Disney Barbie #1	4385	1990	Blonde
Disney Barbie #1	9835	1990	African-American
FAO Schwarz-Winter Fantasy	5946	1990	
Fashion Play Barbie	5766	1990	Blonde
Fashion Play Barbie	5953	1990	African-American
Fashion Play Barbie	5954	1990	Hispanic
Friendship Berlin Wall Barbie	5506	1990	aka German Friendship
Happy Birthday Barbie	7913	1990	Blonde
Happy Birthday Barbie	9561	1990	African-American
Happy Holidays Barbie	4098	1990	Blonde
Happy Holidays Barbie	4543	1990	African-American
Hawaiian Fun Barbie	5940	1990	
Hills-Evening Sparkle Barbie	3274	1990	
Home Pretty Barbie	2249	1990	
Dolls of the World-Brazilian	9094	1990	
Dolls of the World-Nigerian	7376	1990	
JC Penney-Evening Elegance Barbie	7057	1990	
Kmart-Fashion Friend	7019	1990	Swimsuit version
Kmart-Fashion Friend	7026	1990	Party Dress version
On the Go Barbie	1007	1990	
Porcelain-Solo in the Spotlight	7613	1990	1961 Barbie doll reproduction
Porcelain-Sophisticated Lady	5313	1990	
Sears-Lavender Surprise Barbie	5588	1990	African-American
Sears-Lavender Surprise Barbie	9409	1990	Blonde
Stars and Stripes Air Force Barbie	3360	1990	
Summit Barbie	7027	1990	Blonde
Summit Barbie	7028	1990	African-American
Summit Barbie	7029	1990	Asian
Summit Barbie	7030	1990	Hispanic
Target-Party Pretty Barbie	5955	1990	
TRU-Winter Fun Barbie	5949	1990	

DOLL	MATTEL NO.	YEAR	VARIATION/COMMENT
Wal-Mart-Dream Fantasy Barbie	7335	1990	
Western Fun Barbie	2930	1990	African-American
Western Fun Barbie	9932	1990	Blonde
Western Fun Giftset	5408	1990	w/Horse Sun Runner
Western Fun Nia	9933	1990	
Wet 'N Wild Barbie	4103	1990	
Wholesale Clubs-Party Sensation Barbie	9025	1990	
Winn Dixie-Pink Sensation Barbie	5410	1990	
Woolworth-Special Expressions	5504	1990	Blonde
Woolworth-Special Expressions	5505	1990	African-American

◆1991

DOLL	MATTEL NO.	YEAR	VARIATION/COMMENT
All American Barbie	3712	1991	w/Barbie's horse/Giftset
All American Barbie	9423	1991	w/Reeboks
American Beauty Queen	3137	1991	Blonde
American Beauty Queen	3245	1991	African-American
Ames-Hot Looks Barbie	5756	1991	
Ames-Party in Pink Barbie	2909	1991	
Applause-Beauty Belle	4553	1991	
Applause-Holiday	3406	1991	
Ballerina Music Box-Swan Lake	1648	1991	
Bath Magic Barbie	5274	1991	Blonde
Bath Magic Barbie	7951	1991	African-American
African-American Barbie	7134	1991	African-American
Blonde Barbie	7123	1991	Blonde
Bob Mackie Platinum	2703	1991	
Bob Mackie Starlight Splendor	2704	1991	African-American
Costume Ball Barbie	7123	1991	Blonde
Costume Ball Barbie	7134	1991	African-American
Cute 'N Cool Barbie	2954	1991	
Disneyland Visit Giftset	3177	1991	Barbie, Ken & Skipper
Dolls of the World-Czechoslovakian	7330	1991	
Dolls of the World-Eskimo	9844	1991	
Dolls of the World-Malaysian	7329	1991	
Dolls of the World-Parisian	9843	1991	
Dolls of the World-Scottish	9845	1991	
Dream Bride Barbie	1623	1991	
Dream Wardrobe Giftset	3331	1991	
FAO Schwarz-Night Sensation	2921	1991	
Friendship Berlin Wall	2080	1991	
Friendship Berlin Wall III Red	3677	1991	
Happy Holidays Barbie	1871	1991	
Hills-Moonlight Rose Barbie	3549	1991	
Home Shopping Club-Evening Flame Barbie	1865	1991	
Ice Capades Barbie	9847	1991	Second edition
JC Penney-Enchanted Evening	2702	1991	
Lights & Lace Barbie	9725	1991	
McGlynn's Bakery-Barbie	1511	1991	Blonde
McGlynn's Bakery-Barbie	1534	1991	African-American
Mermaid Barbie	1434	1991	

DOLL	MATTEL NO.	YEAR	VARIATION/COMMENT
My First Barbie	9942	1991	Blonde
My First Barbie	9943	1991	Hispanic
My First Barbie	9944	1991	African-American
Porcelain Treasures-Gay Parisienne	9973	1991	1959 Barbie doll reproduction
Radio Shack-Earring Magic	N/A	1991	includes Software Pak
Sears-Southern Belle	2586	1991	
Service Merchandise-Blue Rhapsody	1362	1991	
Shopko-Venture-Blossom Beauty	3142	1991	
Ski Fun Barbie	7511	1991	
Spiegel-Sterling Wishes	3347	1991	
Stars and Stripes Marine Corps Barbie	7549	1991	Blonde
Stars and Stripes Marine Corps Barbie	7594	1991	African-American
Stars and Stripes Marine Corps Barbie & Ken Giftset	4704	1991	Blonde
Stars and Stripes Navy Barbie	9693	1991	Blonde
Stars and Stripes Navy Barbie	9694	1991	African-American
Supermarket-Sweet Spring Barbie	3208	1991	
Supermarket-Trail Blazin' Barbie	2783	1991	
Target-Cute 'n Cool Barbie	2954	1991	
Target-Golden Evening Barbie	2587	1991	
TRU-School Fun Barbie	2721	1991	Blonde
TRU-School Fun Barbie	4111	1991	African-American
TRU-Sweet Romance Barbie	2917	1991	
United Colors of Benetton Barbie (#1)	9404	1991	First in series
Wal-Mart-Ballroom Beauty Barbie	3678	1991	
Wedding Day for Midge-Barbie	9608	1991	
Wedding Day for Midge-Giftset	9852	1991	Six doll set
Wholesale Clubs-Bathtime Giftset	N/A	1991	
Wholesale Clubs-Jewel Jubilee Barbie	2366	1991	
Winn Dixie-Southern Beauty Barbie	3284	1991	
Woolworth-Special Expressions	2582	1991	Blonde
Woolworth-Special Expressions	2583	1991	African-American

◆1992

DOLL	MATTEL NO.	YEAR	VARIATION/COMMENT
Ames-Denim 'N Lace Barbie	2452	1992	
Ballerina Music Box-Nutcracker	5472	1992	
Bath Blast Barbie	3830	1992	African-American
Bath Blast Barbie	4159	1992	Blonde
Birthday Party Barbie	3388	1992	Blonde
Birthday Party Barbie	7948	1992	African-American
Birthday Surprise Barbie	3679	1992	Blonde
Birthday Surprise Barbie	4051	1992	African-American
Bob Mackie Empress Bride	4247	1992	
Bob Mackie Neptune Fantasy	4248	1992	
Caboodles Barbie	03157	1992	
Classique-Benefit Ball Barbie	1521	1992	
Dolls of the World-English	4973	1992	
Dolls of the World-Jamaican	4647	1992	
Dolls of the World-Spanish	4963	1992	
Fancy Frills Barbie	3474	1992	
FAO Schwarz-Madison Avenue	1539	1992	

DOLL	MATTEL NO.	YEAR	VARIATION/COMMENT
Fashion Play Barbie	2713	1992	Blonde
Fashion Play Barbie	3860	1992	Hispanic
Fun to Dress Barbie	3240	1992	Blonde
Fun to Dress Barbie	4809	1992	Hispanic
Happy Holidays Barbie	1429	1992	Blonde
Happy Holidays Barbie	2396	1992	African-American
Hills-Blue Elegance Barbie	1879	1992	
Holiday Sensation Fashion Barbie	7809	1992	
JC Penney-Evening Sensation Barbie	1278	1992	
Kmart-Pretty in Purple Barbie	3117	1992	Blonde
Kmart-Pretty in Purple Barbie	3121	1992	African-American
Meijers-Something Extra Barbie	863	1992	
My First Barbie	2483	1992	Blonde
My First Barbie	2570	1992	African-American
My First Barbie	3839	1992	Blonde
My First Barbie	3861	1992	African-American
My First Barbie	3864	1992	Hispanic
My Size Barbie	2517	1992	Blonde

She can do anything! A representative assortment of popular athletic Barbie dolls.

DOLL	MATTEL NO.	YEAR	VARIATION/COMMENT
My Size Barbie	11212	1992	African-American
Osco-Picnic Pretty	3808	1992	
Porcelain-Crystal Rhapsody	1553	1992	
Porcelain-Plantation Belle Barbie	7526	1992	
Pretty Surprise Barbie	9823	1992	
Rappin' Rockin' Barbie	3248	1992	
Rollerblade Barbie	2214	1992	
Rollerblade Giftset	7142	1992	
Sears-Blossom Beautiful Barbie	3817	1992	
Sears-Dream Princess Barbie	2306	1992	
Service Merchandise-Satin Nights Barbie	1886	1992	
Sharin' Sisters Giftset	5716	1992	
Shopko-Venture-Party Perfect Barbie	1876	1992	
Snap N Play Barbie	3550	1992	Blonde
Snap N Play Barbie	3556	1992	African-American
Snap N Play Giftset	2262	1992	Blonde
Sparkle Eyes Barbie	2482	1992	Blonde
Sparkle Eyes Barbie	5950	1992	African-American
Spiegel-Regal Reflections Barbie	4116	1992	
Stars and Stripes Desert Storm Army	1234	1992	Blonde
Stars and Stripes Desert Storm Army	5618	1992	African-American
Stars and Stripes Desert Storm Army Giftset	5626	1992	Blonde
Stars and Stripes Desert Storm Army Giftset	5627	1992	African-American
Supermarket-Party Premiere Barbie	2001	1992	
Supermarket-Pretty Hearts Barbie	2901	1992	
Supermarket-Red Romance Barbie	3161	1992	
Target-Dazzlin' Date Barbie	3203	1992	
Target-Pretty in Plaid Barbie	5413	1992	
Target-Wild Style Barbie	0411	1992	
Teen Talk Barbie	1612	1992	African-American
Teen Talk Barbie	5745	1992	Blonde
Totally Hair Barbie	1112	1992	Blonde
Totally Hair Barbie	1117	1992	Brunette
Totally Hair Barbie	5948	1992	African-American
Troll Hair Barbie	10257	1992	
TRU-Barbie for President	3722	1992	Blonde
TRU-Barbie for President	3940	1992	African-American
TRU-Cool 'N Sassy Barbie	1490	1992	Blonde
TRU-Cool 'N Sassy Barbie	4110	1992	African-American
TRU-Fashion Brights Barbie	1882	1992	Blonde
TRU-Fashion Brights Barbie	4112	1992	African-American
TRU-Radiant in Red Barbie	1276	1992	Red
TRU-Radiant in Red Barbie	4113	1992	Hispanic
TRU-Spring Parade Barbie	2257	1992	African-American
TRU-Spring Parade Barbie	7008	1992	Blonde
United Colors of Benetton Shopping Barbie	4873	1992	Second in the series
Wal-Mart-Anniversary Star Barbie	2282	1992	
Wholesale Clubs-Fantastica Barbie	3196	1992	Hispanic
Wholesale Clubs-Peach Blossom Barbie	7009	1992	
Wholesale Clubs-Rollerblade Giftset	N/A	1992	
Wholesale Clubs-Royal Romance Barbie	1858	1992	

DOLL	MATTEL NO.	YEAR	VARIATION/COMMENT
Wholesale Clubs-Sparkle Eyes Giftset	7131	1992	
Wholesale Clubs-Sun Sensation Barbie Giftset	1390	1992	
Wholesale Clubs-Very Violet Barbie	1859	1992	
Woolworth-Special Expressions	3197	1992	Blonde
Woolworth-Special Expressions	3198	1992	African-American
Woolworth-Special Expressions	3200	1992	Hispanic
Woolworth-Sweet Lavender Barbie	2522	1992	Blonde
Woolworth-Sweet Lavender Barbie	2523	1992	African-American

◆1993

DOLL	MATTEL NO.	YEAR	VARIATION/COMMENT
Ames-Country Looks Barbie	5854	1993	
Angel Lights Barbie	10610	1993	
Barbie Loves to Read Giftset	10507	1993	
Bob Mackie Masquerade Ball	10803	1993	
Classique-City Style Barbie	10149	1993	
Classique-Evening Extravaganza Barbie	11622	1993	Blonde
Classique-Evening Extravaganza Barbie	11638	1993	African-American
Classique-Opening Night Barbie	10148	1993	
Disney Fun #1	10247	1993	Second in series
Dolls of the World-Australian	3626	1993	
Dolls of the World-Italian	2256	1993	
Earring Magic Barbie	2374	1993	African-American
Earring Magic Barbie	7014	1993	Blonde
Earring Magic Barbie	10255	1993	Brunette
FAO Schwarz-Rockette Barbie	2017	1993	
Fountain Mermaid Barbie	10393	1993	Blonde
Fountain Mermaid Barbie	10522	1993	African-American
Fun to Dress Giftset	3826	1993	
Glitter Beach Barbie	3602	1993	
Great Era-Flapper Barbie	4063	1993	
Great Era-Gibson Girl Barbie	3702	1993	
Happy Holidays Barbie	10824	1993	Blonde
Happy Holidays Barbie	10911	1993	African-American
Hollywood Hair Barbie	2308	1993	
Home Shopping Club-Winter Princess Barbie	10655	1993	
JC Penney-Golden Winter Barbie	10684	1993	
Kool Aid-Wacky Warehouse Barbie (#1)	10309	1993	
Little Debbie Barbie	10123	1993	
Locket Surprise Barbie	10963	1993	Blonde
Locket Surprise Barbie	11224	1993	African-American
McDonalds Birthday Fun Set	11589	1993	
Meijers-Shopping Fun Barbie	10051	1993	
My First Barbie	2516	1993	Blonde
My First Barbie	2767	1993	African-American
My First Barbie	2770	1993	Hispanic
Naf Naf Barbie	10997	1993	
DOW-Native American I Barbie	1753	1993	
Nostalgic-35th Anniversary Barbie	11590	1993	Blonde
Nostalgic-35th Anniversary Barbie	11782	1993	Brunette
Nostalgic-35th Anniversary Giftset	11591	1993	Blonde

DOLL	MATTEL NO.	YEAR	VARIATION/COMMENT
Paint 'N Dazzle Barbie	10039	1993	Blonde
Paint 'N Dazzle Barbie	10057	1993	Dark Auburn
Paint 'N Dazzle Barbie	10058	1993	African-American
Paint 'N Dazzle Barbie	10059	1993	Brunette
Porcelain-Gold Sensation Barbie	10246	1993	
Porcelain-Royal Splendor Barbie	10950	1993	
Porcelain-Silken Flame Barbie	1249	1993	
Romantic Bride Barbie	1861	1993	Blonde
Romantic Bride Barbie	11054	1993	African-American
Sea Holiday Barbie	5471	1993	
Sears-Enchanted Princess Barbie	10292	1993	
Secret Hearts Barbie	3836	1993	African-American
Secret Hearts Barbie	7902	1993	Blonde
Warehouse Clubs-Secret Hearts Giftset (Barbie & Ken)	10929	1993	
Service Merchandise-Sparkling Splendor	10994	1993	
Sharin' Sisters Giftset	10143	1993	
Spiegel-Royal Invitation Barbie	10969	1993	
Stars and Stripes Airforce Barbie & Ken Set	11581	1993	Blonde
Stars and Stripes Airforce Barbie & Ken Set	11582	1993	African-American
Stars and Stripes Airforce Thunderbirds	11552	1993	Blonde
Stars and Stripes Airforce Thunderbirds	11553	1993	African-American
Supermarket-Back to School Barbie	10217	1993	
Supermarket-Be Mine Barbie	11182	1993	
Supermarket-Holiday Hostess Barbie	10280	1993	
Supermarket-Spring Bouquet Barbie	3477	1993	
Swim 'N Dive Barbie	11505	1993	Blonde
Swim 'N Dive Barbie	11734	1993	African-American
Target-Baseball	4583	1993	
Target-Golf Date	10202	1993	
TRU-Dream Wedding Giftset	10712	1993	Blonde
TRU-Dream Wedding Giftset	10713	1993	African-American
TRU-Love to Read Barbie	10507	1993	
TRU-Malt Shoppe Barbie	4581	1993	
TRU-Moonlight Magic Barbie	10608	1993	Caucasian w/dark hair
TRU-Moonlight Magic Barbie	10609	1993	African-American
TRU-Police Officer Barbie	10688	1993	Blonde
TRU-Police Officer Barbie	10689	1993	African-American
TRU-School Spirit Barbie	10682	1993	Blonde
TRU-School Spirit Barbie	10683	1993	African-American
TRU-Spots N Dots Barbie	10491	1993	
Twinkle Lights Barbie	10390	1993	Blonde
Twinkle Lights Barbie	10521	1993	African-American
Wal-Mart Superstar Barbie	10592	1993	Blonde
Wal-Mart Superstar Barbie	10711	1993	Brunette Ethnic
Western Stampin' Barbie	10293	1993	Blonde
Western Stampin' Barbie	10539	1993	African-American
Wholesale Clubs-Beach Fun Giftset	11481	1993	
Wholesale Clubs-Festiva Barbie	10339	1993	Hispanic
Wholesale Clubs-Hollywood Hair Giftset	10928	1993	
Wholesale Clubs-Island Fun Giftset	10379	1993	Barbie & Ken
Wholesale Clubs-Paint 'N Dazzle Giftset	10926	1993	

DOLL	MATTEL NO.	YEAR	VARIATION/COMMENT
Wholesale Clubs-Secret Hearts Giftset	10929	1993	
Wholesale Clubs-Wedding Fantasy Giftset	10924	1993	
Wholesale Clubs-Winter Royale Barbie	10658	1993	
Woolworth-Special Expressions	10048	1993	Blonde
Woolworth-Special Expressions	10049	1993	African-American
Woolworth-Special Expressions	10050	1993	Hispanic

◆ 1994

DOLL	MATTEL NO.	YEAR	VARIATION/COMMENT
American Stories-Colonial Barbie	12578	1994	
American Stories-Pilgrim Barbie	12577	1994	
American Stories-Pioneer Barbie	12680	1994	
Baywatch Barbie	13199	1994	Blonde
Baywatch Barbie	13258	1994	African-American
Bedtime Barbie	11079	1994	Blonde
Bedtime Barbie	11184	1994	African-American
Bicycling Barbie	11689	1994	Blonde
Bicycling Barbie	11817	1994	African-American
Birthday Barbie	11333	1994	Blonde
Birthday Barbie	11334	1994	African-American
Bloomingdale's-Savvy Shopper Barbie	12152	1994	Nicole Miller
Bob Mackie Queen of Hearts	12046	1994	
Camp Barbie	11074	1994	Blonde
Camp Barbie	11831	1994	African-American
Classique-Uptown Chic Barbie	11623	1994	
Dance N Twirl Barbie	11902	1994	Blonde
Dance N Twirl Barbie	12143	1994	African-American
Dolls of the World Giftset	12043	1994	
Dolls of the World-Chinese	11180	1994	
Dolls of the World-Dutch	11104	1994	
Dolls of the World-Kenyan	11181	1994	
Dr. Barbie	11160	1994	Blonde w/baby (varied)
Dr. Barbie	11814	1994	African-American w/baby (varied)
Dress N Fun Barbie	10776	1994	Blonde
Dress N Fun Barbie	11102	1994	Hispanic
Dress N Fun Barbie	11103	1994	African-American
Easter Fun Barbie	11276	1994	
Enchanted Seasons-Snow Princess Barbie	11875	1994	
Erte Stardust	10993	1994	
FAO Schwarz-Shopping Spree Barbie	12749	1994	
FAO Schwarz-Silver Screen Barbie	11652	1994	
Glitter Hair Barbie	10965	1994	Blonde
Glitter Hair Barbie	10966	1994	Brunette
Glitter Hair Barbie	10968	1994	Redhead
Glitter Hair Barbie	11332	1994	African-American
Gold Jubilee Barbie	12009	1994	LE of 5,000
Great Era-Egyptian Queen Barbie	11397	1994	
Great Era-Southern Belle Barbie	11478	1994	
Gymnast Barbie	12127	1994	Blonde
Gymnast Barbie	12153	1994	African-American
Hallmark Victorian Elegance Barbie	12579	1994	First in series

DOLL	MATTEL NO.	YEAR	VARIATION/COMMENT
Happy Holidays Barbie	12155	1994	Blonde
Happy Holidays Barbie	12156	1994	African-American
Hills-Polly Pocket Barbie	12412	1994	
Hills-Sea Pearl Mermaid Barbie	13940	1994	
Hollywood Legends-Ken as Rhett-*Gone with the Wind*	12741	1994	
Hollywood Legends-Scarlett-*Gone with the Wind*-Drapery Dress	12045	1994	
Hollywood Legends-Scarlett-*Gone with the Wind*-BBQ	12997	1994	
JC Penney-Night Dazzle Barbie	12194	1994	
Jewel & Glitter Barbie	11185	1994	
Kool-Aid-Wacky Warehouse Barbie	11763	1994	Second Kool-Aid
Kraft Treasures Barbie	11546	1994	
My First Barbie (Ballerina)	11294	1994	Blonde
My First Barbie (Ballerina)	11340	1994	African-American
My First Barbie (Ballerina)	11341	1994	Hispanic
My First Barbie (Ballerina)	11342	1994	Asian
My First Barbie (Ballerina)	13064	1994	Blonde
My First Barbie (Ballerina)	13065	1994	African-American
My First Barbie (Ballerina)	13066	1994	Brunette
My Size Bride Barbie	12052	1994	Blonde
My Size Bride Barbie	12053	1994	African-American
DOW-Native American II Barbie	11609	1994	
Porcelain-Silver Starlight Barbie	11305	1994	
Porcelain-Star Lily Bride	12953	1994	
Quinceanera Teresa	11928	1994	
Sears-Silver Sweetheart Barbie	12410	1994	
Service Merchandise-City Sophisticate Barbie	12005	1994	
Spiegel-Theatre Elegance Barbie	12077	1994	
Sun Jewel Barbie	10953	1994	
Supermarket-Holiday Dreams Barbie	12192	1994	
TRU-Astronaut Barbie	12149	1994	Blonde-25th Apollo
TRU-Astronaut Barbie	12150	1994	African-American-25th Apollo
TRU-Emerald Elegance Barbie	12322	1994	Caucasian
TRU-Emerald Elegance Barbie	12323	1994	Hispanic
Wal-Mart-Country Western Star Barbie	11646	1994	Blonde
Wal-Mart-Country Western Star Barbie	12097	1994	Hispanic
Wal-Mart-Country Western Star Barbie	12096	1994	African-American
Wal-Mart-Tooth Fairy Barbie	11645	1994	
Warehouse Clubs-Me & My Mustang Giftset		1995	
Warehouse Clubs-Beach Fun	11481	1994	
Warehouse Clubs-Bed Time Giftset	12184	1994	
Wholesale Clubs-Seasons Greetings Barbie	12384	1994	
Wholesale Clubs-Western Stampin' Giftset	11020	1994	
Winter Princess Series-Evergreen Princess Barbie	12123	1994	
Winter Sports Barbie	13516	1994	

◆ 1995

DOLL	MATTEL NO.	YEAR	VARIATION/COMMENT
Ballroom Beauties-Starlight Waltz	14070	1995	1st in series
Ballroom Beauties-Starlight Waltz	14954	1995	1st in series-LE 1500 Disney
Birthday Barbie	12954	1995	Blonde
Birthday Barbie	12955	1995	African-American

DOLL	MATTEL NO.	YEAR	VARIATION/COMMENT
Birthday Barbie	13253	1995	Hispanic
Bloomingdale's-Donna Karan Barbie	14452	1995	Brunette
Bloomingdale's-Donna Karan Barbie	14595	1995	Blonde
Bob Mackie-Goddess of the Sun	14056	1995	
Bubble Angel Barbie	12443	1995	Blonde
Bubble Angel Barbie	12444	1995	African-American
Butterfly Princess Barbie	13051	1995	Blonde
Butterfly Princess Barbie	13052	1995	African-American
Career Collection-Firefighter Barbie	13472	1995	African-American
Career Collection-Firefighter Barbie	13553	1995	Blonde
Career Collection-Teacher Barbie	13914	1995	Blonde
Career Collection-Teacher Barbie	13915	1995	African-American
Children's Collector Series-Barbie as Rapunzel	13016	1995	First in series
Christmas Holiday-Holiday Caroling Barbie	13966	1995	Blonde
Classique-Midnight Gala Barbie	12999	1995	
Cut 'N Style Barbie	12639	1995	Blonde
Cut 'N Style Barbie	12642	1995	African-American
Cut 'N Style Barbie	12643	1995	Brunette
Cut 'N Style Barbie	12644	1995	Red Head
Dance Moves Barbie	13083	1995	Blonde
Dance Moves Barbie	13086	1995	African-American
Christian Dior Barbie	13168	1995	
Dolls of the World Giftset (Irish, German, Polynesian)	13939	1995	
Dolls of the World-German	12698	1995	
Dolls of the World-Irish	12998	1995	
Dolls of the World-Native American III Barbie	12699	1995	
Dolls of the World-Polynesian	12700	1995	
Dr. Barbie	14309	1995	w/3 babies
Dr. Barbie	14315	1995	w/3 babies
Supermarket-Easter Party Barbie	12793	1995	
Enchanted Seasons-Spring Bouquet Barbie	12989	1995	
FAO Schwarz-Circus Star Barbie	13257	1995	
FAO Schwarz-Jeweled Splendor Barbie	14061	1995	
Flying Hero Barbie	14030	1995	Blonde
Great Era-Elizabethan Queen Barbie	12792	1995	
Great Era-Medieval Lady Barbie	12791	1995	
Hallmark-Holiday Memories	14106	1995	
Happy Holidays	14123	1995	Blonde
Happy Holidays	14124	1995	African-American
Hills-Sea Pearl Mermaid	13940	1995	
Hollywood Legends-Maria-*Sound of Music*	13676	1995	
Hollywood Legends-Dorothy-*Wizard of Oz*	12701	1995	
Hollywood Legends-Scarlett-*Gone with the Wind*-Red	12815	1995	
Hollywood Legends-Scarlett-*Gone with the Wind*-White	13254	1995	
Hot Skatin' Barbie	13511	1995	Blonde
Hot Skatin' Barbie	13512	1995	African-American
JC Penney-Royal Enchantment	14010	1995	
Mattel 50th Anniversary Porcelain Barbie	14479	1995	
My First Barbie Princess	13064	1995	Blonde
My First Barbie Princess	13065	1995	African-American

DOLL	MATTEL NO.	YEAR	VARIATION/COMMENT
My First Barbie Princess	13066	1995	Hispanic
My First Barbie Princess	13067	1995	Asian
My Size Princess Ballerina Barbie	13767	1995	Blonde
My Size Princess Ballerina Barbie	13768	1995	African-American
Nostalgic-Busy Gal	13675	1995	
Nostalgic-Solo in the Spotlight	13534	1995	Blonde
Nostalgic-Solo in the Spotlight	13820	1995	Brunette
Porcelain Bride-Starlily Bride	12953	1995	
Ruffle Fun Barbie	12433	1995	Blonde
Ruffle Fun Barbie	12434	1995	African-American
Ruffle Fun Barbie	12435	1995	Hispanic
Supermarket-Easter Party	12793	1995	
Supermarket-School Time Fun Barbie	13741	1995	
Sears-Ribbons and Roses	13911	1995	
Service Merchandise-Ruby Romance	13612	1995	
Sharin' Sisters Giftset	10143	1995	
Slumber Party Barbie	12696	1995	Blonde
Slumber Party Barbie	12697	1995	African-American
Spiegel-Shopping Chic Barbie	14009	1995	
Strollin' Fun Barbie & Kelly	13742	1995	Blonde
Strollin' Fun Barbie & Kelly	13743	1995	African-American
Supermarket-Caroling Fun	13966	1995	
Supertalk Barbie	12290	1995	Blonde
Supertalk Barbie	12379	1995	African-American
Sweet Dreams Barbie	13611	1995	Blonde
Sweet Dreams Barbie	13630	1995	African-American
Target-Steppin' Out Barbie	14110	1995	
Travelin' Sisters Giftset	14073	1995	
Tropical Splash Barbie	12446	1995	
TRU-Pog Barbie	13239	1995	Blonde
TRU-Purple Passion Barbie	13554	1995	Blonde
TRU-Purple Passion Barbie	13555	1995	African-American
TRU-Sapphire Dream Barbie	13255	1995	First in series
TRU-Sunflower Barbie	13489	1995	
Valentine Barbie	12675	1995	
Wal-Mart-Country Bride Barbie	13614	1995	Blonde
Wal-Mart-Country Bride Barbie	13615	1995	African-American
Wal-Mart-Country Bride Barbie	13616	1995	Hispanic
Warehouse Clubs-Denim 'N Ruffles Giftset	12371	1995	
Wholesale Clubs-Winter's Eve	13613	1995	
Wedding Party Barbie Giftset	13557	1995	
Wessco-International Traveler Barbie	13912	1995	
Western Stampin' Barbie-Western Star Horse (red)	13478	1995	
Winter Princess Series-Peppermint Princess	13598	1995	

◆1996

DOLL	MATTEL NO.	YEAR	VARIATION/COMMENT
American Stories-Civil War Nurse	14612	1996	
American Stories-Native American w/papoose	14715	1996	
American Stories-Pioneer Shopkeeper	14756	1996	
Andalusia Barbie-Flamenco	15780	1996	

DOLL	MATTEL NO.	YEAR	VARIATION/COMMENT
Avon Winter Velvet	15571	1996	Blonde
Avon Winter Velvet	15587	1996	African-American
Avon-Spring Blossom Barbie	15201	1996	Blonde
Avon-Spring Blossom Barbie	15202	1996	African-American
Ballroom Beauties-Midnight Waltz	15685	1996	Blonde
Ballroom Beauties-Midnight Waltz	16705	1996	Brunette-Internet Exclusive
Barbie Millicent Roberts Giftset	16080	1996	
Birthday Fun Kelly Giftset	15610	1996	
Bloomingdales-Bloomies Barbie	16290	1996	
Bloomingdales-Calvin Klein Barbie	16211	1996	
Bob Mackie-Goddess of the Moon	14105	1996	
Career Colleciton-Pet Doctor Barbie	15302	1996	African-American
Career Collection-Pet Doctor Barbie	14603	1996	Blonde
Career Collection-Teacher Barbie	16210	1996	Hispanic
Children's Collector Series-Barbie as Little Bo Peep	14960	1996	
Chuck E. Cheese Barbie	14615	1996	
Classique-Starlight Dance (Cynthia Young)	15461	1996	Blonde
Classique-Starlight Dance (Cynthia Young)	15819	1996	African-American
Coca-Cola Fashion Classic Series-Soda Fountain Sweetheart	15762	1996	
Couture Collection-Portrait in Taffeta #1	15528	1996	
Disney Fun #3	13533	1996	
Dolls of the World-Ghanaian	15303	1996	
Dolls of the World-Giftset-Japanese, Norwegian, Indian	15283	1996	
Dolls of the World-India	14451	1996	
Dolls of the World-Japan	14163	1996	
Dolls of the World-Mexico	14449	1996	
Dolls of the World-Native American IV	15304	1996	
Dolls of the World-Norway	14450	1996	Look for red flower variation vs. pink
Empress Sissy Barbie	15846	1996	
Enchanted Seasons-Autumn Glory	15204	1996	
Erte #2	14109	1996	
Escada	15948	1996	
FAO Schwarz-Antique Rose-Floral Signature Collection	15814	1996	
FAO Schwarz-Liberty Belle	14664	1996	
Foam and Color	14457	1996	Pink
Foam and Color	15098	1996	Yellow
Foam and Color	15099	1996	Blue
GAP Barbie	16449	1996	Blonde
GAP Barbie	16450	1996	African-American
Great Eras-Grecian Goddess	15005	1996	
Great Eras-Victorian Lady	14900	1996	
Hallmark Sweet Valentine Barbie	14880	1996	
Hallmark-Yuletide Romance	15621	1996	
Happy Birthday Barbie	14649	1996	White
Happy Birthday Barbie	14662	1996	African-American
Happy Birthday Barbie	14663	1996	Hispanic
Happy Holidays Barbie	15647	1996	African-American
Happy Holidays Barbie	15646	1996	Blonde
Hills-Teddy Fun Barbie	15684	1996	
Holiday Porcelain-2nd edition-Holiday Caroler	15760	1996	
Hollywood Legends-Barbie as Eliza Doolittle Evening Gown	15550	1996	

DOLL	MATTEL NO.	YEAR	VARIATION/COMMENT
Hollywood Legends-Barbie as Eliza Doolittle-Ascot	15497	1996	
Hollywood Legends-Barbie as Eliza Doolittle-Flower Girl	15498	1996	
Hollywood Legends-Barbie as Eliza Doolittle-Pink	15501	1996	
In-Line Skater Barbie	15473	1996	
JC Penney-Arizona Jeans Barbie	15441	1996	
JC Penney-Foam 'n Color Giftset	16567	1996	
JC Penney-Winter Renaissance	15570	1996	
Jewel Hair Mermaid	14586	1996	White
Jewel Hair Mermaid	14587	1996	African-American
Kool-Aid Wacky Warehouse #3	15620	1996	
Little Debbie #2	14616	1996	2nd in series
Macy's-City Shopper (Nicole Miller)	16289	1996	1st in series
Mercantile Stores-Special Occasion	15831	1996	
My First Tea Party	14592	1996	White
My First Tea Party	14593	1996	African-American
My First Tea Party	14875	1996	Hispanic
My First Tea Party	14876	1996	Asian
My Size Barbie	15909	1996	White
My Size Barbie	15910	1996	African-American
Nostalgic-Enchanted Evening Barbie	14992	1996	Blonde
Nostalgic-Enchanted Evening Barbie	15407	1996	Brunette
Nostalgic-Francie (Gad About)	14608	1996	
Nostalgic-Poodle Parade (American Girl)	15280	1996	
Ocean Friends (Barbie & Keiko)	15428	1996	Blonde
Ocean Friends (Barbie & Keiko)	15429	1996	African-American
Olympic Gymnast Barbie	15123	1996	Blonde
Olympic Gymnast Barbie	15124	1996	African-American
Olympic Gymnast Barbie	15125	1996	Redhead
Oshogatsu Barbie Japanese New Year	14024	1996	
Pink Splendor (Cynthia Young)	16091	1996	
Pop Culture-Star Trek Giftset-Barbie and Ken	15006	1996	
Porcelain Bride-Romantic Rose Bride	14541	1996	
Presidential Porcelain-Evening Pearl Barbie	12825	1996	Brunette
Pretty Hearts Barbie	14473	1996	Blonde
Pretty Hearts Barbie	14474	1996	African-American
Pretty Hearts Barbie	14475	1996	Hispanic
Price/Costco-Silver Royale	15952	1996	
Russell Stover Easter Barbie-Checkered pattern	14617	1996	
Russell Stover Easter Barbie-Print	14956	1996	
Sears-Evening Flame Barbie	15533	1996	
Service Merchandise-Sea Princess Barbie	15531	1996	
Shopping Fun Giftset	15756	1996	White
Shopping Fun Giftset	15757	1996	African-American
Songbird Barbie	14320	1996	Blonde
Songbird Barbie	14484	1996	African-American
Sparkle Beach Barbie	13132	1996	
Spiegel-Shopping Chic	14009	1996	Blonde
Spiegel-Shopping Chic	15801	1996	African-American
Spiegel-Summer Sophisticate	15591	1996	
Strollin' Sisters (Barbie & Shelley)	13742	1996	
Supermarket-Easter Basket	14613	1996	

DOLL	MATTEL NO.	YEAR	VARIATION/COMMENT
Supermarket-Graduation Class of '96	15003	1996	
Supermarket-Holiday Season	15581	1996	Blonde
Supermarket-Holiday Season	15583	1996	Ethnic
Supermarket-Valentine	14641	1996	
Target-City Style Barbie	15612	1996	
Target-Pet Doctor Barbie Brunette	16458	1996	Brunette exclusive for Target
Target-Valentine	15172	1996	
TRU-Crystal Splendor	15136	1996	Blonde
TRU-Crystal Splendor	15137	1996	African-American
TRU-Dr. Barbie-Career Collection	15803	1996	Blonde
TRU-Dr. Barbie-Career Collection	15804	1996	African-American
TRU-Got Milk? Barbie	15121	1996	Blonde
TRU-Got Milk? Barbie	15122	1996	African-American
TRU-Got Milk? Barbie	15123	1996	Hispanic
TRU-International Pen Friend	13558	1996	
TRU-Pink Ice	15141	1996	
TRU-Radiant in Rose	15061	1996	Blonde
TRU-Radiant in Rose	15140	1996	Ethnic
Twirling Ballerina	15086	1996	Blonde
Twirling Ballerina	15087	1996	African-American
U.S. Military Outlets-Daisy Barbie	15133	1996	
Wal-Mart-Sweet Magnolia	15652	1996	Blonde
Wal-Mart-Sweet Magnolia	15653	1996	African-American
Wal-Mart-Sweet Magnolia	15652	1996	Hispanic
Wal-Mart-Skating Star	15510	1996	Blonde
Wal-Mart-Skating Star	16691	1996	African-American
Wal-Mart-Skating Star	15511	1996	Hispanic
Walt Disney World Barbie-25th Anniversary	16525	1996	
Warehouse Clubs-Fifties Fun	15820	1996	
Warehouse Clubs-Rose Bride Barbie	15987	1996	
Warehouse Clubs-Winter Fantasy	15334	1996	Blonde
Warehouse Clubs-Winter Fantasy	15530	1996	Brunette
Wessco-International Traveler #2	16158	1996	
Winter Holiday Giftset	15645	1996	
Winter Princess-Jewel Princess	15826	1996	

◆ 1997

DOLL	MATTEL NO.	YEAR	VARIATION/COMMENT
101 Dalmatians Barbie	17248	1997	Blonde
101 Dalmatians Barbie	17601	1997	African-American
American Stories-American Indian	17313	1997	Last in series
American Stories-Patriot	17312	1997	Last in series
Ames/Meijer-Ladybug Barbie	N/A	1997	
Angel Princess	15911	1997	Blonde
Angel Princess	15912	1997	African-American
Artist Series-Water Lily (Claude Monet)	17783	1997	
Avon-Mrs. PFE Albee	17690	1997	
Avon-Spring Petals	18656	1997	Blonde
Avon-Spring Petals	18657	1997	African-American
Avon-Spring Petals	18658	1997	Brunette
Avon-Winter Rhapsody	16353	1997	Blonde

DOLL	MATTEL NO.	YEAR	VARIATION/COMMENT
Avon-Winter Rhapsody	16873	1997	Brunette
Avon-Winter Rhapsody	16354	1997	African-American
Ballroom Beauties-Moonlight Waltz	17763	1997	Blonde
Barbie and Ginger	17116	1997	Blonde
Barbie and Ginger	17369	1997	African-American
Barbie Loves Pop Culture-Barbie Loves Elvis Giftset	17450	1997	
Barbie Millicent Roberts-Perfectly Suited Giftset	17567	1997	
Bill Blass Barbie	17040	1997	
Billions of Dreams	17641	1997	
Birthday Barbie	15998	1997	Blonde
Birthday Barbie	15999	1997	African-American
Birthday Barbie	16000	1997	Hispanic
BJs Wholesale Club-Sparkle Beauty Barbie	17251	1997	
Bloomingdale's-Ralph Lauren Barbie	15950	1997	
Blossom Beauty Barbie	17032	1997	Blonde
Blossom Beauty Barbie	17033	1997	African-American
Bob Mackie-Jewel Essence Collection-Amethyst Aura	15522	1997	
Bob Mackie-Jewel Essence Collection-Diamond Dazzle	15519	1997	
Bob Mackie-Jewel Essence Collection-Emerald Embers	15521	1997	
Bob Mackie-Jewel Essence Collection-Ruby Radiance	15520	1997	
Bob Mackie-Jewel Essence Collection-Sapphire Splendor	15523	1997	
Bob Mackie-Madame du Barbie	17934	1997	
Bubbling Mermaid	16131	1997	Blonde
Bubbling Mermaid	16132	1997	African-American
Career Collection-Dentist Barbie	17255	1997	Blonde
Career Collection-Dentist Barbie	17478	1997	African-American
Children's Collector Series-Barbie as Cinderella	16900	1997	
Christian Dior #2-50th Anniversary	16013	1997	
Classic Ballet Series-Sugarplum Fairy	17056	1997	
Classique-Romantic Interlude	17136	1997	Blonde
Classique-Romantic Interlude	17137	1997	African-American
Coca-Cola-After the Walk Barbie	17341	1997	
Cool Shoppin' Barbie	17487	1997	
Couture Collection-Serenade in Satin	17572	1997	
Disney Convention-Midnight Princess	18486	1997	Brunette
Disney Fun #4	17058	1997	
Dolls of the World-Arctic Barbie	16495	1997	
Dolls of the World-French	16499	1997	
Dolls of the World-Puerto Rican Barbie	16754	1997	
Dolls of the World-Russian Barbie	16500	1997	
Enchanted Seasons-Summer Splendor	15683	1997	
FAO Schwarz-Barbie as George Washington	17557	1997	
FAO Schwarz-Barbie at FAO	17298	1997	
FAO Schwarz-Lily, Floral Signature Collection	17556	1997	
Flower Fun	16063	1997	Blonde
Flower Fun	16064	1997	African-American
GAP-Barbie & Kelly Giftset	18547	1997	Blonde
GAP-Barbie & Kelly Giftset	18548	1997	African-American
Grand Ole Opry Country Rose Barbie	17782	1997	
Grand Premiere (Official Barbie Collectors Club Doll)	16498	1997	
Great Eras-Chinese Empress	16708	1997	

DOLL	MATTEL NO.	YEAR	VARIATION/COMMENT
Great Eras-French Lady	16707	1997	
Hallmark-Holiday Traditions	17094	1997	
Hallmark-Sentimenal Valentine Barbie	16536	1997	
Happy Holidays Barbie	17833	1997	African-American
Happy Holidays Barbie	17832	1997	Blonde
Hills-Hula Hoop Barbie	18167	1997	
Holiday Porcelain-Holiday Ball of the Past	18326	1997	
Hollywood Legends-Barbie as Glinda the Good Witch in *The Wizard of Oz*	14901	1997	
Hollywood Legends-Barbie as Marilyn in *Gentlemen Prefer Blondes* (Pink)	17451	1997	
Hollywood Legends-Barbie as Marilyn in *Gentlemen Prefer Blondes* (Red)	17452	1997	
Hollywood Legends-Barbie as Marilyn in *The Seven Year Itch* (White)	17155	1997	
Hollywood Legends-Ken as Scarecrow-*The Wizard of Oz*	16497	1997	
Hollywood Legends-Ken as the Cowardly Lion-*The Wizard of Oz*	16573	1997	
Hula Hair Barbie	17048	1997	African-American
Hula Hair Barbie	17047	1997	Blonde
JC Penney-Arizona Jeans Barbie #2	18020	1997	
JC Penney-Evening Majesty Barbie	17235	1997	
JC Penney-Moonlight Waltz	17763	1997	
Kay-Bee-Glamour Barbie	18594	1997	Blonde
Kay-Bee-Glamour Barbie	18595	1997	African-American
Macy's-Anne Klein Barbie	17603	1997	
Masquerade Ball (Limited Edition)	18667	1997	
Military-Ponytails Barbie	18141	1997	Blonde
Military-Ponytails Barbie	18142	1997	African-American
My First Barbie-Jewelry Fun	16005	1997	Blonde
My First Barbie-Jewelry Fun	16006	1997	African-American
My First Barbie-Jewelry Fun	16007	1997	Hispanic
My First Barbie-Jewelry Fun	16008	1997	Asian
Oshogatsu Barbie-#2	16093	1997	
Runway Collection-In the Limelight-Byron Lars	17031	1997	African-American
Russell Stover Holiday	18199	1997	
Sears-Blue Starlight	17125	1997	
Service Merchandise-Dream Bride	17153	1997	Blonde
Share a Smile Barbie	17247	1997	
Shoppin' Fun Barbie and Kelly	15756	1997	Blonde
Shoppin' Fun Barbie and Kelly	15757	1997	African-American
Show Parade Barbie with Star Stampin' Horse	15059	1997	Blonde
Spiegel-Winner's Circle	17441	1997	
Splash 'n Color	16169	1997	Blonde
Splash 'n Color	16174	1997	African-American
Splash 'n Color	16172	1997	Hispanic
Supermarket-Back-to-School Barbie	17099	1997	
Supermarket-Birthday Surprise	16491	1997	
Supermarket-Easter Barbie	16315	1997	
Supermarket-Graduation	16487	1997	
Supermarket-Valentine Fun	16311	1997	
Sweet Moments	17642	1997	

DOLL	MATTEL NO.	YEAR	VARIATION/COMMENT
Talk with Me Barbie	17350	1997	
Target-35th Anniversary	16485	1997	Blonde
Target-35th Anniversary	17608	1997	African-American
Target-City Style Barbie	18952	1997	
Target-Happy Halloween Giftset	17238	1997	
TRU-Barbie & Kelly Gardening Set	17242	1997	
TRU-Crystal Splendor	15137	1997	African-American
TRU-Crystal Splendor	15136	1997	Blonde
TRU-Emerald Enchantment	17443	1997	
TRU-Harley-Davidson Barbie	17692	1997	
TRU-Career Collection-Paleontologist Barbie	17240	1997	Blonde
TRU-Career Collection-Paleontologist Barbie	17241	1997	African-American
TRU-Oreo Barbie	669458	1997	
TRU-Sapphire Sophisticate	16693	1997	Brunette
TRU-Sapphire Sophisticate	16692	1997	African-American
TRU-Share a Smile Barbie	17247	1997	
TRU-Wedding Fantasy Barbie Giftset	17243	1997	
University Barbie-Auburn University	17699	1997	
University Barbie-Clemmons	17753	1997	
University Barbie-Duke	17750	1997	
University Barbie-Georgetown	17749	1997	
University Barbie-North Carolina State University	17194	1997	
University Barbie-Oklahoma State University	17752	1997	
University Barbie-Penn State University	17698	1997	
University Barbie-University of Arizona	17751	1997	
University Barbie-University of Florida	17700	1997	
University Barbie-University of Georgia	17192	1997	
University Barbie-University of Illinois	17755	1997	
University Barbie-University of Miami	17794	1997	
University Barbie-University of Michigan	17398	1997	
University Barbie-University of Nebraska	17193	1997	
University Barbie-University of Tennessee	17554	1997	
University Barbie-University of Texas	17792	1997	
University Barbie-University of Virginia	17754	1997	
University Barbie-University of Wisconsin	17195	1997	
Vintage Reproductions-Fashion Luncheon	17382	1997	
Vintage Reproductions-Wedding Day Set	17119	1997	Blonde
Vintage Reproductions-Wedding Day Set	17120	1997	Redhead
Wal-Mart-35th Anniversary	17616	1997	Black
Wal-Mart-Skatin' Star	17244	1997	
Warehouse Clubs-Sixties Fun	17252	1997	
Warehouse Clubs-Winter Fantasy II	17249	1997	Blonde
Warehouse Clubs-Winter Fantasy II	17250	1997	Brunette
Wedding Flower Porcelain-Blushing Orchid Bride	16962	1997	
Wessco-Carnival Cruise Lines	17868	1997	
Winter Princess-Midnight Princess	17780	1997	
Workin' Out Barbie	17317	1997	

*New York Nights— Barbie dolls
in gowns (left to right):
Classique Opening Night
Barbie, Classique Benefit Ball
Barbie, Toys 'R Us Sapphire
Dream Barbie, Winter Princess
Evergreen Princess Barbie,
Spiegel Royal Invitation Barbie
(front): Spiegel Theater
Elegance Barbie*

BIBLIOGRAPHY

Advertising Age, "Barbie Grows Up," v63, p30, June 1, 1992.

Advertising Age, "Mattel Fashions Barbie Boutique," v62, p3, July 1, 1991.

AdWEEK, "Barbie to Petra: You're No Friend of Mine," v32, p16, August 15, 1991.

AdWEEK, "Ethnic Barbie Struts her Stuff on TV," v40, p4, July 23, 1990.

AdWEEK, "Mattel's Barbie Ties Charity Drive to Worldwide Summit," v40, p47, November 5, 1990.

AdWEEK's Advertising Week, "Barbie at 30," v30, p20, February 13, 1989.

Allentown Morning Call, "Barbie Mania," pB1, October 30, 1996.

Antiques and Collecting, "Barbie is Thirty," v94, pp22-5, September, 1989.

Architectural Digest, "BillyBoy in Paris," v46, pp94+, September 1989.

Associated Press, "Chador-Clad Doll is Iran's Answer to Barbie," October 24, 1996.

BillyBoy. Barbie—Her Life & Times.* New York: Crown, 1987.

Bryan, Sandra. Barbie—The Eyelash Era. Self-published, 1989.

Business Week, "Looking for a Few Good Boy Toys," p116, February 17, 1992.

Business Week, "Why Do All Those Street Kids Love Mattel?" p130, October 28, 1991.

Business Week, "Mattel Struggles," p76+, May 9, 1989.

Business Week, "Dollhouse in Order," p66-7, August 28, 1989.

Business Week, "Barbie Is Her Best Friend," p80, June 8, 1992.

Chicago Tribune, "Barbie Goes for Gold," p10, September 1, 1996.

Chicago Tribune, "Iran Takes on Barbie with its New Sara Doll," p4, October 25, 1996.

Chicago Tribune, "These Chairs Were Designed with Only Barbie in Mind...." p1, May 26, 1996.

Chicago Tribune, "Despite Middle Age on the Horizon, Barbie Just Keeps Getting Better and More Popular," p11, May 26, 1996.

Chicago Tribune, "Ken at 35: Vintage Toy No Boy," p3, March 1,4 1996.

Cleveland Plain Dealer, "Soon the Japanese Can Dress Like Barbie," December 19, 1996.

Cleveland Plain Dealer, "You've Come a Long Way, Barbie," March 10, 1996.

Columbus Dispatch, "Ugh, You Beautiful Doll, At 35 Ken's Tired of Playing Second Banana to Barbie," p01E, March 27 1996.

Dallas Morning News, "Barbie's Ken Will Get Updated Look--Again," p3C, April 6, 1996.

Dallas Morning News, "Girl, 8, Helps Design Barbie CD-ROM," p1C, November 25, 1996.

Detroit News, "Big-Hair Barbie: Stylist Makes Sure America's Doll is Perfectly Tressed," August 39, 1996.

DeWein, Sibyl St. John. *Collectible Barbie Dolls, 1977-79.*

DeWein, Sibyl and Evelyn *Ashabraner. Barbie Dolls & Collectibles.* Collector Books, 1992.

Eames, Sarah Sink. *Barbie Fashion, 1959-1972.* Collector Books, 1990.

Education Digest, "Barbie Doesn't Add Up," v58, pp72-4, December 1992.

Financial Times, "Why grown men dream of a future with Barbie," p13, September 17, 1992.

Financial Week, "Eternally Yours, Barbie," v161, pp36-7, September 1, 1992.

Forbes, "Barbie Does Budapest," v147, pp66+, January 7, 1991.

Forbes, "Brink of Bankruptcy," v136, pp50-1+, August 12, 1985.

Forbes, "Is There a Doctor in the House?" pp218-220, May 28, 1990.

Forbes, "Stick With the Doll that Brung Ya," v145, pp218-19, May 28, 1990.

Forbes, "Barbie Does Silicon Valley," v 154, pp84-5, September 26, 1994.

Forbes, "Barbie at 30," v142, pp248-9, November 14, 1988.

Fortune, "Putting Barbie Back Together Again," v102, pp84-88, September 8, 1980.

Fortune, "Earring Magic," v126, p56, September 21, 1992.

Forward, "A Doll's Evolution From German Tramp to American Princess," March 24, 1995.

Gannett News Service, "Set Your Phasers on 'Purchase:' 'Star Trek' Barbie Beams into Stores," June 21, 1996.

Hobbies, "Barbie Doll Boom," v90, pp32-6, June 1985.

Hollywood Reporter, "Digital Barbie and Kinetic Ken," p5, February 9, 1996.

Houston Chronicle, "Barbie's Main Man," p1, April 11, 1996.

Houston Chronicle, "Furriers Feel Heat Over Mink-Clad Barbie Doll," p13, January 20, 1997.

Houston Chronicle, "Toys-to-Computer Surge is Child's Play," June 26, 1996.

Interview, "Our Barbies, Ourselves," v21, p36, December 1991.

Investor's Business Daily—Executive Update, "What Makes Barbie A Girl's Favorite Doll," April 12, 1995.

Jacobs, Laura. *Barbie in Fashion.* New York: Abbeville Press, 1994.

The Licensing Book, "Nicole Miller Barbie Doll Hits Macy's in Time for the Holidays," p39, December 1996.

Los Angeles Magazine, "King Barbie," v39, pp62-8, August 1994.

Los Angeles Times, "Barbies Can Come Out, but They Can't Play," p21, November 19, 1992.

Los Angeles Times, "The Man Who Would Be Ken," p1, August 2, 1994.

Los Angeles Times, "Barbie's Inventor Has Seen Her Grow From Hunch to Hit to Ageless," p8, December 15, 1994.

Los Angeles Times, "Missing Part? No Need to Throw Out the Barbie With the Bathwater," p2, September 29, 1996.

Los Angeles Times, "Woman to Run House That Barbie Built," pA1, August 23, 1996.

Los Angeles Times, "Why Wall Street Has a Crush on Barbie," p1, January 26, 1996.

Los Angeles Times, "Barbie's Mane Man," pE-1, August 26, 1996.

Los Angeles Times, "Beverly Hills Barbies, Rodeo Drive Goes Ga-Ga Over Auction Featuring Popular Doll," pB-1, December 9, 1996.

M2 Presswire, "Mattel Launches Multimedia Company," February 13, 1996.

Mandeville, A. Glenn. *Doll Fashion Anthology.* Hobby House Press, 1993.

Manos, Susan. *The Wonder of Barbie.* Collector Books, 1990.
Manos, Susan. *The World of Barbie Dolls.* Collector Books, 1990.
Marketing News, "Mattel Chief Followed Her Instincts and Found Success," v26, p15, March 16, 1992.
Marketing News, "Toy Companies Release 'Ethnically Correct' Dolls," v25, p1, September 30, 1991.
Marketing News, "New Line of Barbie Dolls Targets Big, Rich Kids," v30, p6, June 17, 1996.
Miller's Barbie Collector, various issues.
Miller's Price Guide, 1997.
Money, "Barbie Looks Like A Billion Bucks," v22, p82, May 1993.
Ms., "Is There a Barbie Doll in Your Past?" v8, p102, September 1979.
New Republic, "Bedtime Barbie," v 212, pp12-13, January 9-16, 1995.
New Choices, "All Dolled Up," v31, pp93-4, April 1991.
Newsday, "Beam Me Up, Barbie," pB37, October 15, 1996.
Newsweek, "Hot Date: Barbie and G.I. Joe," v113, p59, February 20, 1989.
Newsweek, "Barbie at 24," v102, p10+, September 12, 1983.
Newsweek, "Finally, Barbie Doll Ads Go Ethnic," v116, p48, August 13, 1990.
Newsweek, "Honey, They Blew Up Barbie," v120, p42, July 27, 1992.
New York Times, "Toy Makers Meet The Inner Child, Ages 21 and Up," p12, December 27, 1992.
Orange County Register, "Ken's Midlife Crisis," pE01, April 15, 1996.
Orange County Register, "Take Back Your Mink," February 25, 1997.
PC Week, "Mattel Debuts in Software Market with Focus on Girls," February 12, 1996.
People, "Barbie Turns 30," v31, p186-7, March 6, 1989.
People, "Volley of the Dolls," v36, p95, September 9, 1991.
People, "Barbie, Meet Brenda," v37, p120-1, February 17, 1992.
People, "Barbie Bashing," v40, p67, August 9, 1993.
Philadelphia, "Oh, You Beautiful Doll," June 1993, pp31-2.
Phoenix Gazette, "Ken is Finally His Own Man," pA2, April 4, 1996.
Pittsburgh Post-Gazette, "Barbie's Main Guy Turns 35," pB-1, April 11, 1996.
Playthings, "Mattel Brings In-Line Skating Fun to Doll Market," v90, p78, February 1992.
Rana, Margo. *Barbie Exclusives.* Collector Books, 1994.
Robins, Cynthia. *Barbie-30 Years of America's Doll.* Contemporary Books, 1989.
St. Louis Dispatch, "Barbie Togs Clothing for Real Women in Japan Modeled on Doll," January 5, 1997.
Sarasohn-Kahn, Jane. "Barbie Goes to Work," Barbie Bazaar, September/October 1994.
Sarasohn-Kahn, Jane. "Barbie in Cyberspace," Miller's Barbie Collector, November/December 1994.
Sarasohn-Kahn, Jane. "Barbie 2009: You've Come a Long Way, Barbie," Baltimore National Barbie Convention, August 1993.
Time, "Barbie Boots Up," p48, November 11, 1996.
US News & World Report, "Mattel Gets All Dolled Up," v115, pp74-6, December 13, 1993.
US News & World Report, "Teen Talk Barbie," v113, p25, September 12, 1992.
US News & World Report, "Barbie's New World," v111, p22, September 30, 1991.
US News & World Report, "Valley of the Dolls?" v109, pp56-9, December 3, 1990.
USA Today, "Investors Seek Comfort in Toy Companies," February 8, 1996.
Unity Marketing, "Collectible Doll Market Posts $1.4 Billion in Sales," Press Release, September 18, 1996.
Utne Reader, "What a Doll!" p46+, March-April 1992.
WWD, "Byron Lars in Deal for Collectible Barbie," p13, March 25, 1996.
Wall Street Journal, The, "Barbie, Miss America Make Up and Settle Dispute Over Looks," pC18, August 27, 1992.
Wall Street Journal, The, "Educators Give Barbie a Good Dressing-Down," pB1, September 25, 1992.
Wall Street Journal, The, "Girls, Parents Not Only Ones Buying 'Earring Magic Ken' Doll," August 30, 1992.
Wall Street Journal, The, "Christmas '96: Barbie, Dressed to Kill, Beats CD-ROM Rivals," pB1, December 18, 1996.
Wall Street Journal, The, "Mattel's New Chief Executive Displays Knack for Kids' Tastes," March 5, 1997.
Wall Street Journal, The, "Makeover Artist: She Reinvented Barbie; Now, Can Jill Barad Do The Same for Mattel?" pA1, March 5, 1997.
Wall Street Journal, The, "Avon's New Calling: Sell Barbie in China," pB1, May 1, 1997.
Washington Informer, "Why Didn't Black Barbie Dolls Sell Well This Christmas?" January 3, 1996.
Washington Post, "It's a Bird! It's a Plane! It's Barbie!" pN13, June 9, 1995.
Washington Post, "Fits of Pink," pB02, May 16, 1997.
Washington Post, "Barbie Doll: Japan's New Look," pA20, December 16, 1996.
Washington Post, "If Only Barbie Could Bend Her Knees," pT05, June 6, 1996.
Washingtonian, "Child's Play," pp149-150, December 1994.
Westenhauser, Kitturah. *The Story of Barbie.* Collector Books, 1993.
Wired, "Gender Blender," p189, November 1996.
Working Woman, "Moving Beyond Barbie," v18, pp46-8, December 1993.
Working Woman, "Mistress of the Universe," v10, p160, September 1983.
Working Woman, "It's How You Play the Game," v15, pp88-91, May 1990.
Working Woman, "When Toys Mean Business," v12, pp133-4+, May 1987.
Working Woman, "Going Where No Woman Has Gone Before," November/December 1996.

INDEX

ABOUT THE AUTHOR

Jane Sarasohn-Kahn has been writing since her mother bought a thirty-pound IBM Selectric typewriter for her to work with in 1964. When not collecting Barbie dolls, Jane is a management consultant and economist who works globally with organizations on matters relating to the future of health care and technology. She has published articles in more than 40 business journals and collectibles magazines on topics ranging from health care reform and global business to Barbie collecting. She also writes a monthly column, "Notes from a Friend of the Barbie Doll," for *Toy Trader* magazine.

Jane holds an M.A. in Economics, an M.H.S.A. in Public Health, a B.A. in Economics and a B.A. in Journalism, all from the University of Michigan. She is married to an international banker who lovingly brings her Barbie dolls discovered in the course of his worldwide travels. They have a daughter who is more fun to dress than the Barbie doll.

PHOTOGRAPH BY MICHAEL